WALKING THE GR7
IN ANDALUCÍA

About the Authors

Kirstie Shirra is a freelance writer and environmental campaigner. Climbing mountains since she could walk, she has travelled throughout Europe and the Americas but always ends up back in the wonderful mountains of north-west Scotland where she lives with her husband Pete. Kirstie has also written *Scotland's Best Small Mountains* for Cicerone and regularly writes for walking publications.

Michelle Lowe is a writer, researcher and campaigner who loves walking. Based in Edinburgh with her husband Charlie she has spent time living, travelling and trekking in Ecuador, Peru, Nepal and Europe. When not walking she likes making pots.

Born and living in Málaga (in the south of Spain), **Miguel Ángel Santaella** is an environmental health engineer and nurse who helped the authors with the GPS routes. He has traveled and walked almost all countries in Asia, New Zealand, Central Europe and Spain. He is the creator of the www.rutasyviajes. net website which posts GPS routes for each stage of the GR7, as well as other walking routes. His passions are trekking and hiking.

Other Cicerone guides by the authors
Scotland's Best Small Mountains (Kirstie Shirra)

WALKING THE GR7
IN ANDALUCÍA

by Kirstie Shirra and Michelle Lowe
with Miguel Ángel Santaella

2 POLICE SQUARE, MILNTHORPE, CUMBRIA LA7 7PY
www.cicerone.co.uk

Printed in China on behalf of Latitude Press Ltd.
A catalogue record for this book is available from the British Library.
Text and photographs © Michelle Lowe and Kirstie Shirra 2013
1:50,000 map bases property of the National Geographic Institute of Spain

Acknowledgements

Huge thanks to Charlie, Pete and Liz for accompanying us on our adventures in the Panda and on the route; Jonathan and Lesley Williams for helping us by rewalking some of the Alpujarran section; Miguel Ángel Santaella for all his help with GPS routes, Ozi Explorer and walking sections; and to Francisco Jiménez Richarte from the Federación Andaluza de Montañismo for patiently answering all our questions. Thanks also to Juan Holgado and to all the readers who sent in helpful comments on the first edition of this book with special thanks to Ivan and Sue Godfrey, Arthur Hugh, Frank Gledhill, Giles Heywood, Phil Olsen, J Bouwman, R S Bingley, George Masson, Julia Herrod, Patrick and Susan Elvin, Anita Beijer and Mike Gaches.

Advice to Readers

While every effort is made by our authors to ensure the accuracy of guidebooks as they go to print, changes can occur during the lifetime of an edition. If we know of any, there will be an Updates tab on this book's page on the Cicerone website (www.cicerone.co.uk), so please check before planning your trip. We also advise that you check information about such things as transport, accommodation and shops locally. Even rights of way can be altered over time. We are always grateful for information about any discrepancies between a guidebook and the facts on the ground, sent by email to info@cicerone.co.uk or by post to Cicerone, 2 Police Square, Milnthorpe LA7 7PY, United Kingdom.

Front cover: The pretty mountain village of Trévelez in the Alpujarras (Granada, Southern Fork)

CONTENTS

Route symbols on maps

12a   route and stage number

◀   direction of route

Los Barios   town where a stage starts/finishes

⊕   start point

⊕   finish point

⊕   stage finish/start point

For all other symbols, see the IGN 1:100,000 maps from which the route maps are derived.

Map scale
1:100K (1cm=1km)

0 ————————— 1 mile

0 ——————— 1 ——————— 2km

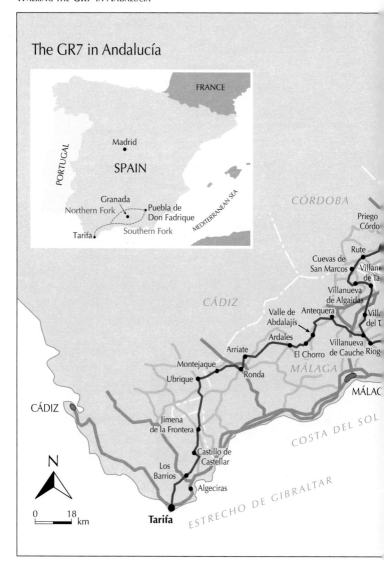

The GR7 in Andalucía

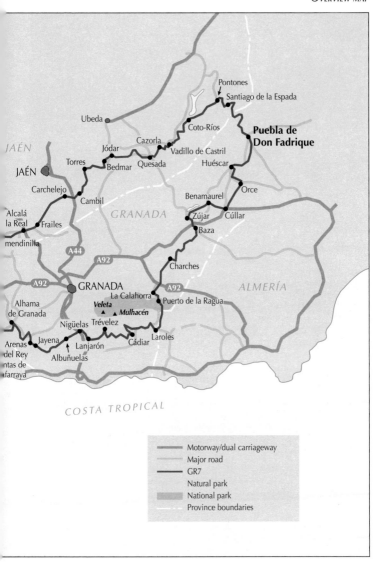

In the gorge on the approach to Alhama (Stage 14B)

PUBLISHER'S PREFACE

We walked several stages of the route to help Kirstie and Michelle with the new edition. Walking the GR7 in Andalucía is a fantastic experience, with good weather, varied and dramatic landscapes, ancient villages and plenty of cultural, historical and geological points of interest. It has all the ingredients of a great route, and more. The GR7 should not however be seen as an easy option.

There are three main challenges for the walker to take on board. Firstly, the landscape itself. Washington Irvine in his *Tales from the Alhambra* described the land he crossed between Seville and Granada as 'harsh and empty, with no Italian softness'. It hasn't really changed at all. It is still somewhere where large armies would starve and small ones be defeated. Tracks become concrete roads, and get washed away. Tarmac roads degrade into tracks, then get resurfaced in concrete, all within a few months. Riverside paths get washed out and replaced, or not. All in all, a kilometre seems further in Andalucía than in most other parts of Europe!

Secondly, the villages. Some sections of the route pass through a large number of small villages. These are very beautiful and offer plenty of opportunities of refreshments and interesting detours. But the complexity of their entrances and especially their exits need extra time and a real feel for the complexities of Moorish village design! I would also think it wise to expect some of the accommodation not to survive the recession and unemployment that is affecting Spain so severely at the moment.

Thirdly, the GR7 route itself. The waymarking varies dramatically across the length of the route and is far from the level of an established French GR route. Some sections have not been well maintained and marking can be sparse where needed and placed idiosyncratically. A guidebook to a route of this length can only pick the main threads where small villages may be surrounded by 50km or more of farm tracks, otherwise it risks becoming enormous, and so useless. This challenge, allied with the quality of Spanish maps, which is not great, mean that even with the best and most accurate route description, route finding will sometimes be a challenge. You will need to develop some insight into the innermost thought processes and dreams of the route setters and markers to stay on trail!

We suggest that experienced walkers and those with some prior experience walking in Spain, will get most from the route. It is also useful to speak some Spanish, as very little English is spoken in the less touristy parts of the route. That said, for those with a spirit of adventure, we highly recommend the route for its wild remote country, beautiful villages and warm hospitality.

Expect to get 'mislaid' occasionally and expect surprises, nearly all good!

Jonathan and Lesley Williams

Looking across Torres to the mountains (Northern Fork, Jaén province, Stages 22A and 23A)

INTRODUCTION

The Embalse de Negratín and open plains between Baza and Zújar (Southern Fork, Granada province, Stage 29B)

With white sand beaches, pine forests, semi-arid desert badlands, snow-capped peaks, fertile plains, traditional agricultural villages, lush expansive river valleys, olive groves and rolling hills of cork woodland, the 1183km of the GR7 in Andalucía take you on a journey through one of the most geographically varied regions on the Iberian peninsula, and possibly even Europe.

This scenically diverse route starts at the southernmost tip of Spain on the coast at Tarifa, and meanders through the province of Cádiz before splitting into two in the Málaga province. Both routes are part of the official GR7 so the walker has the choice of taking the Northern Fork, which heads through Córdoba and Jaén provinces, or the Southern Fork, which passes through Almería and Granada. The whole northern route is 717.8km long and takes 34 to 41 days. The southern route is 735km and takes 35 to 42 days. The routes rejoin at Puebla de Don Fadrique, the last town in the Andalucían section of the GR7 and the end of this guide. From here the route continues into the region of Murcia. On its journey through Andalucía, the GR7 crosses through seven stunning natural parks and the Sierra Nevada national park, home to mainland Spain's highest peak, Mulhacén.

Andalucía has many faces. It is perhaps most famous among holidaymakers for its coastline – a haven for sunseekers but now somewhat spoilt by overdevelopment. The GR7 offers the opportunity to see another of its faces. You will explore little-visited hidden gems, enjoy the natural parks and visit unspoilt peaceful villages. And you can take part in positive rural tourism, supporting small communities by staying and eating in family-run hotels, restaurants and guesthouses.

The GR7 is also a great journey through history and cultures of the past and present. As the southernmost part of Spain, Andalucía is the cultural and geographical borderland between Europe and Africa, connecting the Mediterranean with the Atlantic Ocean. It is infused with romance as the place of the Moors' last stand and has long been an inspiration to artists and writers. Grand fortresses and watchtowers bring to life aspects of the eight centuries of Arab rule and there are also some internationally significant prehistoric sites.

ABOUT ANDALUCÍA

Andalucía is the most southerly of Spain's 17 autonomous communities and has both Mediterranean and Atlantic coastlines. It has its own regional administration, the Junta de Andalucía, based in its capital, Sevilla, and its other major cities are Granada and Córdoba. At 87,300km² it is Spain's second largest region and is divided into eight provinces, six of which the GR7 passes through.

Despite being the most populous of the autonomous communities (with 8.4 million people), much of the land is still uncultivated or being farmed in traditional ways. About half of Andalucía is mountainous, a third of it at altitudes greater than 600m and including 46 peaks over 1000m. It is home to two of the highest peaks of the Iberian peninsula in the Sierra Nevada mountains: Mulhacén (3481m) and Veleta (3398m).

Thanks to regional and national government initiatives over the last two decades, Andalucía now has a significant programme of environmental protection with almost a fifth of its area under some form of protection. There are 24 natural parks, 29 natural reserves, 32 natural areas and two national parks – the route passes through one of these, the Sierra Nevada, as well as through seven natural parks.

Historically, Andalucía has been a poor region, particularly as a result of the *latifundio* land ownership system, dating back to the Roman era, in which a few rich gentry owned vast tracts of land worked by poverty-stricken landless peasants. Until recently there were far sharper, more rigid class distinctions in Andalucía than in the north of the country, and often class relations were marked by conflict, with many rebellions over the years.

CULTURE

Andalucians have a rich and distinct culture and a strong sense of regional identity. They are known for being gregarious and for enjoying parties and crowds. The area is particularly famous for being the home of both flamenco and bullfighting.

Flamboyant flamenco music – a fusion of Arabic, Jewish and other styles of music – originated in the southwest of the region in the 18th century and is still hugely popular today.

Bullfighting is thought to have originated in the Roman era and there are still more than 150 bullrings in Andalucía,

La Calahorra castle (Southern Fork, Granada province, Stage 27B)

including the famous one in Ronda. The bullfighting season, which lasts from Easter Sunday to October, is popular in Andalucía and much less controversial than it is in the north of Spain.

Andalucía is also known for its colourful *fiestas* and *ferias* (local festivals and fairs). Most villages have their own *fiesta* (and usually more than one). The main religious event is *Semana Santa* (Holy Week), when you will encounter processions with crowds bearing huge effigies of Jesus and Mary. *Carnaval* in February or March is also important, with parties and fancy dress parades – especially in Cádiz. The main village *ferias* are usually in the summer. They originated from regional cattle markets and now often involve bullfighting, a fairground, parade and all-night singing, music, dancing and drinking.

The area is also known for having retained many of its traditional arts and crafts and these are now flourishing again with the advent of tourism. In many of the villages you will find workshops for pottery, leatherwork, rugmaking, furniture, copper, gold and silverwork, wickerwork and handmade musical instruments.

ANDALUCIAN CUISINE

The region's food has been influenced by many cultures and especially Arabian cuisine, in dishes using citrus fruits, almonds, spices, mint, and also pastries and cakes.

In the villages you will visit the food tends to be simple and often based on meat (including game and ham, especially in the high mountain villages where it is cured), seafood or cheese (sheep, goat, cow and combinations of the three). Fresh local ingredients are usually on offer in the restaurants,

Olive groves en route just after Guaro (Southern Fork, Málaga province, Stage 13B)

including olives, lots of olive oil, oranges, lemons, chestnuts, avocados and game.

Typical Andalucian dishes include stews using the famous *rabo de toro* (oxtail stew), fried fish, *gazpacho* (refreshing cold tomato soup), *jamón serrano* (mountain-cured ham) and olives. Desserts are not a great feature of the menus – there will usually be *flan* (*crème caramel*) and ice cream on offer. Sometimes you will come across traditional deserts including *pestiños de miel* (honey-coated pastry fritters), *amarguillos* (almond macaroons) and *polvorónes* (almond cookies). Bread, generally white, is usually provided with your meal and most villages have their own bakeries.

There are a few vegetarian options on offer in most bars and restaurants. However, be aware that apparently vegetarian dishes may contain chopped ham or seafood. *Gazpacho, revueltos* (scrambled egg), cheese and lots of egg and potatoes are likely to be your standard diet as a vegetarian.

Tapas

In many bars the main food on offer is *tapas*, often sitting warming on the bar in a glass display cabinet. These are snacks but can be combined to make up a full meal. One or two portions of *tapas* are sometimes offered free with your drinks. You can also ask for larger portions of them: a whole plateful is a *ración* and half a plateful is a *media ración*.

Wines and liquors

Andalucía has a long tradition of wine production (possibly dating back to the Phoenicians). It is popular and cheap

COMMON TAPAS

alcachofas	artichokes
alioli	garlicky oil/mayonaise paste usually served on bread or with potatoes, fish or meat
boquerones	anchovies (often marinated in garlic olive oil and vinegar)
chocos fritos	fried battered squid
chopitos	baby squid
chorizo al vino	chorizo sausage slowly cooked in wine
ensaladilla	Russian salad of boiled vegetables with tuna, olives and mayonnaise
gambas	prawns
habas con jamón	broad beans with ham
pinchos	mini kebabs (usually pork or chicken)
patatas bravas	fried potatoes, served with a tomato salsa and mayonnaise
queso con anchoas	cheese with anchovies
rajo	pork seasoned with garlic and parsley
revuelto de esparragos	scrambled egg with asparagus
tortilla de patatas	omelette containing fried chunks of potatoes and sometimes onion
tortillitas de camarones	battered prawns

and you can order it in bars by the glass (*copa*) or bottle (*botella*). Almost every village has its own local wine, but not all of them are great! Make sure you try the sherry and the other liquors of the region, such as the *anís* made in Rute.

LANGUAGE

If you speak Spanish it will be a great help in your travels in Andalucía, as in most of the villages you'll pass through on the route very little English is spoken (although it is more commonly spoken in tourist areas, especially the Alpujarras). Even if you don't speak

any Spanish it is worth getting hold of a phrase book and having a go as people will appreciate the effort. Appendix B is a glossary of Spanish words that will be useful en route.

HISTORY

Andalucía's location on the edge of Europe and Africa has made its history active, colourful and often bloody since prehistoric times. Its fertile land has also made it desirable territory for farming communities throughout history. The key periods in Andalucian history are outlined below.

17

Prehistoric Andalucía

During the Palaeolithic era (the last Ice Age to 8000BC) there were significant numbers of hunter–gatherer peoples living in Andalucía. Orce, in the Granada province, is famous for a bone fragment found in 1982 which holds a disputed status as a fragment of the oldest known human in Europe (possibly over a million years old) (Stage 32B). Along the route there are a few sites where you can see cave paintings, such as the Cueva de Ardales (Stage 7) and other caves near Ronda. You can also visit some of Spain's best known dolmens (large tombs made of rocks constructed in the Chalcolithic age) near Antequera (Stage 10).

8th to 7th centuries : Tartessos

In the eighth and seventh centuries BC the Tartessos culture flourished in western Andalucía. It is thought to have been very rich, with advanced gold and iron-working techniques. It was influenced by Phoenician (from present-day Lebanon) and later Greek traders, who exchanged perfumes, ivory, jewellery, oil, wine and textiles for Andalucian silver and bronze.

6th to 1st centuries : Iberians

From the sixth century BC the Phoenicians and Greeks were pushed out of Andalucía by the Iberians or Carthaginians from further north in Spain.

1st century to 5th century : Romans

The Iberians came into conflict with the growing power base of Rome and southern Spain was fought over by the two groups. In 206BC the Romans finally beat the Iberians and soon after built Itálica, the first Roman town in Spain, near modern-day Sevilla. Andalucía became wealthy under the Romans, with Rome importing many Andalucian products such as wheat, vegetables, grapes, olives, copper, silver, lead and fish.

5th to 8th centuries: Visigoths

Throughout the third, fourth and fifth centuries the central authority of Rome waned and Germanic tribes invaded the territories of the Roman empire, including the Iberian peninsula. Rome was taken over by the Visigoths in AD410 and they then went on to occupy the Iberian peninsula. The Visigoths maintained many Roman institutions and did not mix with the Spanish population until the period of Muslim rule and so the Visigoth language left little trace on modern Iberian languages.

8th to 15th centuries: Al-Andalus

The Arabs and Islam spread through the Middle East and North Africa in the eighth century, and in AD711 Arabs (Moors) landed at Gibraltar. Over the next few years they took almost all of Spain (except for areas of the northwest and Basque areas in the Pyrenees).

The Moors ruled throughout a vast area called Al-Andalus which encompassed parts of North Africa, Spain and Portugal. Their heartland was modern-day Andalucía. They were in power across most of the Iberian peninsula for four centuries and continued to be a dominant force for another three, developing the most advanced society in western Europe at the time.

The Moors left behind them beautiful palaces, mosques, gardens, bathhouses and universities, and in rural areas they left impressive irrigation

Gate to the Alcazaba, Antequera (Málaga province, Stage 10)

systems and new crops such as oranges, lemons, sugar cane and rice.

Throughout the period of Arab rule, internal conflict was rife between the rulers (made up of various Muslim groups), the Berbers (North African commoners who were often given poor quality land), and the Christians, who were allowed freedom of worship but paid extra taxes. Throughout this period power shifted from one Arab dynasty to another, including the Omayyades, Almoravides, Almohades and Nasrides. There was also near-constant conflict on its borders with Christians, although for a long time they posed little threat to Al-Andalus, which was far stronger in terms of population, economy, culture and military might. As time went on intermarriage between powerful families living in the Christian north and in the Muslim south of Spain became commonplace.

8th to 15th centuries: Reconquista

The *Reconquista*, the Christian takeover of Spain, was a long, drawn-out process with internal fighting between Christian realms as well as between Christians and Muslims. Over the centuries, the Christian and Muslim populations became increasingly intermingled, making it less of a Christian crusade than a series of local, territorial conflicts.

In 1212 a coalition of Christian kings drove the Muslims from the centre of Spain. However, the Nasrid Emirate of Granada, whose domain included the modern provinces of Granada, Málaga and Almería as well as parts of Cádiz, Córdoba, Jaén and Sevilla, continued to be extremely powerful as a vassal state to the Christian kingdom until 1492.

The Treaty (or Capitulation) of Granada to the Catholic monarchs, King Fernando II of Aragon and Queen

Isabella of Castile, was ratified at the end of 1491 by Boabdil of Granada (Abu 'Abd Allah Muhammad). It guaranteed rights to the Moors, including religious tolerance, in return for their unconditional surrender. Boabdil received the Alpujarras (through which the GR7 passes) as a fiefdom but only stayed a year or so.

For the first time since the Visigoth era, the Catholic monarchs then united most of modern Spain religiously, politically and economically under one rule and brought Spain into power and prominence in Europe. The promised religious tolerance didn't last long. Muslims were forced to convert to Christianity or deported to Africa and Jews were also persecuted. In 1499, Cardinal Cisneros, the leader of the Spanish Inquisition, forced about 50,000 Moors in Granada into mass baptisms. Islamic books were burnt, the Arabic language banned and Muslims' land confiscated.

After a quashed rebellion that started in 1500 in the Alpujarras, people who refused baptism or deportation to Africa were killed and there was a mass exodus of Muslims and Jews. In 1567 a second Alpujarran rebellion led to all *Moriscos* (Muslims converted to Christianity) being deported.

16th and 17th centuries: Sevilla, empire and the Golden Age

Through the conquest of most of South America and the West Indies Spain began to establish itself as an empire, with huge quantities of gold and silver being sent back to Spain. Sevilla was the premier city in Spain until the 17th century, one of the richest and largest in Europe and a world trade hub. This opened Andalucía up to new European ideas and artistic movements and its cities flourished. Rural Andalucía, however, remained extremely poor, with a handful of rich landowners controlling large tracts of land on which they just kept sheep. Few peasants owned any land or property.

The Golden Age soon came to an end, with economic losses and mismanagement leading to a trade deficit. A decline in silver shipments combined with poor harvests led to the death of about 300,000 people, which, combined with the expulsion of the *Moriscos*, caused underpopulation and several economic collapses.

18th century: the Enlightenment and the Bourbons

In the 18th century, the French Bourbon Dynasty, which is Spain's ruling family again today, took control of Spain and the country enjoyed a limited economic recovery. Spanish ports traded with the Americas, stimulating the growth of Málaga, and new settlers from other parts of the country came to boost Andalucía's population.

19th century: Napoleonic Wars – the Reformation

Spain initially sided against France in the Napoleonic Wars. The Spanish were defeated along with the French at the decisive Battle of Trafalgar in 1805, prompting the Spanish king to reconsider his alliance with France. This led Napoleon Bonaparte, Emperor of France, to invade Spain in 1808 and depose the king, thereby starting the Spanish War of Independence in which the Spanish people fought guerrilla-style against the

French, finally driving them out with support from the British and Portuguese armies led by the Duke of Wellington.

Cádiz withstood a two-year siege by Napoleon's army to become the last bastion of Spain's anti-monarchist, liberal movement. During the French occupation the national parliament was based there, and, in 1812, that parliament declared the first Spanish constitution, which proclaimed the people's sovereignty and reduced the power of the monarchy, nobility and church.

However, Ferdinand VII revoked the new constitution and continued to rule in an authoritarian style, temporarily reinstating the Inquisition. While he and his liberal opponents struggled in Spain, revolution then broke out in the Spanish colonies. Taking advantage of Spain's weakness, they won their independence.

In 1836 and 1855, to reduce the national debt, successive liberal governments auctioned off church and municipal lands, allowing the rich to build up bigger estates and plunging peasants deeper into poverty as they lost vital grazing land. Andalucía had a sharply divided population of rich landed gentry and poor landless seasonal workers who were mostly desperately poor and illiterate. In 1873 Spain briefly became a republic – a federation of 17 states – but it immediately came under attack from all sides and collapsed when the monarchy was reinstated by the army less than a year later.

Early 20th century: Rebellion, dictatorship, republic and civil war

At the beginning of the 20th century, Andalucian peasants staged various brutally crushed uprisings against their miserable conditions. In 1910 an anarchist union, the CNT, was founded in Sevilla and grew to almost 100,000 Andalucian members in just nine years.

After a period of military dictatorship between 1923 and 1930, a second Spanish republic was established in 1931 but fractious, rapidly changing governing coalitions led to serious political unrest. In 1933, a right-wing government was elected and violence erupted between left-wing groups and the government, and in 1936 the country slid into civil war.

The vicious conflict between Nationalists and Republicans led to over 350,000 deaths including massacres of civilians and prisoners. In Andalucía, communist and socialist groups tried to bring about anarchist revolution, seizing land, killing church officials and burning churches. About 100 agrarian communities were established.

On 1 April 1939, this brutal war ended with the downfall of the Republic and General Francisco Franco's installation as dictator. Franco formed an alliance between all the right-wing parties and banned the left-wing and Republican parties and trade unions. About 100,000 people are thought to have been killed after he took power.

1939–1975: the Franco dictatorship

During Franco's rule, Spain remained largely economically and culturally isolated from the outside world. Although supposedly neutral in World War II, Franco lent his support to the Nazis, as a result of which, after the war, Spain suffered the effects of an international blockade. The 1940s were known as the hunger years, with peasants in poor areas Andalucía barely managing to survive.

With the latter years of Franco's rule came some economic and political liberalization, the so-called Spanish Miracle, including the launch of mass foreign tourism on Andalucía's coast. However Spain remained far behind the rest of Europe.

1975 to the present day: democracy and economic boom then bust

Franco ruled until he died on 20 November 1975, when King Juan Carlos came to power. He oversaw the shift to a new democratic state and a liberalization of society. In 1982 the centre-left PSOE were elected. Felipe González became Prime Minister and governed for 14 years.

In 1982, devolution created a regional government in Andalucía, which the PSOE also controlled. Both national and regional government took positive steps to tackle poverty in the 1980s with grants, community work schemes, social security support and some land reform to tackle the unjust ownership system.

By the 1990s, the PSOE were in decline and they lost the 1996 elections to centre-right Partido Popular, which then governed for eight years. In 2004, after their unpopular decision to support the Iraq war, and three days after the Madrid bombings of 11 March, they were unseated in favour of a new socialist government. The Spanish Socialist Workers' Party governed from 2004 to 2011, winning a second term in 2008. They implemented liberal secular policies including promoting women's rights, changing the abortion law, and legalising same-sex marriage. The Partido Popular took power again in November 2011 in the midst of the recession.

CURRENT ISSUES

Economic Crisis

Until 2008, Andalucía experienced a huge boom in tourism and industry and benefitted from EU subsidies for agriculture. However, the international financial crisis of 2008 hit Spain's economy hard. The construction industry, upon which the economy was very dependent, collapsed, as did property values. Economic growth stopped and unemployment soared. The national Government has implemented severe austerity measures, cutting spending and laying off workers. Andalucía now has high unemployment and in the rural areas, through which the GR7 passes, life can be tough. Tourism has been impacted by the financial crisis and over a fifth of the population still relies on agriculture for income.

Immigration

Modern-day Andalucía is still the gateway between Europe and Africa and home to a significant proportion of Spain's one million Muslims. There are many Moroccan migrant workers and frequent reports of illegal immigrants' desperate and often tragic attempts to cross the Straits of Gibraltar. Illegal immigrants are open to exploitation and, in rural areas, there are many stories of immigrants being paid low wages and working in poor conditions in intensive vegetable cultivation. Although the area has a rosy reputation for positive racial integration,

Countryside on the way to Los Barrios (Cádiz province, Stage 1)

in the context of heightened European-wide anxiety about immigration and terrorism, the issue is becoming more politicised and debates more heated.

Drought

The combination of two water-intensive activities – agriculture and tourism – is taking a heavy toll in Andalucía. This is especially true of the tourist coast, where a vast increase in the number of swimming pools and heavily watered golf courses is having a serious environmental impact.

It is also causing problems inland in some of the villages that you will visit on the GR7. Land which was once fertile is now parched and barren. The Junta de Andalucía has a ten-year plan to combat desertification, including the reforestation of mountains, financial aid for farmers and education programmes to inform the public about environmentally friendly farming methods and water conservation. There are also ongoing debates about controversial plans to divert water from the north to the south.

WILDLIFE

The animal and plant life of Andalucía is heavily influenced, and made unique, by its location at the meeting point between Africa and Europe and by the area's geographic diversity. The meeting of the cold Atlantic and the warm Mediterranean at Tarifa make for a distinctive climate which is abundant in bird, reptile, mammal and plant life.

Andalucía sits on one of two key migration routes for birds between Europe and Africa and is a paradise for

23

birdwatchers. There are over 250 species which are resident all year round in Andalucía, with more wintering there. Of the resident species, 13 are birds of prey, one of which is the Spanish Imperial Eagle, which, as its name suggests, is only found in Spain. There are also golden eagles, black vultures (Europe's largest bird), griffon vultures and red kites. You are also likely to come across storks nesting on top of telegraph poles and church towers in the spring. In terms of smaller birds, the most distinctive and exotic to look out for is the golden oriole, which has a bright yellow body.

Lizards are extremely common in Andalucía and you will see and hear them all along the route. Some of the rustling you hear may also be one of the 13 different types of snake that can be found in Spain, five of which are venomous (see 'Safety and emergencies'). One

Storks nesting

of the most common to Andalucía is the ladder snake which is not venomous and named for the pattern along its back.

Walking among the wildflowers

Mammals you may spot include red and roe deer, red squirrels, foxes – including the distinctive grey Spanish fox – and mountain goats or ibex. The wild boar is also common along much of the GR7 route but it is nocturnal and so harder to spot. Wolves still live in Andalucía in small numbers and are now mainly found in northern Córdoba.

Andalucía is also host to 5000 species of plants and trees. Several types of oak, pine, ash, alder, willow and poplar trees are all common, with some very large forests. Wild olive trees survive alongside the huge olive plantations, which in total cover more than 4500km of Andalucía. The plant life is unusually varied owing to the great geographic diversity. Lower regions are dominated by olives and pastures with other trees occupying higher slopes alongside beautiful and aromatic wild herbs such as rosemary, thyme and lavender.

NATIONAL AND NATURAL PARKS

The route of the GR7 passes through eight natural or national parks: Los Alcornocales and Sierra de Grazalema in Cádiz province; Sierra Subbética in Córdoba province; Sierras de Cazorla, Segura y las Villas and Sierra Mágina in Jaén province; and Sierras de Tejeda, Almijara y Alhama, Sierra Nevada (a national park) and Sierra de Baza in Granada province.

In 1918, Spain was one of the first countries in Europe to establish national parks and the mainland is now home to ten, encompassing over 1200km^2 of land. The national parks are designated as areas of important ecological,

scientific and educational value that, on the whole, have remained untouched by human intervention or developments. Throughout Spain there are also numerous natural parks. These are protected ecosystems or areas of outstanding natural beauty which are managed by autonomous regions, such as Andalucía. Most tend to be areas of wilderness, with little in the way of settlements or infrastructure.

The geography of the parks varies greatly across Spain, from forest to salt plains, but those through which the GR7 passes tend to be dominated by mountains (the Parque Natural de Los Alcornocales being the exception), from the rocky limestone peaks of the Sierra de Grazalema in Cádiz province, to the lush slopes of the Sierra Subbética in Córdoba province and the pines and aridity of the Sierra de Baza in Granada province.

Descriptions of the plants and animals to be found in each park are given in information boxes within the relevant province chapters. If you want to detour off the GR7 to explore further, most parks have their own tourist office or offices with full details of walks, along with other park information.

ABOUT THE GR7

The GR7 is one of many waymarked long-distance routes across Europe known as 'GR', which in Spain stands for Gran Recorrido. Wherever possible they avoid tarmac roads and traffic, instead taking ancient routes including old trade routes, caminos reales (wider routes now protected by royal decree), bridlepaths and even goat tracks. There

Cortijo Auta (Southern Fork, Málaga province, Stage 13B)

is a total of 1183km of waymarked GR7 route through the provinces of Cádiz, Málaga, Córdoba, Jaén, Granada and Almería, and the route is described here from west to east.

The GR7 is the Spanish part of a much longer trans-European route, the E4, which you will sometimes see mentioned on signboards. This passes through Andalucía, Murcia, Valencia and Cataluña before leaving Spain for France, Switzerland, Germany, Austria, Hungary, Romania, Bulgaria, Greece and Cyprus. The E4 is over 10,000km long and one of 11 long-distance European walking routes (E1–11) which link existing national and local route networks.

The GR7 in Andalucía is a long-distance and challenging route and it is possible to walk the entire length of it (on one of the two routes) in around 40 days. However, it is also varied and versatile and can be broken into shorter sections of many different kinds, offering something for most walkers. While there are many long, strenuous days, ranging from 15 to 35km, there are also plenty of short sections that could make pleasant day trips or be combined for longer routes. Most sections do not travel far from facilities and civilisation, but there are options to walk longer sections through natural parks with enticing diversions to climb peaks or explore some of Spain's most beautiful wild spaces further. In some of these more remote sections, or to shorten longer days, a tent becomes essential. Otherwise accommodation can be found on the rest of the route, and the remote sections avoided by using public transport if desired. The route is suitable for walkers of a reasonable level of fitness and there are only a few sections with very steep ascents. However, the possibility of high temperatures, the weight of a tent and the need to be able to navigate in certain places should be taken into account when deciding which sections to walk and when.

Waymarking

The route is marked with red-and-white markings which appear on specific signposts, small markers and often on convenient landmarks, such as rocks or trees. The signposts show the next place on the route and, often, the estimated time to get there. The route was created and marked in 1996–1999 by the *Federación Andaluza de Montañismo* (FAM), the regional mountaineering agency, in partnership with other bodies. Since then, the maintenance and marking of the route has been carried out by different agencies at local and regional levels. In some places, lack of resources has meant that the waymarking has barely been refreshed since this date. In other areas the marking is excellent. As a result, the quality and consistency of the marking is very varied from province to province and from section to section. You will often notice a sudden change in marking when crossing a provincial boundary. Some stages require good navigation skills, patience and detective work to find the route after years without maintenance of the signs, and other sections have been rerouted along roads by FAM, to avoid disputes over access or poorly maintained sections.

This guide will help the walker make decisions about which sections to walk, dividing the route into potential day stages, detailing all the facilities available and summarising the terrain, height and landscape. It also indicates

A typical GR7 signpost

where waymarking is particularly poor and occasionally suggests alternatives where the route is very hard to follow due to lack of signage. A summary of all the routes, including this information, can be found in Appendix A.

Deciding which sections to walk

Walkers need to decide which of the two GR7 routes in Andalucía to take. Both are part of the official waymarked route, which divides at Villanueva de Cauche in Málaga province. The Northern Fork heads through Córdoba and Jaén provinces whilst the Southern Fork passes through Almería and Granada. The routes rejoin at Puebla de Don Fadrique, the last town on the GR7 in Andalucía. The final section of the Southern Fork from La Calahorra onwards has not been promoted or maintained and is more of a challenge to follow.

The book is divided into three sections: Part 1 describes the first section of the route, before the split; Part 2 describes the Northern Fork; and Part 3 describes the Southern Fork. It is possible to walk the entirety of the 717.8km northern route (Part 1 plus the Northern Fork) in 34 to 41 days. The southern route (Part 1 plus the Southern Fork) is 735km long and takes 35 to 42 days to walk. The table below summarises these routes.

Northern Fork

The Northern Fork takes you into beautiful unspoilt areas not yet on the tourist trail, along winding tracks and paths through the olive groves, mountains and natural parks of Córdoba and Jaén.

In Córdoba you follow pretty, old woodland paths in the Parque Natural de la Sierra Subbética, with stunning views across the Subbética mountains,

Route	walking days	distance (km)	hours	possible tent days
PART 1	**13–17**	**269.5**	**78h00**	**2**
Cádiz province	6–9	161.5	46h00	2
Málaga province	7–8	108.0	32h00	
PART 2: NORTHERN FORK	**21–24**	**448.3**	**118h25**	**3**
Málaga province	5–6	107.4	25h40	1
Córdoba province	3	55.5	16h30	
Jaén province	13–15	285.4	76h15	2
NORTHERN ROUTE TOTAL (Part 1 & Northern Fork)	*34–41*	*717.8*	*196h25*	*5*
PART 3: SOUTHERN FORK	**22–25**	**465.5**	**130h30**	
Málaga province	2	46.0	11h30	
Granada province	20–23	419.5	119h	3
SOUTHERN ROUTE TOTAL (Part 1 & Southern Fork)	*35–42*	*735.0*	*208h30*	*5*

Viewpoint overlooking Villanueva de Tapia (Southern Fork, Málaga province, Stage 13A)

and visit the small town of Rute, famed for its liqueur – *anís* – and Priego de Córdoba, a striking historic town on a plateau. In Jaén the route takes you through the most important mountain ranges in the province: the Sierra Sur, the Sierra Mágina and the Sierras de Cazorla, Segura y las Villas. You get a taste of the beautiful natural wild spaces in the province, especially in the sections which pass through the largest natural park in Andalucía, the Parque Natural de Cazorla, Segura y las Villas and the Parque Natural de la Sierra Mágina.

You also pass through picturesque historic towns and villages including Alcalá la Real, dominated by its eighth-century castle, and the vibrant and beautiful Cazorla. The route then crosses over into the Granada province to join

up with the Southern Fork of the GR7 in Puebla de Don Fadrique.

Southern Fork

At the divide in Málaga province, the Southern Fork heads into the hills along the foot of the Sierra de las Cabras and down into the province of Granada. The route in Granada is best known for the section in the Alpujarras, with its pretty winding ancient paths joining the dots between tiny whitewashed Berber villages and breathtaking views of snowy peaks. However its less-walked sections are also memorable – from the wild green expanses of three natural parks to the immense sun-baked desert landscapes of the *altiplano*.

En route you pass through towns and villages with a rich history, including the beautiful town of Alhama de Granada

29

View of Tajo del Gomer and Doña Ana (Southern Fork, Málaga province, Stage 13B)

with its dramatic gorge and relaxing *balneario* (spa bath) and the villages of the Alpujarras, such as Lanjarón. This fork also crosses briefly into Almería province, through Bayárcal, its highest village at 1255m, and then climbs further over the pine-forested pass of Puerto de la Ragua (2000m). From here it crosses the arid plains of the Marquesado del Zenete then takes you up into the rugged mountains of the Sierra de Baza on its way to Puebla de Don Fadrique and the end of the GR7 in Andalucía.

WEATHER AND WHEN TO GO

The climate in Andalucía is Mediterranean and the hottest and driest of anywhere in Spain. Although it varies slightly depending on whether you are inland or on the coast, in general it is very hot and dry in the summer months, especially July and August. Temperatures can exceed 40°C inland and it is best

to avoid walking during this period. Winters are mild on the coast and cool inland, but along the route there is very little in the way of tourist infrastructure open during winter (with the exception of the ski resorts in the Sierra Nevada). The best times to go therefore are spring and autumn, March to June and September to October.

While the Sierra de Grazalema natural park in Cádiz province is noted as one of the wettest places in Spain, the likelihood of consistent rainfall over consecutive days on most of the route is low even in the spring and autumn months. Temperatures in the spring and autumn are warm and make for very pleasant walking although it can still get very hot, especially in June when it may be better to avoid walking in the middle of the day. Conversely, in the higher sections of the route (the Sierra Mágina and the Cazorla, Segura y las Villas natural park in Jaén and in the Alpujarras in

Granada in particular) the temperature, though warm during the day, can plummet overnight and it is worth having a warm sleeping bag if you plan to camp.

Aside from the temperature, the abundant wildflowers make spring a wonderful time to visit Andalucía (see 'Wildlife').

Most Spanish people take their holidays over Easter and in July or August and at other times many places can be extremely quiet, the natural parks, in fact, almost empty, and accommodation should be available (see 'Where to stay').

HOW TO GET THERE

You can to travel to Spain from the UK relatively inexpensively by train, plane or ferry.

By train

The quickest way is to take the Eurostar from London to Paris and then a connecting sleeper train from Paris to Madrid. From there you can take a train or another sleeper to Algeciras for the start of the route at Tarifa, or a train or bus to other destinations on the route. For more information on train travel in Spain contact RENFE (tel 902 320 320 www.renfe.es) or on international rail travel from www.raileurope.com or www.seat61.com.

By air

Several airlines fly to Gibraltar or Málaga from various UK cities including www.ryanair.com, www.easyjet.com, www.britishairways.com, www.monarch.co.uk and www.flybe.com. Easyjet also fly to Almería from London. You can find out connection times for buses to Tarifa or other towns on the route from Gibraltar at www.ctmcg.es. There are also good connections from Málaga, and Almería which can be found at www.alsa.es.

Viewpoint in the Sierra de Almijara on route to Albuñuelas (Southern Fork, Granada province, Stage 17B)

Bubión is a typical white-washed village (Southern Fork, Granada province Stage 21B)

By boat

Brittany ferries run from Plymouth or Portsmouth to Santander and from Portsmouth to Bilbao, both in the north of Spain (www.brittany-ferries.co.uk), and these may be a good option if you want to take your car and do sections of the route.

Details of how to get to the start of the route in each province can be found in the respective chapters.

How to get back

There are local transport links connecting most places on the route back to Granada, Jaén or Málaga, from where you can get home (see above). From Puebla de Don Fadrique, the endpoint of both the Northern and Southern Forks, there are two buses a day to Granada (one on Sundays). See the start of each of the three parts of the book for details of bus times and routes.

WHERE TO STAY

The accommodation you will encounter along the route varies considerably. In most areas, accommodation of all types is plentiful but on a few sections of the route there are some quite long stretches without anywhere to stay and you really need to take a tent and camping gear, or make use of public transport, taxis or hitching to skip a section or divert to places with accommodation. The following seven routes are those where it would be useful or essential to have a tent.

Cádiz
- Tarifa – Los Barrios (45km, useful – you can otherwise deviate to Facinas or return to Tarifa by bus from crossroads on N340 and return by bus the following morning)
- Jimena de la Frontera – Ubrique (35km and 1160m of ascent, useful – you can hitch the final 10km)

Málaga
- Villanueva del Trabuco – Villanueva de Tapia (30.6km, useful – can shortcut to reduce to 22.6km)

Jaén
- Frailes – Carchelejo (35.5km and 1755m of ascent, essential)
- Jódar – Quesada (34.4km, useful, camping allowed at Hornos de Peal)

Granada
- Jayena – Albuñuelas (31.1km, useful, could be skipped by bus)
- La Calahorra – Narváez (53.5km and 1660m of ascent, essential)

The rest of the route can easily be walked between hostels and hotels, although, if you do choose to take a tent, there are also options throughout for camping (official campsites are in the place boxes and the route summary table in Appendix A). There are more campsites on the Southern Fork than the Northern Fork.

Hotels have a star rating from one to five, according to facilities. The stars are supposed to indicate price bands but are set by local authorities and vary from province to province. *Pensiones* and *hostales* are also star-rated, from one to three. We have indicated the prices in the accommodation listed according to the least expensive high season price for one night for two people (either sharing a room or camping). The price of single rooms varies significantly, with some hotels charging the same price or almost the same price as for a double room and other charging as little as half. Prices

Approaching Puebla de Don Fadrique (Southern Fork, Granada province Stage 34B)

are also dramatically lower in the low season.

- (A) Budget – under €40
- (B) Mid range – €41–70
- (C) Expensive – €71–100
- (D) Luxury – over €101

Accommodation is only likely to be booked up in August, Easter and for other local fiestas. However, if you're doing a long day and planning to arrive late, you may want to call ahead to have the comfort of knowing a bed is waiting for you.

TYPES OF ACCOMMODATION

Albergue – A basic hostel often with dormitories, but sometimes only available to groups and need to be booked in advance.

Apartamento – self-catering flats often let for a minimum period of two days.

Camping – There are three types of camping ground:

- Free permitted camping areas in national and natural parks, often without any facilities but sometimes with a drinking fountain and benches. Further information on this is provided, where available, in each of the natural park information boxes.

- Registered campsites for which you have to pay. These are divided into three categories according to facilities, from showers and toilets to swimming pools, bar/restaurants, shop and laundry. Many campsites also have bungalows.

- It is also worth asking about camping on private land as people are often amenable to you putting up a tent, as long as you ask permission first.

Casa rural – country houses let out as whole self-catering houses or by the room. Many of them are tastefully renovated traditional buildings. They are often family-run businesses and can have real character. Those let on a whole-house basis are often only available for a minimum of two nights but it is worth asking if you only want a night.

Hostal – simple small guesthouse or hotel with fewer facilities and services and therefore generally cheaper than a hotel (and not to be confused with a hostel).

Hotel – likely to be slightly more expensive and more comfortable than a hostal with the same number of stars.

Pensión – standard budget accommodation, usually small places offering rooms for the night, often above a bar.

Refugio – hostel in mountain areas and natural parks; as with *albergues* not always open access. They sometimes need booking ahead and are only for groups.

FACILITIES

Depending on which section of the route you are walking, the frequency of refreshment stops, accommodation and other facilities varies quite significantly. It is possible to walk the vast majority of the route in manageable day walks which take you from one village with accommodation and food to another. In some sections of the route, particularly the Alpujarras, you will pass through several villages each day, all with drinking fountains, and most with cafés, bars and grocers.

However, there are a few sections which are more remote, mainly those which go through natural parks. These require you to stock up on supplies and carry a tent. If you prefer not to carry camping gear these sections can be avoided by taking public transport (see each section for details of bus times and routes). You can check the facilities available on each route and in each village using the symbols in the information boxes and route descriptions. They are also summarised in the table in Appendix A.

Most facilities (shops, pharmacies, tourist offices and museums) are closed for a long lunchtime *siesta* of at least two hours. There is some variation but common opening hours are 9.30am–2pm and 5–8pm, although bakers and bars will often be open as early as 6.30am if you want to pick up bread or grab a quick coffee first thing. Most shops close on Saturday afternoons and shops and many bars close on Sundays, with some also closed on Mondays. There is a plethora of local public holidays, some of which can be specific to individual villages and so hard to predict. It

is best to have a little extra food in case you are caught out and find everything unexpectedly shut for the day, and also worth asking locals whether there are any upcoming fiestas. Where there is no dedicated tourist information office, the town hall (*ayuntamiento*) is the best place to go for information about services and facilities in a town or village. They will often have lists of accommodation and transport information and can advise on health centres and so on.

MAPS AND GUIDES

The maps provided in this book are intended as a guide and, due to the limitations of space, can only give an indication of the route. Anyone walking the GR7, or any part of it, must take detailed topographical maps and/or a GPS with maps and routes. It is also worth noting that many road numbers have been changed and differ from map to map so don't be surprised if roads you come to have a different name to that shown on your map/in this guide. We have used the most up-to-date road numbers as of 2012 but these differ from those shown on some of the maps recommended below.

For hard copy maps, the best option is the 1:25,000 *Servicio Geografico del Ejercito* (Spanish Military Survey) maps. You can buy the maps cheaply online from Spain at www.tiendaverde.es or www.libreriadesnivel.com or from the UK at www.stanfords.co.uk. Leave at least a month for delivery from both. If you can't wait that long, you may be able to buy them in person from Stanfords in London (12–14 Long Acre, Covent Garden; tel 020 7836 1321 to

En route to Arenas (Southern Fork, Granada province, Stage 15B)

check stock); The Map Shop in Upton-on-Severn (15 High Street, Upton upon Severn, Worcestershire WR8 0HJ; tel 0800 085 40 80); or from Cartográfica del Sur in Madrid (C/Valle Inclán 2, tel 958 204 901). Other maps are available for the natural and national parks and for the Alpujarras. These can be purchased from the relevant park offices (see information boxes in the relevant sections).

More up-to-date maps are available electronically. 1:10,000 maps (*Ortofotografía digital de Andalucía en color* (Fecha de vuelo, 2007)) are available to download or buy on disk from the Andaluician Regional Authority at www.juntadeandalucia.es. 1:25,000 maps can be downloaded from the IGN (National Geographic Institute). You can find and download them at http://centrodedescargas.cnig.es.

The Federación Andaluza de Montañismo (FAM), in collaboration with local partners in each area, has published guides in Spanish to the provinces of Córdoba (pre-2006), Cádiz (2006), Málaga (2008) and Jaén (2008). These are available for a small administration charge plus postage by emailing ofitec@fedamon.com or can be downloaded from www.fedamon.com. The hard copy guides come with sketch maps for each stage, but some sections which have changed are now out of date. There are also a few guides in Spanish for parts of the Granada section produced by the Diputación de Granada (1998, 1999, 2000). The most up-to-date (available in English) is from Alhama de Granada to Cádiar and can be downloaded from www.gr7-granada.com for a charge.

Although the FAM guides have not been updated since they were published, the agency does update its GPS routes which can be downloaded from their website. They also have a section with updates and warnings from other walkers. Up-to-date GPS tracks for the whole route can also be downloaded free from the website www.rutasyviajes.net. (See the box at the back of this guide for full instructions.)

WHAT TO TAKE

What you take will vary according to the season in which you are travelling, but, even in summer, be prepared for cold mornings and evenings at high altitude and the occasional rain storm.

Essentials

- Comfortable clothes – several thin layers for dealing with temperature changes throughout the day and at different altitudes
- Comfortable rucksack (try not to overpack and keep the weight down)
- Waterproof jacket and trousers
- Waterproof rucksack cover (not essential) and plastic bags for organising the contents of your rucksack and keeping them dry
- Strong waterproof walking boots with ankle support and good grip (ideally ones that you have already worn in)
- Sandals
- Maps
- Compass
- Whistle
- Torch and headlamp
- Food (have emergency supplies even if you expect to pass through villages with shops and beware the 2–5pm siesta when most shops are shut)

On the Serrato-Ardales road (Cádiz province, Stage 7)

- A water bottle big enough to carry plenty of water (fountains along the route are marked but there is no guarantee that they will have water in summer)
- Sun protection (hat, sunglasses and sun cream are essential)
- First aid kit and toiletries, including a good selection of plasters and blister products, painkillers, insect repellent and antihistamine and ankle supports
- Supply of euros and a credit card
- Tent and camping equipment (essential for a few sections of the GR7, if you are not planning to skip them)

Useful extras
- Water purification tablets
- Walking poles to ease the weight of your pack and to fend off dogs
- A pedometer for check your own progress against the descriptions
- A mobile phone for emergencies – there is reception along much of the route
- Camera
- Lightweight binoculars
- GPS, if you plan to use the downloaded tracks (see 'Maps and Guides')

SAFETY AND EMERGENCIES

In general, Andalucía is a very safe place to travel through. You do not need any vaccinations and if you are an EU citizen you will be covered for healthcare by your European Health Insurance Card (EHIC), available free online or from the Post Office. You should still get travel insurance to cover you for the cost of any medications that you may be prescribed and also to cover you for theft or loss of belongings.

Bites and stings
There are five types of venomous snakes in Spain. The only one that you might come across in Andalucía is the Lataste's viper. Distinguished by its triangular head and distinctive zigzag pattern, it is grey and short (around 50cm) and lives in dry, rocky areas, away from human habitation. It is thankfully rare but if you are unlucky enough to be bitten, seek medical attention immediately as its bite can be fatal and you will need to be treated with a serum (stocked by most Spanish medical centres).

In the more forested sections of the route look out for hairy reddish-brown caterpillars. They can cause an allergic skin reaction if you touch them. There are also scorpions in parts of Andalucía and their sting can be extremely painful but not fatal. Check your boots in the morning!

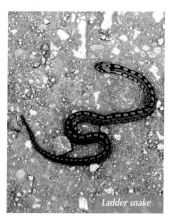

Ladder snake

Bathing pools on the Río Borosa on route to Coto-Ríos (Northern Fork, Jaén province, Stage 29A)

Dogs

Many rural houses and farms in Andalucía have at least one guard dog to scare people away from the property. This means that you are likely to encounter unfriendly dogs at some point on your trip. In general, they will do little more than bark at you and they will usually back down if you bend to pick up a small stone. For the occasional dog that looks as if it might do more than bark it is sensible to carry a walking pole.

For women travellers

While instances of attacks on women in Spain are low, there is a more overtly masculine culture in Spain than in Britain and men are more likely to whistle, sound their car horns and shout comments at you. Try to take sensible precautions to keep yourself safe: don't walk about in towns or cities in the dark by yourself; carry a phone with you if possible; don't accept lifts from strangers; and, if you are wild camping near a town or village, choose your pitch carefully and don't let strangers know where it is.

General walking safety tips

- Tell someone where you are going.
- Keep to a clear path and avoid taking shortcuts unless you are absolutely confident that you know where you are going.
- Be aware that the weather can change rapidly. Bad weather including fog, rain and storms can come in quickly and unexpectedly.
- Be aware that dry river beds and streams can quickly flood in storms.
- Help to protect and maintain the area you are walking through.
- Carry a whistle and torch (the international distress call is six long blasts

39

(or torch flashes at night) evenly spaced over a minute, followed by a minute's pause, and repeated until an answer is received. The answer is three signals per minute.)

Police

There are three different police forces in Spain:

The *Guardia Civil* wear green uniforms and are responsible for national security and customs.

The *Policía Nacional* normally wear a black uniform and white shirts and are responsible for guarding public buildings, the royal family and government figures. They also respond to crimes so you should contact them in the event of any trouble.

The *Policía Municipal* wear blue and white uniforms and spend most of their time controlling local traffic and giving parking tickets, but can be a good source of local information. If you are a victim of theft the local *Policía Municipal* office is also the place to go to report the crime and get the police report that you will need to claim on your insurance.

Emergency contacts

The main number to call in any type of emergency is the European emergency number – 112. This is the urgent police, fire brigade or ambulance number and is also the number to call if you are lost in the mountains as they will connect you to local rescue teams.

Other useful numbers:

- *Policía Nacional* tel 091
- *Policía Municipal* tel 092
- *Guardia Civil* tel 062

- Rapid response health line (24 hours), tel 902 111 444
- Duty pharmacies, tel 010
- British Consular Emergency Service, tel 902 109 356
- British Embassy General Enquiries, tel 917 146 300

Communications

The international code for Spain is 0034, which should be dialled before all the phone numbers given in this book if calling from the UK. The cheapest way to call local numbers from your mobile is to buy a local sim card. Don't rely on having mobile reception on remoter sections of the route, however. The numbers given include the area code. Most villages now have somewhere with wi-fi access or an internet café.

USING THIS GUIDE

The main body of the book is made up of detailed route descriptions. As covered in more detail in 'About the GR7' above, the route descriptions are divided into three parts: Part 1 covers the route in the provinces of Cádiz and Málaga up until the point where the route divides; Part 2 describes the Northern Fork, which continues through Córdoba and Jaén provinces; and Part 3 describes the Southern Fork, which passes through Almería and Granada. Both routes rejoin at Puebla de Don Fadrique, the last town in the Andalucian section of the GR7.

Within these three parts the book is divided into provinces, each with an introduction giving an overview of the route within that province, transport to and within the province, and further

The view south between Guaro and Ventas de Zafarraya (Southern Fork, Málaga province, Stage 13B)

tourist information and information on walking in the area (the small section of the route that crosses into Almería province is included in the Granada province section). These province introductions, combined with the overall introduction to the book and the route summaries in Appendix A, should provide you with the information you need to choose the sections that you would like to walk.

Within each province the route is divided into stages which, in the main, can be walked in a day and always end at a place with accommodation. These sections vary in length, reflecting the location of towns and villages along the route and also the strenuousness of the walking. A handful of stages are longer than can easily be walked in a day. To walk these stages, which are highlighted in the 'Where to stay' section

above, you would need to have a tent, or be prepared to take a shortcut, hitch or take public transport to get to other accommodation. Conversely, there are many stages which include places with accommodation along the way. Details of these are included to give you the flexibility to plan short days or rest days, or put together your own itinerary.

All towns and villages with accommodation have their facilities outlined in an information box. Each box describes the local facilities, sites and sources of further information. Sometimes a range of prices for accommodation indicates seasonal fluctuations or a choice of rooms. Facilities – such as drinking fountains, bars and campsites – situated in places not large enough to merit an information box are highlighted in blue in the body of the text.

41

Walking on to the last stop on the GR7 in Andalucía (Southern Fork, Granada province, Stage 34A)

In many places there is no tourist information office, but often town halls will provide you with local information. Where this is the case, the telephone number for the town hall has been included. Facilities are described in text boxes at the relevant locations.

The timings given in the route headings are based on a person of average fitness. They do not include rests, which should be added in, as a five-hour route could be a full day out, especially in hot sunshine. The descriptions also include timings given on GR7 posts to give an indication of where you are on a route, although these seem to vary in accuracy depending on which area you are in. The text indicates where the timings appear inaccurate.

The route descriptions identify the different types of terrain that the route follows. A 'path' refers to something that is not suitable for vehicles and, generally, single file. A 'track' may be suitable for some 4x4 vehicles and a 'road' is either tarmac or concrete and suitable for all vehicles.

Where the route description refers to places or features shown on the sketch map, these features are highlighted in the text in **bold**.

1 CÁDIZ AND MÁLAGA
TARIFA TO VILLANUEVA DE CAUCHE
CÁDIZ PROVINCE

Montejaque – looking back from the road to Ronda (Stage 6)

43

CÁDIZ PROVINCE

In the Alcornocales Natural Park on route from Jimena de la Frontera to Ubrique (Stage 4)

HIGHLIGHTS OF THE ROUTE IN CÁDIZ PROVINCE

- the 6km stretch of white sand and blue sea that starts the route in Tarifa
- the many birds of prey and vultures circling overhead in the thermals near the coast
- the abundant cork oak groves of the Parque Natural de los Alcornocales
- the imposing limestone crags of the Parque Natural de las Sierras de Grazalema
- the whitewashed mountainside villages, famous throughout Andalucía

The GR7 starts its trip eastwards in Cádiz province where, from Tarifa on the coast, it travels over 160km through striking and ever-changing landscapes.

From Tarifa, at the most southwesterly point of Spain, where the Atlantic meets the Mediterranean, the route takes you through beautiful rolling hills, up to the dramatic Ojén mountains and into the Parque Natural de los Alcornocales, home to one of the world's largest cork oak groves.

You pass through the small town of Los Barrios and then, within the park, you visit the village of Castillo de Castellar, almost entirely located within a medieval fortress perched on a hilltop. From there you carry on to Jimena de la Frontera, dominated by its Arab castle, and then into the wilderness of the Cortes de la Frontera before arriving in the once-Roman town of Ubrique.

The route then crosses the Parque Natural de las Sierras de Grazalema, famous for the rare Spanish fir, caves and spectacular limestone gorges and cliffs. The park is home to the beautiful whitewashed villages of Benaocaz and Villaluenga del Rosario, which you visit before crossing spectacular limestone peaks to enter the Málaga province, just before the village of Montejaque.

TRAVEL

It is possible to get to the start of the route in Tarifa by a variety of means. By train, Algeciras (a very regular 30min bus journey away) is the closest station, with trains going there direct from Granada (4h30) and Madrid (6h or 11h) or from Málaga, Córdoba and Sevilla if you change at Bobadilla. Buses also run regularly from these destinations to Algeciras, or direct to Tarifa from Sevilla (3h) and Málaga (2h).

Within Cádiz province, the Algeciras–Granada train route (three or four trains daily) passes through San Roque-La Línea, Almoraima and Jimena de la Frontera, and some trains also stop in Los Barrios, all of which are on, or very near, the GR7 route.

There are numerous local bus services to and from almost all of the places highlighted on the GR7 route. Contact the bus companies for further information. Most villages also have taxi companies – these are highlighted in the place information boxes.

MORE INFORMATION

Trains
In Spain: www.renfe.es, tel 902 320 320. For international rail travel: www.raileurope.com or www.seat61.com.

Buses
Comes: www.tgcomes.es, tel 902 199 208.

TOURIST INFORMATION

Provincial tourist information office: Pza. de Madrid, s/n. Estadio Ramón de Carranza (Fondo Sur), 4ª Planta – 11011 Cádiz, tel 956 807 061/956 807 223, www.cadizturismo.com.

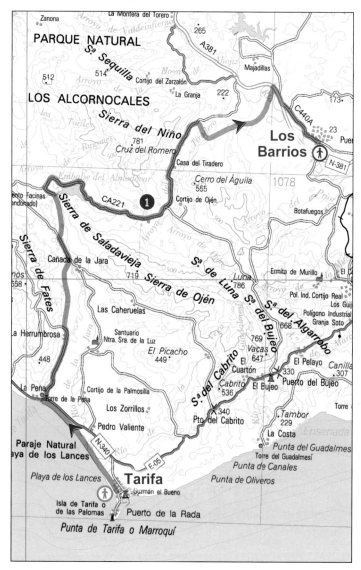

TARIFA TO MONTEJAQUE (161.5KM)

STAGE 1
Tarifa – Los Barrios

Start	Tarifa tourist information office
Distance	45km
Time	12h
Highest point	241m
Height gain	820m
Height loss	810m
Note	Unless you want a very long day, a tent is recommended (see below).

A long beach walk along clean white sands, trying to resist the lure of swimming in the tempting blue sea, followed by a gentle climb up into green hills and shady cork oak groves. Lots of road and track walking.

As this walk makes a very long day a tent is recommended. Alternatively, you can return by bus to Tarifa, detour to Facinas (10km round trip) or walk a very short first day along the beach to one of the accommodation options at the end of the beach, followed by a long second day.

TARIFA 86M POPULATION 17,850

Accommodation, campsite, restaurant/bar/café, drinking fountain, food shop, ATM, telephone, PO, pharmacy, tourist information, transport.

Accommodation and food
There are lots of places to eat – a mix of international restaurants including many with Arabic and Asian influences – and also plenty of hotels, but it is worth booking in summer months. There are three campsites which you pass along the beach (all open all year). **Camping Río Jara** (A) is a large campsite just off the beach after about 4km, has its own shop and restaurant, tel 956 68 05 70, www.campingriojara. com. **Melting Pot Hostel** (A) Very friendly and helpful, just near the start of the route, C/Turriano Gracil 5, tel 956 682906 www.meltingpothostels.com/tarifa.

La Casa Amarilla (B), Central with colourful large rooms, some with lounge and balcony, around traditional courtyard, C/Sancho IV El Bravo 9, tel 956 681 993 www.lacasaamarilla.net.

Further information
Tourist Information Office: Paseo de la Alameda, tel 956 680 993, www.aytotarifa.com.

Transport
Regular buses to and from Málaga, Sevilla, Cádiz and other destinations and other local destinations leave from the bus station at the north end of C/Batalla del Salado in the north of the town. Taxi firms include: tel 675 604 594, tel 956 799 077.

A busy windsurfing and kite surfing resort with a picturesque old town and spectacular views across to Africa from the viewpoint at the top of town. It's worth spending a night here to relax on the beautiful white sand beaches and explore the old town, including the Arab castle of Guzmán el Bueno, the recently restored eighth-century Jerez Gate, the Gothic San Mateo church and the municipal museum.

The walk starts at the tourist office in the centre of **Tarifa**, where there's a signboard with information about the footpath. Head towards the sea, going up the Av. de la Constitución, turning left on the Av. de Andalucía and then second right along a road that brings you to the C/de la Almadraba and down to the **Playa de los Lances**, which is to the right and north of the old stone pier.

Walk along the beach and cross the **Río de la Jara** after about 2.5km. ◄ From here you can walk along a track next to pine trees above the beach. About 6km from the start, just before the Club Mistral Windsurfing Centre, turn right up a track which heads inland through some pine trees and soon brings you to the main **N340** coast road. Don't get confused by the tracks to the earlier windsurfing centre or hotels.

The easiest and most pleasant option is to paddle across.

When you come to the road, turn right and walk for less than 100m until you reach the first turning on your left. Here there is a GR7 sign, next to the Hotel Peña, directing you up a smaller road which winds its way around the side of the Sierra de Enmedio, with the peak of **La Peña** at 448m up to the left.

Keep to this small well-marked road, ignoring all small tracks off it. It is a reasonably good small tarmac road which gradually becomes more gravelly and takes you into more remote and picturesque countryside. ▶ You will pass by lots of cork trees with their barked stripped off, a sight common in this area, which is part of the Parque Natural de los Alcornocales.

The route is straightforward to follow. The only point to watch out for is when, after just under 5km, the main track heads east downhill to the CA9210 road – you don't want to go this way. Instead, keep to the smaller track and continue contouring north round the hillside.

2km after this junction, be careful not to miss a small path off the track down to the right. You stay on this as it crosses a stream and passes a working flour mill. Continue on the same path as it gets wider and comes out on the CA9210, a short distance before the pass, the Puerto de la Torre del Rayo. Turn left up it.

At the pass, stay on the main road, ignoring a smaller track off to the left, and follow the road for just under 1.5km until you reach a track on the right (signposted Saladavieja). Take this track through the beautiful countryside of the **Sierra de Ojén**, with a good chance of seeing birds of prey in the crags up to the right. ▶

This section is less well marked, but if you keep to the main track you shouldn't get lost. You should pass a water works building and then cross a small river with the dam of the **Embalse de Almodóvar** up to your right. Continue following the track up from the other side of the river through a few farms until you reach the CA221 road (19km from Tarifa). Turn right along the road and around the far side of the reservoir, heading east.

> If you wish to **detour into Facinas**, where there is a *pensión*, head left along this road and follow if for 5km to the village, ignoring turnings including one back to the left about halfway along.

From here markings are few and far between, but you stay on the obvious CA221. Keep going through oak woodland, heading towards pasture land and after 7.5km you will reach the beautiful Puerto de Ojén. ▶ Carry on, at first downhill, passing the **Cerro del Águilla** on your right, until

The wind farm you are looking down on to the east is one of the largest in Europe.

The area through which you're passing boasts over 18 species of raptors including short-toed eagle, booted eagle, griffon vulture, tawny owl, eagle owl, buzzard, goshawk and sparrowhawk.

There is an old inn here (only very occasionally open), once the meeting point for horsemen and merchants passing between Cádiz and Algeciras.

Puerto de Ojén

you reach a small track with a gate off to the right after about 6.5km. **Note:** here the official route of the GR7 goes right through the gate but there have been reports of the route being blocked.

Official route

To continue on the official route, if you find it not to be blocked, go through the gate and take the path that goes downhill, not the one which runs alongside the fence. From here the route is hard to find through a maze of little paths. Keep a close eye for frequent markings and small stone cairns. After about 5–10min you should pass through a marked gap in a fence.

A couple of small paths run from here until another fence, and both end up at the same gate. Go through this and carry on along a marked but overgrown path with the Arroyo del Raudal to your right. A little path takes you down to, and across, the stream where you may need to paddle depending on the season. If you miss the path to the stream you will very quickly reach a GR7 sign indicating that you've gone the wrong way.

Across the stream (2.75km from turning off the track) pass the Molino de Enmedio, a water wheel mill. The path quickly turns into a wider track and, when you reach a junction, you turn left. There are then no markings for a while but you continue on this track. You will pass a shady picnic area on your left and then leave the park, passing the Cortijo Jaramillo. The track then crosses the Río Palmones and passes under the **A381** motorway. Here you will find yourself on the C440A road at the Venta del Frenazo (tel 956 620814) (4.5km from the Molino de Enmedio).

To get to Los Barrios turn right for an uninspiring 3.5km walk down the road. 300m after the venta you will see a turning to the left. This is the start of the next section of the route and if you choose to head into **Los Barrios** to sleep or for refreshments, you will need to return to here to rejoin the route. To get in to Los Barrios continue to the roundabout and take the CA9207 in to the town, arriving eventually on the Paseo de Coca.

Alternative route

Alternatively, if the route is blocked it would be easier to continue on the same main track (CA221). Follow the track for a further 6.5km until you come out onto the C440A road which runs next to the A381 motorway. Turn right and, taking care, go along this busy road for an uninspiring 6.5km walk into the centre of Los Barrios. After 2.5km you pass the Venta del Frenazo (956 620814), from where you can follow the route above.

LOS ALCORNOCALES NATURAL PARK

The Parque Natural de los Alcornocales (1678km^2) contains the Iberian peninsula's biggest cork oak woodland and plays a large part in making Spain the world's second largest cork producer, after Portugal.

Wildlife

As well as cork, the park is also home to some of the last remains of sub-tropical forest in Europe, the only others to be found in Turkey. In the humid microclimates of the canutos – deep, narrow valleys carved out by streams – are tropical trees and vegetation such as wild olives, pyrean oaks, rare ferns, laurel, hazel, alder and rhododendron, giving an insight into what parts of Europe would have looked like in primeval times.

Forty years ago the park would have been home to bears and wolves, but these have now been hunted to extinction and you are more likely to see red and roe deer and smaller mammals such as otters, foxes and polecats. Wild boar also inhabit the park but, as they are nocturnal, you're less likely to come across them.

The park has 226 species of birds from 56 families – including several species of eagle. It is a perfect habitat for them, with its huge forests and rocky outcrops and is situated in an ideal location for a stop-off on the migratory route to Africa.

Cork
Cork comes from the cork oak tree, *Quercus suber*. It is the only tree which is able to sustain cork being taken from it. The bark is harvested from mature trees, those at least 25 years old, just once every nine years in the spring or summer. Specialised workers cut the oak's cork, *pela*, and create piles of cork, *panas*, which you can see waiting to be transported for sorting as you pass through cork groves.

Cork production has been happening in this way for up to 3000 years and nowadays the main use of cork, which is a very sustainable resource, is for bottle corks, which make up 60 per cent of the market.

Further information
There are two park visitor centres, both tel 956 679 161.

LOS BARRIOS 23M POPULATION 22,850

Accommodation, restaurant/bar/café, drinking fountain, food shop, ATM, telephone, PO, pharmacy, tourist information, transport.

Accommodation and food
A mix of eateries including tapas, pizzas, Chinese and fast food and a choice of places to stay including: **Hotel Real** (B) modern, smart and near the centre with 20 rooms, free wi-fi and meals available in cosy restaurant downstairs, Av Pablo Picasso 7, tel 956 620 024 www.hotelreallosbarrios.com; **Hotel Montera** (B) Pleasant modern hotel with pool, free wi-fi and restaurant on the southern edge of town, Av Carlos Cano, tel 856 220 220, www.hotelmontera.com.

Further information
Tourist information: Paseo de la Constitución 15, tel 956 58 25 04
www.losbarrios.es

Transport
There are bus connections to Algeciras and Ronda local towns including Castellar and Jimena. Taxi firms include: tel 609 592 029/956 620 076.

A charming small town centred around two plazas, one busy with cafés and bars, and the other, the Plaza de la Iglesia, the focus of the old town with the old church and tower, grand town hall and casino. It is also known for being the start of the bull route and has many bull farms in the vicinity. There is a good natural history museum (C/Calvario 14, tel 956 621 169).

STAGE 2
Los Barrios – Castillo de Castellar

Start	Paseo de Coca, Los Barrios
Distance	33km
Time	9h30
Highest point	250m
Height gain	750m
Height loss	520m

Good hill tracks start the route, followed by a long road walk with the reward of the beautiful view of the hill-top castle of Castellar to end the day.

The first 3.5km of this stage retraces your steps from the day before. Leave from the west of Los Barrios to come to a petrol station on a roundabout at a motorway exit. Take the service lane which leaves from here, the C440A. Follow this road until you come to a junction, where you turn right. Once on this new road you stay on it, ignoring all turnings. You go through the gate to some military barracks (*el acuartelamiento de Charco Redondo*) and continue until you come to a gate marked *campo de tiro* (shooting range) and you have to turn right to climb on a dirt track.

Go through a new gate which blocks vehicle access to the estate and from here you climb, following the 'Parque Natural' signs which mark the Parque Natural de los Acornocales boundary running along the left hand side of the track. When you reach the top, you are rewarded with

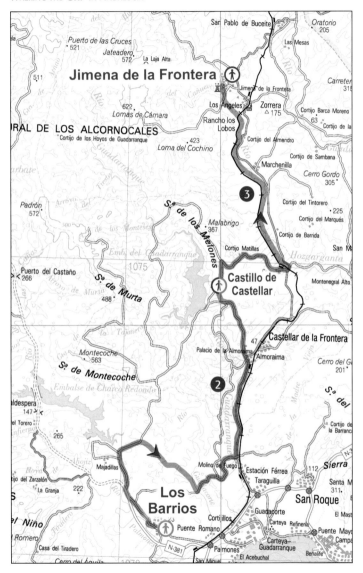

spectacular views including the **Embalse de Charco Redondo** in the distance.

Keep following the same track and you'll come to a sign telling you that you have come 2h20 from Los Barrios. Continue on the right here, climbing until you reach the next pass marked with a sign, Castellar 5h50. ▸

Take the right fork and follow the route downhill. The track is bordered by fences to livestock and arable fields. You arrive at a rubbish dump and come out at junction. You take the track to the left which runs along the landfill's perimeter fence. Just when the fence ends, you will see a gate about 30m away on the right. Go through this and head downhill on the track to the left. The terrain from here is rougher and the track is in poor condition. Arrive at the junction with a more open track with a sign, Los Barrios 4h and Castellar 4h30. Turn right and stay on this wide level track until you hit the CA5121 road. ▸

Turn left along the road and stay on this same road (CA5121) passing several junctions. The road climbs over the hill and nearly 5km from the point where you joined the road you reach a bridge over the **Río Guadarranque** and a junction with the busier A405, where there are two bar/restaurants, a pleasant refreshment stop; one of them is also a hotel (Hotel los Timbales (A) 956 786 046).

From here it is a 2h walk along a busy road to **Castellar de la Frontera**, the road again following the park boundary. Make use of the green cycle route on the left where you can to avoid the busy road. ▸ There are a couple of bars along the way that might be open.

After 6km you will reach a junction in **Almoraima**, the area by the station on the outskirts of Castellar which is a protected natural area that is rich in wildlife. ▸ Continue round on the main road to carry on to **Castillo de Castellar** (nearly 7km away) or, if you want to stay in the new town, you can turn off to the right at the junction from which it is a 1km walk.

There are two places called Castellar – the new town Castellar de la Frontera and the old town, Castillo de Castellar. The signs all refer to the former which is 1h40 before the old town on the hill.

You are passing through private land and may come across cattle on the loose.

The plethora of storks' nests on the tops of the electricity pylons are a pleasant distraction.

There is a cork processing centre here and you can see the piles of cork.

CASTELLAR DE LA FRONTERA 25M POPULATION 3187

Accommodation, restaurant/bar/café, drinking fountain, telephone, PO, pharmacy, tourist information, transport.

Accommodation and food
With most tourism focused on Castillo de Castellar, food and accommodation
option are limited, but there are a couple of bars in the town and luxury accommodation on the outskirts.

Hotel la Almoraima (B) is a beautifully restored 17th century convent housing a restaurant and 23 rooms, Ctra. Algeciras-Ronda, tel 956 693 002, www.
laalmoraimahotel.com. **NH Castellar** (C) is a large luxury hotel with swimming pool, tennis courts, and sauna on the way into Castellar, Ctra Castellar-
Almoraima, tel 956 693 018, www.nh-resorts.com/nuestros-resorts/nh-castellar.

Further information
Town hall: Pza de Andalucía, 956 693 001, www.castellardelafrontera.es.

Transport
Buses run to Algeciras, La Línea and to Jimena and other local towns.

This neat modern town 8km from Castillo de Castellar was planned and built in
the late 1960s to provide better living conditions for families living in the historic
but cramped Castillo. Many moved to Castellar in 1971 and the wide streets and
modern houses are a big contrast to its hilltop neighbour.

To carry on to **Castillo de Castellar** continue round to the left
on the main road. After 10 minutes you arrive at a roundabout and follow signs for Castillo de Castellar. Follow the
road (CA5131), but to cut out a section of road walking look
out for a small fork off to the right between the Km2 and Km3
signs, marked with a sign claiming 1h to Castillo de Castellar.
This pretty route through the trees brings you back onto the
road further up, where you can turn left for La Jarandilla
campsite, or continue along the road past the *venta* (bar) of
the same name.

After the bar, at Km4 on the road take a marked shortcut up to the left, which brings you back onto the road
briefly at Km8 before you leave it again on the right (signposted Castillo de Castellar 25min) to follow on the historic cobbled route up to the castle. After a steep climb with
panoramic views, you rejoin the road just at the entrance
to the village and from here make the final climb up to the
castle gates.

The eponymous castle of Castillo de Castellar

CASTILLO DE CASTELLAR 240M POPULATION 200

Accommodation, campsite, restaurant/bar/café, drinking fountain, food shop, telephone, transport.

Accommodation and food
There are lovely rooms and camping to choose from and a couple of places to eat, a few local bars including **Bar Al Andalus** and a restaurant inside the castle walls: **Complejo Turístico de Castellar** (B), 18 stylish hotel rooms and 9 well equipped pretty whitewashed houses inside the castle walls, C/Rosario, tel 956 693 150, www.tugasa.com.

Further information
Visit the Natural Park info centre if you are around in office hours.

Transport
Buses run to Algeciras, La Línea and to Jimena and other local towns.

This beautiful hilltop village has been inhabited since prehistoric times and has a rich history as a medieval fortress and throughout the conflict between the Christians and the Muslims. It has impressive views down over the Embalse de Guadarranque. In 1983, the Government declared village and castle a 'Historical and Artistic Monument' and invested in their restoration.

57

STAGE 3
Castillo de Castellar – Jimena de la Frontera

Start	Castle in Castillo de Castellar
Distance	20.5km
Time	6h
Highest point	250m
Height gain	170m
Height loss	340m

After leaving behind the castle of Castillo, the route to Jimena is a long flat one following the railway line most of the way through rural landscapes with the opportunity of seeing many eagles overhead.

See map in Stage 2.

From here you will catch glimpses of the huge Embalse de Guadarranque to the west above which the castle is perched.

You'll follow this almost all the way into Jimena: if in doubt, where the track divides stick to the branch closest to the railway line.

From the castle head back to the road, which is now called the CA512, and follow it out in the opposite direction from which you arrived and down, ignoring a smaller track to the left which takes you down to an old fountain. ◄ After 1.5km you reach the Finca Boyd and the tarmac comes to an end, but the unpaved road continues downhill to the right and on into the trees.

Follow this track, which is very rough and stony in places, looking out for birds of prey. After 15min you arrive at two gates. Go through the left hand one and follow a heavily eroded track gently downhill all the way to another farm (about 1h10 after leaving Castillo). Here you pass through another gate and follow a broad track across flat farmland. Take a left hand fork and head across a vast flat field towards the railway line before turning right, and walking at least 1.5km in what seems to be the wrong direction. Then turn left and about 7km from Castillo you reach the railway line near the old Castellar **train station**. Cross the railway tracks and turn left along a path running next to the train line. ◄ After about 8km, all unmarked, you come to a signpost (Jimena 1h30, Castellar 4h30).

Here the wide track that you were on crosses the railway, but you turn off down a narrow path to the right that continues alongside the railway. After crossing a small stream

with a broken wooden bridge you reach another sign (1h15) directing you along a wider track. Keep following the railway, but don't cross it until you reach a mark near Rancho los Lobos (about 2km after joining the wider track). Follow this to the left and soon cross the railway line. **Jimena de la Frontera** appears on the hill in front of you and you remain on the same road as its winds towards the **Río Hozgarganta**. Cross this and take the left fork road (almost straight ahead) climbing very steeply up into the village (C/de Pasada de Alcala). If you don't want to enter the village, turn left 100m after the bridge and follow the signposted Río Hozgarganta footpath round the back of the village to rejoin the road on the other side at the white cross on the hill.

Approaching Jimena de la Frontera

JIMENA DE LA FRONTERA 200M POPULATION 10,500

Accommodation, campsite, restaurant/bar/café, drinking fountain, food shop, cashpoint, telephone, PO, pharmacy, tourist information, transport.

Accommodation and food

A selection of *casas rurales*, a few *hostales* and a campsite:

Camping los Alcornocales (A). Just off the road out of the village on the GR7 route, this large campsite has a bar–restaurant, shop, swimming pool and power, tel 956 640 060, www.campinglosalcornocales.com. **Casa Henrietta** (B) has 12 characterful rooms, sun terrace and tapas restaurant. C/Sevilla 44, tel 956 648 130, www.casahenrietta.com. **Casa Rural Posada la Casa Grande** (B) is Norwegian-run with a good atmosphere. C/Fuente Nueva 42, tel 956 64 11 20/622 16 79 44, www.posadalacasagrande.es. **Hostal el Anón** (B) has 12 rooms, rooftop swimming pool, sun terrace and restaurant with home-cooked food, including great vegetarian options. A vibrant place with an American owner who is knowledgeable about walking and bird watching in the area. C/Consuelo 34, tel 956 640 113, www.hostalanon.com.

Further information
Town hall: C/Sevilla 61, tel 956 640 254, www.jimenadelafrontera.es.

Transport
Several trains a day stop at Jimena on the line between Algeciras and Granada. Buses run to Algerciras and local towns.

Taxis: tel 956 640 293/956 640 187.

Dominated by its castle, an Arab fortress built on Roman ruins, Jimena is a delightful ancient village built on a steep hillside and looking down over fertile green valleys with orange groves and cork forested hills. Many British residents enjoy its sunshine and relaxed pace of life. From the castle you can see as far as Algeciras and Gibraltar.

STAGE 4
Jimena de la Frontera – Ubrique

Start	Centre of Jimena de la Frontera
Distance	35km
Time	10h
Highest point	840m
Height gain	1160m
Height loss	995m
Note	A tent is essential if you wish to break the journey

A beautiful route almost entirely on small paths taking you far from civilization to lofty passes and remote cork tree groves. With almost 40km separating the two places, you will either need to wild camp en route to avoid a very long day, or plan to hitch a lift or call a taxi when you arrive at the road, about 10km from Ubrique.

Leaving Jimena de la Frontera

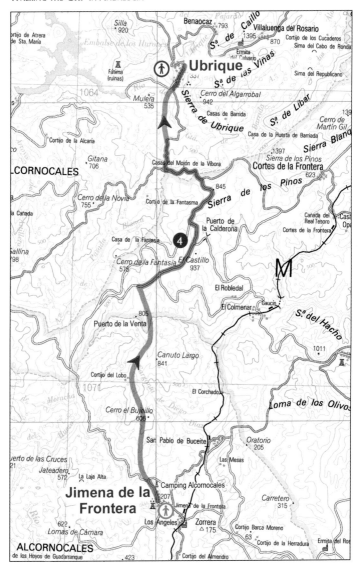

To get onto the route to Ubrique, leave Jimena on the main road north. Just after you pass **Camping Alcornocales** you will reach a junction in the road and directly opposite is the well-marked GR7 path heading steeply uphill. Climb this initially cobbled path, which is known as the Sendero Vereda Ubrique – Asomidallas, until you reach a wide track after about a kilometre. Cross over and carry on up the hillside as marked, following the line of the stone wall. Be sure to look back at the great views of Jimena.

When you reach the brow of the hill, a GR7 signpost (Jimena 1h, Ubrique 9h) and a wider track go through the gate and carry on upwards on small paths, keeping the stone wall close on your left until you come to a second gate through which is a wider track again. ▶ Follow this, and when you come to an unmarked junction take the right fork. Pass one turning on the right but take the second one (which has a post further on).

At the next junction, about 1.5km further on, you don't take either of the forks, but instead head steeply up to the right again following a wall. The rocky tops of the Altos de Paneron and Cerro de Marín, which you are aiming for, are up to your right. The path here is vague and disappears entirely in places among the rocks, but after about 10min of ascent there is a gate on your right with a GR7 post clearly visible.

Go through the gate and follow the now clear track left up to the top of the hill. Follow a signpost (Ubrique 7h30) left along the top of a shoulder with stunning views over the barren hills on either side.

The track brings you to two gates, take the left one and carry on down through cork oaks. You'll then reach a gate marked 'private property', but this is the route so go through. After a short distance you will come to a post directing you right into some more dense woodland and onto an attractive path.

▶ At the only uncertain divide take the left fork to emerge a few minutes later at the **Puerto de la Venta** with a gate ahead of you. Go through the gate and then downhill gently through more corks. The scenery opens out a bit when you reach a sign for Ubrique (6h).

Contour round the hillside on a wide track and then head left, and westwards, still on the track through pine trees. When you meet another track turn right, crossing into Málaga province, although you leave it again before arriving

Alternatively you can follow the wider track up to this next gate.

This section is well marked.

in Ubrique. There are two more right turns after this and then you arrive at a pass signposted Carrera del Caballo and Ubrique 4h (17km from the start). Carry on from here on the main track, contouring round with **El Castillo** (hilltop with phone masts on it) up to your right.

As you pass by the summit you'll come to a cow shelter, Albergue la Calderone. From there start heading downwards past an annoying sign claiming that it is 4h15 to Ubrique (when the one you walked past half an hour ago said 4h). ◄

> If you have a tent and want to stop for the night, wild camping is permitted in this area.

As you head downwards crossing over an intersection, the distinctive peak of Peñón del Berrueco dominates the horizon, Ubrique lying beyond and to west of it. Ignore two right turns and soon you should reach the A373 Cortes to Alcalá de la Frontera road. Here there is a signpost and board with a route map (Jimena 7h, Ubrique 3h) – but be warned, after a good half hour's walking you will meet another sign saying 2h45.

Turn left and walk on this small road until you reach a 2h45 sign. Here, just before the road junction to Ubrique, you enter the Parque Natural de las Sierra de Grazalema (see information box in Stage 5 below) and head off on a small marked path in front of a bar which cuts out many of the longer loops of the road. Don't worry if you miss a shortcut, just keep following the road direction and you'll come to the next one. This brings you all the way to the southern edge of **Ubrique**, visible nestled among the hills, then join the road into the town itself.

UBRIQUE 337M POPULATION 16,870

Accommodation, restaurant/bar/café, drinking fountain, food shop, cashpoint, telephone, PO, pharmacy, tourist information, transport.

Accommodation and food

Good selection of eateries, but very limited accommodation for such a large place. The only hotels in the town itself are **Hotel Ocurris** (B), clean and smart with the luxury of deep baths: Av. Solís Pascual 51, tel 956 463 939, www.hotelocurris.com; and **Hostal Rosario** (A), reasonable and central with ensuites or shared bathrooms: C/Botica 3, tel 956 461 046.

On the way into Ubrique on the Cortes road, **Hotel Sierra de Ubrique** (B) is a very grand establishment: Ctra Ubrique-Cortes, Km33, 700, tel 956 466 805, www.hotelsierradeubrique.com.

Further information
Tourist Information: C/Moreno de Mora 19 A, tel 956 46 49 00,
www.ayuntamientoubrique.es.

Transport
Buses run to Málaga, Cádiz, Ronda and local destinations. Taxis: tel 608 549
954/610 909 777.

A sizeable town with all the amenities you could need, but still retaining some
of the charm of a typical *pueblo blanco*. If you can manage some more walking,
it is worth heading up to the old town for the views over the whole of Ubrique
and the interestingly named Iglesia de Nuestro Señora de la O (Church of Our
Lady of the O).

Famous for its leather, produced from the livestock which are reared in the
surrounding areas, every other shop seems to sell leather goods.

STAGE 5
Ubrique – Montejaque

Start	Hotel Ocurris in Ubrique
Distance	28km
Time	7h30
Highest point	1044m
Height gain	1230m
Height loss	880m

A spectacular section with steep climbs that are more than worth it for the
stunning views across the limestone crags and spacious valleys of the Sierra de
Grazalema natural park.

Ubrique – Benaocaz (4km, 1h)
From the Hotel Ocurris go up the C/Doctor Solis Pascual and
turn right along the Av. de Manuel de Falla. Turn right along
the Av. de Miguel Riguera and then left to leave Ubrique at
the north end of town on the Camino de Benaocaz, which

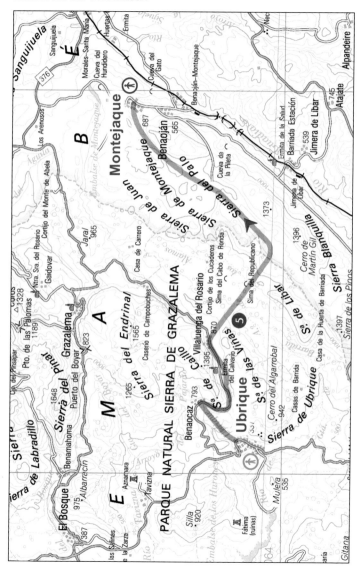

Benaocaz

you will find just behind the grand Convento de Capuchinos. A sign points you uphill to **Benaocaz** and you climb for about 3.5km up a steep roughly cobbled Roman path. When you arrive at the main road cross over to go in to the village or turn right along the road to continue to Villaluenga.

BENAOCAZ 793M POPULATION 750

Accommodation, restaurant/bar/café, drinking fountain, food shop, cashpoint, telephone, PO, pharmacy, tourist information, transport.

Accommodation and food

A few nice cafés, bars and restaurants with sunny outside seating and good views and a limited selection of places to stay:

Los Chozos del Puente del Moro (B), just outside Benaocaz, has thatched circular houses along with a restaurant, swimming pool and gardens: Finca el Lentiscal y Pereo, tel 954 637 205, www.loschozos.com. **Hostal San Antón** (B) is a small, straightforward hostal with 5 rooms: Pza de San Anton 5, tel 956 125 577. **Posada el Parral** (B) is a rustic guesthouse housed in an old mountain refuge with pool, restaurant and terrace with great views: C/de las Laderas del Parral, tel 956 125 565, www.posadaelparral.es.

Further information
Town hall – Plaza de las Libertades, tel 956 125 500, www.benaocaz.es – also
has a list of flats to rent.

A small whitewashed village with pretty, shady little squares and a striking church
tower with red decoration. If you have the energy, it's worth climbing to the top
of the village to see the archaeological ruins and the impressive views. You can
also visit the Museo Historico (c/Jabonería) with information on life in the region
since historic times.

> **Benacoaz – Villaluenga del Rosario (5.5km, 1h20)**
> Leave Benaocaz on either the top or bottom road out of town
> heading south and you'll come to a sign where they meet,
> pointing you along the road (Villaluenga del Rosario 1h20).
> Pass the Santa Fountain on your left and after 1km you reach
> a picnic area on your right. Here a steep path which takes
> you off the road with a signpost (Villaluenga 40min). Where
> the path disappears you rejoin the road and keep climbing,
> though more gently, with the **1395m peak** of Navazo Alto
> of the Sierra del Caíllo to your left, up to the next village,
> passing an outdoor climbing wall on your left as you enter
> **Villaluenga del Rosario**.

VILLALUENGA DEL ROSARIO 1000M POPULATION 485

Accommodation, restaurant/bar/café, drinking fountain, food shop, cashpoint,
telephone, PO, pharmacy, tourist information, transport.

Accommodation and food
A few bars and cafés and one smart restaurant which is part of the only hotel: **Hotel
la Posada** (B), a fairly luxurious place in a beautiful old building, with 6 double
rooms and 1 single, all with air conditioning, TV and telephone, with a restaurant
downstairs with a range of traditional dishes from the area. Well signposted from the
entrance to the village, C/Torre 1, tel 956 126 119, www.tugasa.com/hotel14_1.php.

A picturesque village with a laid back atmosphere and a dramatic setting, the
highest in the province, set among dramatic limestone rock faces. It has the area's
main caving and potholing school and is famous for its award-winning sheep and
goat cheeses, which you can purchase direct from the factory on your way out.
There are various short walks which leave from the village and the area is great
for bird watching – look out for signboards with identification charts on the route.

Villaluenga del Rosario – Montejaque (18.5km, 5h10)
Take the road east and, just as you reach the end of the village and a large sign for a recycling centre, turn off to the
right along a path signposted as the Llanos del Republicano
walking route. Climb the hill on a concrete road, admiring
the views back over the village and the Sierra de Bandera
behind you. Ignore the track off to the right. After the top of
the hill go through a gate and 300m beyond the top of the
hill in the shade of some trees there is a post directing you
down a wide track to the right (Puerto de Correo 2h).

Follow the track down and turn left across an open
field at another signpost (1h30). Go through a big metal
gate and look out for a post to the right (Llanos de Líbar
4km). Follow a small stream on your left as you bend
around steadily to the left. You'll pass by two of the deep
potholes (simas) for which the natural park is famous, the
second, **Sima del Republicano**, by a gate, 600 metres away
down a signposted path. The route soon takes you steeply
uphill through the rocky terrain of the **Sierra de Líbar**, part
of the Parque Natural de las Sierra de Grazalema, towards
the pass, climbing over 200m in height. There is a steep
initial climb followed by a gentler climb and then another

*View of Sierra del
Palo (highest peak
1400m) en route to
Montejaque*

SIERRA DE GRAZALEMA NATURAL PARK

The Parque Natural de la Sierra de Grazalema (517km^2) was Andalucía's first natural park, becoming so in 1984, having been designated a UNESCO Biosphere reserve seven years earlier. Located in both Cádiz and Málaga provinces, it is made up primarily of stunning cliffs and gorges carved out of limestone mountains, the highest of which is El Torreón at 1654m. The nature of limestone, combined with Spain's highest rainfall, means the park is home to some of the largest cave and pothole systems in Spain, with the largest cavern of the Hundidero–Gato system measuring 4km long.

Culturally the area is rich too, with the mountains of the park forming the boundary between the Arab Kingdom of Granada and the Christian Kingdom, Castilla, during the 13th and 14th centuries, although evidence of human occupation dates back much further, evidenced by local cave paintings.

Wildlife
The high rainfall also makes the park rich in vegetation, with over 1300 plant species registered, including the rare Spanish fir, which dates from over 65 million years ago. Discovered in 1837 by a Swiss botanist, it is very resistant to cold and can live at an altitude of up to 1700m.

The park is home to some of Europe's largest griffon vulture colonies as well as black and Egyptian vultures, five types of eagle, ospreys and peregrines along with many smaller birds such as the great spotted woodpecker and hoopoe.

Foxes, badgers, wild boar, wildcats and beech martins can all be found here, as can red and roe deer, which have been reintroduced for hunting.

Further information
Park visitor centre: Cortes de la Frontera, tel 952 154 599.

Park office with maps, permits for restricted areas and information on walking routes: El Bosque, tel 956 727 029.

The views from the top of the pass are dramatic, with the rocky Sierra del Palo and its highest peak at 1400m ahead and the lush valley below.

steep climb before a very gentle ascent through a pass. The path is well marked all the way. ◀ Descending the other side of the hill you cross into Málaga province and come to a signboard and posts but with no information for those heading in this direction. You then pass through a gate and stick to the main (unmarked) path heading downhill before emerging into the expansive and beautiful valley of Llanos de Líbar.

There are no markings here and the path peters out, but stick to the dry stone wall, keeping it on your right, and head towards an old gate where a signpost directs you on to Montejaque, but with the yellow markings of the PRA

252 route. The sign says it is 5h30 but don't despair: the real timing is more like 2h45. Continue along the long flat dirt track and after about 2km you reach an *albergue* (Cortijo de Líbar). ▶

From here there is 3km of gentle downhill walking through shady cork oaks to a sign pointing back to the Cortijo de Líbar and you stay on the main track, which doesn't have many markings but is quite easy to follow. The track crosses a fertile plain, passes a farm on the left and then climbs steadily to a pass. Turn around for spectacular views back over the mountains. There is an initially steep descent down a wide but impressive gorge. Where the route divides, take the right fork which takes you 3.5km downhill under steep cliffs into **Montejaque**, which eventually comes into view just before the entrance to the village where you follow the C/Doctor Gutiérrez towards the centre.

It must be booked ahead in its entirety, but there is a camping area with toilets and picnic benches behind it which is usually available and free to use (tel 952 877 778 to confirm).

MONTEJAQUE 687M POPULATION 1050

Accommodation, restaurant/bar/café, drinking fountain, food shop, cashpoint, telephone, tourist information, transport.

Accommodation and food
A good selection of little places to eat and a few places to stay, mostly upmarket:

Posada del Fresno (B). The owners are wonderful hosts with extensive local knowledge and a great library: C/Miguel de Cervantes 2, Montejaque, tel 952 167 544, www.posadadelfresno.com. **Hotel Palacete de Mañara** (C). Smart with lots of useful information, swimming pool and air conditioning: Pza Constitución 2, tel 952 167 252. **Casas de Montejaque** (C) has luxurious houses set around a swimming pool: C/Manuel Ortega 16, tel 952 168 120, www.montejaque.net, www.casasdemontejaque.net.

Further information
www.montejaque.es.

Montejaque, which comes from the Arabic for 'lost mountain', is a pretty white village and a popular walking base with many shorter routes also departing from here. The centre of the village is the Plaza Constitution with the Santiago el Mayor church and the Hotel Palacete de Mañara, in the mansion that was once the seat of power in the area but also latterly, slightly oddly, a sausage factory.

MÁLAGA PROVINCE

Mountain view on route to Villanueva de Cauche

HIGHLIGHTS OF THE ROUTE IN MÁLAGA PROVINCE

- the dramatic limestone peaks surrounding the pretty village of Montejaque
- Ronda's beautiful architecture and precarious clifftop location
- the magnificent rock faces and gorge of El Chorro
- the 27 spires of Antequera's various churches viewed from the city's castle
- the weird and wonderful landscape of the Parque Natural El Torcal

The GR7 runs for just over 215km through Málaga. This section describes the first 108km of the route, before it divides into two forks. The remaining parts of the route in the province are described in Part 2 and Part 3.

The route enters Málaga over the Puerto del Correo in the Parque Natural de las Sierra de Grazalema, descending into the Montejaque area with its rugged dolomite limestone cliffs. From here it

passes through the spectacularly located Ronda and on into the idyllic mountain villages of El Chorro and Ardales.

At Villanueva de Cauche the route splits into two forks, one (the Northern Fork) heading into the northeast of Málaga province through the olive-ringed villages of Villanueva del Rosario, Villanueva del Trabuco, Villanueva de Tapia, Villanueva de Algaidas, Cuevas Bajas and Cuevas de San Marcos before crossing the Luis de Armiñán bridge over the Río Genil into Córdoba province.

The other (the Southern Fork) heads south into the foothills of the Sierra de las Cabras and down into the province of Granada by way of an old dismantled railway line.

TRAVEL

Ronda (11km) and Antequera (20.5km) are both good places to join or leave the route, with a wide range of public transport options. Other smaller places are also quite well served by local buses and trains.

Trains

The Algeciras–Granada train route (3 or 4 trains daily) passes through Benaoján (very close to Montejaque), Arriate and Ronda. Some trains also stop in El Chorro. For information tel 902 320 320 or visit www.renfe.es.

There are also connections from Ronda with Granada via Antequera and Málaga (1 daily Mon–Sat), Córdoba (2 daily) and Madrid (1 day train, 1 night train).

Antequera is on the line to Granada (6 daily, 1h30), Sevilla (3 daily, 1h45) and Ronda (3 daily, 1h15).

Buses

Several bus companies serve the area with regular buses:

- Comes, tel 952 871 992, www.tgcomes.es: Ronda–Cádiz (5 daily, 2h), Jimena de la Frontera–Algeciras (1 daily, 1h30)
- Los Amarillos, tel 952 187 061, www.losamarillos.es: Ronda–Sevilla (5 daily, 2h30min), Ronda–Ardales– Málaga (every 2h, 1h45)
- Portillo, tel 902 450 550, http://portillo.avanzabus.com: Ronda–Málaga (4 daily, 1h30)
- Automóviles Casado, tel 952 841 957: Antequera–Málaga (every 50min, 1h)
- Alsina Graells 952 841 365, www.alsa.es: Antequera–Granada, Córdoba, Almería
- Useful site for searching buses from over 50 companies: http://autobuses.costasur.com

TOURIST INFORMATION

Central tourist information office: Pl de la Marina 11, 29001, Málaga, tel 951 926 020, www.malagaturismo.com.

OTHER WALKS

There is lots of walking in the hills surrounding Montejaque, including a 3h circuit to the Tavizna gorge, a 2h30 ascent of the peak of Hacho (1075m) and a 14km circular route of the smaller hills around the village. The Parque Natural del Torcal has three marked walking routes.

MONTEJAQUE TO
VILLANUEVA DE CAUCHE (108KM)

STAGE 6
Montejaque – Arriate

Start	MA8402 road heading east from Montejaque
Distance	16.5km
Time	5h
Highest point	761m
Height gain	525m
Height loss	615m

A short route taking you steeply up and over the El Puerto pass and into the historic town of Ronda, where it is worth stopping for a while. Once you've found your way out of Ronda, this route opens out taking you across the wide valley floor to Arriate, though disappointingly mostly on roads.

MONTEJAQUE 687M POPULATION 1050

Accommodation, restaurant/bar/café, drinking fountain, food shop, cashpoint, telephone, tourist information, transport.

Accommodation and food
A good selection of little places to eat and a few places to stay, mostly upmarket:

Posada del Fresno (B). The owners are wonderful hosts with extensive local knowledge and a great library: C/Miguel de Cervantes 2, Montejaque, tel 952 167 544, www.posadadelfresno.com. **Hotel Palacete de Mañara** (C). Smart with lots of useful information, swimming pool and air conditioning: Pza Constitución 2, tel 952 167 252. **Casas de Montejaque** (C) has luxurious houses set around a swimming pool: C/Manuel Ortega 16, tel 952 168 120, www.montejaque.net, www.casasdemontejaque.net.

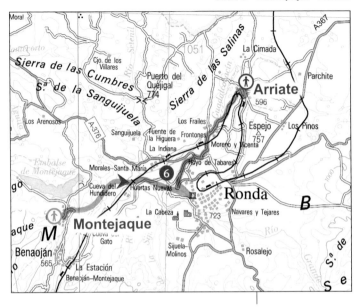

Further information
www.montejaque.es.

Montejaque, which comes from the Arabic for 'lost mountain', is a pretty white village and a popular walking base with many shorter routes also departing from here. The centre of the village is the Plaza Constitution with the Santiago el Mayor church and the Hotel Palacete de Mañara, in the mansion that was once the seat of power in the area but also latterly, slightly oddly, a sausage factory.

Montejaque – Ronda (8.5km, 3h)
Come out of Montejaque on the MA8402 road heading east and downhill. Just under a kilometre out of town you come to a signboard listing the network of local walking routes, including the GR7. Don't be tempted to turn left up this path; carry on down the road another 200m to a sign directing you off the road up the next left to the Ermita de Escarihuela. ▶

This is before the road bends sharp right.

The ancient route – which was the way to Ronda before roads – zigzags steeply upwards. After about 20min you

75

The line was built in the 1890s to allow British garrison officers and their families to visit the countryside from Gibraltar.

should reach the top, El Puerto Ermita de Escarihuela. The route flattens out and passes a farm before descending the other side of the hill. Stick to the main track despite the sparse markings. There is a steep initial descent before the track contours, gently undulating and then bends right to descend to the valley floor where you cross the Algeciras–Bobadilla **railway line**, just over 5km from Montejaque. ◄

Just after it, where the track divides, turn left along the tarmac road. You'll soon pass a guest house, Finca los Gallos, on your left ((B), tel 651 182 051, www.fincalosgallos.es, 4 *casas rurales* to let with pool) and, where you meet the main road, turn left onto it. After about 500m the main road bends left, but you continue straight on along a wide dirt track with houses alongside. At La Indiana, when the track turns into a tarmac road that bends downhill to the right, you go up the marked dirt track next to it.

From here it's one big climb to **Ronda**. Climb up a rough dirt track between scattered houses, cross a wider track and then continue very steeply uphill with a green warehouse and recycling centre on your left. Cross another wide track and continue uphill towards the main road, but do not join it, keep it on your left and continue uphill. When you meet

The famous cliff edge on which Ronda sits

a large stone wall, turn left to continue uphill with the wall on your right as the track turns to tarmac. Great views of the cliffs below Ronda open up on the right and as the tarmac turns into a gravel track you stay left to come into the western side of town on a road that passes a viewpoint and becomes the C/de Jerez (about 1.8km and 25min after La Indiana).

RONDA 744M POPULATION 36,000

Accommodation, campsite, restaurant/bar/café, drinking fountain, food shop, cashpoint, telephone, PO, pharmacy, tourist information, transport.

Accommodation and food

Ronda has a huge number of hotels and restaurants to suit every price range but it's still worth booking in summer months.

Campsite el Sur (A) is situated just over a kilometre from Ronda and has all the facilities you would expect including a swimming pool plus wi-fi: Ctra Algeciras, Km1.5, tel 952 875 939, www.elsur.com. **Pensión González** (A) is a small pleasant budget hostal with clean rooms some with balconies: C/San Vicente de Paúl 3, tel 952 871 445. **Hostal Virgen del Rocío** (A) is a mid-range place on a bustling side street full of restaurants, air conditioning: C/Nuevo 18, tel 952 877 425. **Hotel Don Javier** (C) is a clean, friendly central hotel with decent rooms and a bustling restaurant with outside seating: C/José Aparicio 6, tel 952 872 020, www.hoteldonjavier.com.

If you want to treat yourself, **Parador de Ronda** (D) is a luxury chain hotel right on the famous bridge, the Puente Nuevo: Pza de España, tel 952 877 500, www.paradores-spain.com/spain/pronda.html.

Further information

Andalucía tourist information office: Pza de España 1, tel 952 871 272.

Municipal tourist information office: Paseo Blas Infante, tel 952 187 119, www.turismoderonda.es.

Transport

Bus Station, Plaza Redondo, Train station, Av. Andalucía, tel 952 871 673.

Ronda is perhaps the best known of the *pueblos blancos* in the area, famous for its dramatic location atop cliffs high above the Río Guadalevín valley and straddling the 130m deep El Tajo gorge. It is much bigger and more touristy than the smaller villages surrounding it and the huge crowds of day-trippers can be a shock after the peace and space of the open countryside. But its popularity is well deserved, with beautiful architecture and great views.

Ronda – Arriate (8km, 2h)

Retrace your steps to leave Ronda the same way you came in, by walking north on C/Jerez. Pass the viewpoint where you came in and continue on C/Jerez heading north. Turn left at the point where you meet C/Zahara de la Sierra to go downhill to meet and cross Ctra de Ronda (A374). Here there is a short path through trees to cut off a loop of the road. When you rejoin it turn right along the road for just over 1km until Km28, where you turn off onto a narrow road on the right where there is a GR7 signboard and a various other signs. Continue on this road, which meets and passes under the **railway**, until you reach a junction. This has no GR7 markings but take the right fork and continue on, passing a couple of bars, and you will come into the village of **Arriate** on C/Montejaque and C/de Fuente, passing a drinking fountain as you enter.

ARRIATE 603M POPULATION 4150

Accommodation, restaurant/bar/café, drinking fountain, food shop, cashpoint, telephone, PO, transport.

Accommodation and food

A range of bars and cafés, a couple of expensive hotels before you reach the village itself and a spa hotel in the village.

Hotel Molino del Arco (D) is a luxurious option right on the GR7, en route up to Arriate about 3km before the village: tel 952 114 017, www.hotelmolinodelarco.com.

Hotel la Fuente de la Higuera (D) is another very high quality option on the route but out of the range of most budgets, en route up to Arriate: tel 952 114 355, www.hotellafuente.com. Finally **Hoteles Con Embrujo** (C) is a 16 room recently refurbished hotel and restaurant with a range of spa treatments available including sports massages for aching legs! Plaza de la Constitución 26, tel 952 166 527, www.hotelesconembrujo.com.

Further information

www.arriate.es.

Transport

Taxis: tel 646 955 622/952 165 158.

Arriate, which comes from the Arabic for 'the gardens', was part of the municipality of Ronda until 1630 when residents clubbed together to buy their freedom and create the smallest municipality in Málaga province. The town itself is a quiet *pueblo blanco* with an impressive church spire.

STAGE 7
Arriate – Ardales

Start	Shops at centre of Arriate
Distance	32.7km
Time	9h30
Highest point	894m
Height gain	765m
Height loss	1005m

A mixed route with some beautiful walking along old drovers tracks through remote hilly landscapes interrupted by some tarmac walking and a section next to and along a busy road. This stage can be split by taking a detour to spend a night in nearby Cuevas del Becerro.

Arriate to Serrato (20km, 5h20)
From Arriate's main shopping street descend on C/Albarra (signposted to Setenil) to cross the river and then climb very steeply up C/Casas Nuevas. Before you leave the village, take a street to the right signposted 'Urbanización los Arroyos'. After less than 500m on this street you'll come to a battered old GR7 signpost (8h30 to Serrato).

Climb for just over 2.5km on the quiet old Cuevas del Becerro road, passing lots of olive groves to arrive at **Parchite**, where there is an old railway station. Turn left alongside the railway tracks and, where there is a crossing before you reach the station platform, cross the train tracks and turn right on the other side to pass in front of a building and then head uphill on a wide dirt track. This takes you up through holm oaks and gorse and after 1.8km you emerge on to the **A367** road at Km32.

From here you basically follow the busy road for 5.5km, but there is a path right next to it which is more pleasant than walking on tarmac. To follow this, cross the road and continue up the unmarked dirt track directly opposite. ▶ You follow this through scrub with the road close by on your left and a wire fence on your right. The path peters out at times

It looks blocked by rubble but a small footpath continues alongside the road.

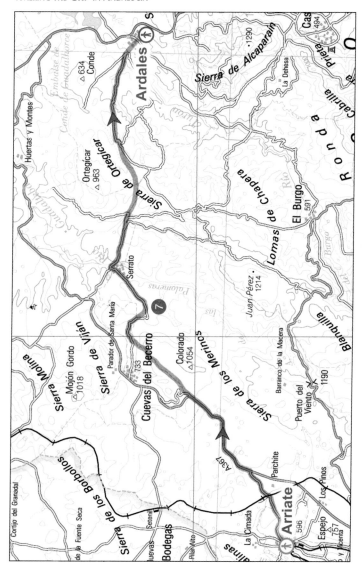

but you continue next to the road, passing military land and then the Ascari Race Resort on your right. Soon after the resort (1.7km and 20min from where you crossed the road) the path becomes more of a track and you continue next to the road for about another 1.5km, until Km29 of the road, where the tall wire fence on your right ends and the track peters out, becoming a path that gets lost in the bushes and leads you to the dry stone wall of the new and controversial golf course which has blocked the GR7 route.

From here, walk up the busy road for the remaining 2km until just after Km27, where you see a sign for Puerto el Saltillo. ▸ Here a large signboard for the *cañada real* directs you off the road to the right and then round to the left. After 500m you see a GR7 post directing you up a track to the right.

Approaching Cuevas del Becerro

This is the high point of the road at 885m.

Cañadas reales are old cattle tracks that were created to allow the movement of cattle between pastures. In total they cover a distance almost 15 times the length of the Spanish railways and have a unique ecological value because, like rivers, they help the migration of a variety of species. There were the main means of getting around Spain for centuries.

Caminos reales, like *cañadas reales*, are centuries-old pathways which were designated as such by royal decree. The decree is still in force today and they are still very much in use by farmers and their animals.

Follow the track as it winds up over a hill through arable fields and then down into olives, with a good view on the left of the **Sierra de Viján**, and soon of the town of **Cuevas del Becerro** below it. After 1.8km (25min) on this track you reach a divide.

At the fork, go left to detour down into Cuevas just over 1km away. Accommodation is available from Bar Alfredo (A) C/Andalucía, 31 (tel 952 163 008) and a number of casas rurales, including Casa el Puente, tel 952 162 092, www.casaelpuente.com. If you do go into Cuevas you can return to the GR7 by taking the cañada real from the northeast end of the village and follow it for less than 1km to rejoin the route.

At the fork, stay right to continue to Serrato. Stay on the main track descending gently and passing under the rocky outcrop of Juan Durán on your right. ◀ After about 2km (25min) from the Cuevas turning you descend to meet a tarmac road and turn right up it (signposted Cañada Real de Serrato). Continue up this quiet old road through arable and olive fields, with the new road running parallel around the hillside up above. Ignore a track up to the left after 20min/about 1.5km on the road and continue on tarmac uphill. Pass another track off to the left, then when the tarmac ends and the road forks into two tracks, take the left fork.

When you join another track (which used to be the GR7 before the golf course was built), you pass a signboard highlighting the bird life in the area. Descend on the main track passing through olives to enter **Serrato** (500m, population 650, restaurant/bar/café, cashpoint, telephone, pharmacy) on C/Ermita just under 10km and 2h30min from joining the cañada real off the A367. As you enter the village you pass a GR7 sign pointing back the way you have come (stating Arriate 9h).

You are heading towards the dramatic Sierra de Viján with an *atalaya* (defensive tower) and the big cave below it visible high on the hill.

Serrato – Ardales (4h10, 12.7km)

To continue from Serrato to Ardales, head down to the lower part of the village looking for C/Andalucía or C/Riachuelo.

At the edge of the village, where they meet, there is a drinking fountain, a GR7 display board with its information panel (currently) missing and a sign to Ardales (4h).

From here turn left on to a gravel track and then right onto the MA 5400, a quiet tarmac road. Walk east and uphill on the road for 2km where you will find a track to the left.

The track takes you downhill and into the hill country of the Serranía de Ronda, away from most signs of civilisation. After about 300m ignore a turning to the right and, at the bottom, where the track divides, take the right fork to start climbing again. As you near the top, there is an unmarked junction in the track: turn right and continue all the way to the top of the pass, where you will be rewarded with great views of the valleys to come and of the **Embalse del Conde de Guadalhorce**. A sign indicates that Ardales is 3h downhill from this point.

As you head downhill on the same track cross over another track and then turn left at the next two, well-marked,

Serrato

The track here heads through an amazing patchwork of fields with neat rows of almonds and olive trees all around.

junctions. ◀ Then, 6.5km after you left the main road, you get your first view of Ardales in front of you. From here the route is very straightforward, though lacking shade, heading directly for the village. As you pass a sign saying Ardales is 1h away, ignore a smaller track off to the left. You'll then arrive at the bottom of the village. To enter **Ardales**, cross the Roman Molino bridge over the **Río Turón** and then go through the underpass beyond.

ARDALES 450M POPULATION 2600

Accommodation, restaurant/bar/café, drinking fountain, food shop, cashpoint, telephone, PO, pharmacy, tourist information, transport.

Accommodation and food

A few lively bars and a range of places to eat including the hotels:

Hotel Restaurante el Cruce (B) has clean rooms with comfy beds and nice big balconies – although a bit near a big road – and a good restaurant downstairs. On the GR7 route out of town, across the bridge from the centre: Ctra Ardales-Campillos 2, tel 952 459 012. **La Posada del Conde** (C) is an upmarket establishment with comfortable rooms overlooking the reservoir. Air conditioning, heating, TV and its own restaurant offering traditional dishes: Pantano del Chorro, tel 952 112 411/800 www.hoteldelconde.com. **Apartamentos Ardales** (C) has luxurious flats with swimming pool just off the main square: C/El Burgo, tel 952 459 466, www.apartamentosardales.com.

Further information

www.ardales.es, www.cuevadeardales.com.

A pleasant, compact town most known for the discovery of Neolithic and Copper Age artefacts here. Just on the outskirts of the town is the Cueva de Ardales, a paeliolithic cave complex famous for its geology, including massive stalagmites, and its history of human occupation evidenced by its impressive cave paintings. Depending on the season the cave can be visited on various days by calling the Museo de Ardales (Av. De Malaga, tel 952 458 046) or ask in the town hall in the central plaza.

STAGE 8
Ardales – El Chorro

Start	MA446 in the centre of Ardales
Distance	15.8km
Time	5h
Highest point	583m
Height gain	580m
Height loss	840m

Great walking with the route talking you across hilltops and then down a wonderful steep zigzagging mountain path into the gorge where the small but quirky village of El Chorro sits.

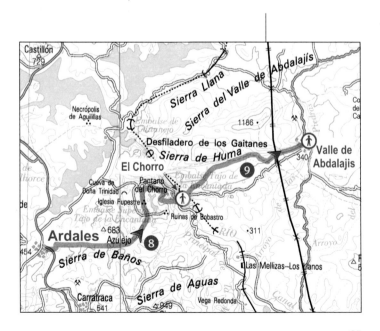

Ardales

There is a big display board for the Sendero to El Chorro.

Leave the centre of Ardales heading north along the MA446 towards the tourist information office and across the bridge. ◄

Turn right at Hotel el Cruce and, after 800m, take the first left, signposted 5h to El Chorro, just after passing beneath a bridge and before the slip road onto a busy road above. This starts out as tarmac but soon becomes a concrete track. Climb the hill on this track, ignoring side tracks off to houses and where the road forks go right.

When you reach the top follow the road along a ridge and round the shoulder of the hill and, where the track divides again (just over 2km since you left the main road), fork left onto a tarmac minor road (GR7 signpost). ◄

To the right is the Cueva de Ardales.

Follow this tarmac road through pines, broom, gorse and rosemary for 1.5km, ignoring several turnings. Do not turn sharp right on a very good gravel track before the top of the hill, but turn right onto a marked gravel track 200m after the top of the hill. Stick to this main track, descending to cross the Arroyo del Granado and then climbing up again. Meet another track and go left along it. Descend again keeping to this main track and not taking any of the side tracks. When the path levels out you will pass two tracks to the right, the second signed to Finca los Gamos but keep left and continue down through pines until you reach another small road (MA448) (4km after leaving the tarmac road).

Turn right along the road and after a few hundred metres you arrive at a ticket office where you can purchase a ticket for a detour to visit the interesting archaeological site of **Bobastro**.

> **Bobastro** is the ruins of the fortified village which the famous dissident Omar Ibn Hafsun used as his base to lead a revolt against the caliphal government in Córdoba between 879 and 918AD. Climb on the road for just over a kilometre and then turn off left at a bend in the road and onto a forest track. Here a sign points back to Ardales, saying 6h – 3h30 is closer to the truth.

Continue along through the shady pines and take the first left with a reservoir wall above you to your right. The track takes you north around the reservoir (**Embalse Tajo de la Encantada**) and through the Paraje Natural del Desfiladero de los Gaitanes. When you reach a tarmac road, which leads to a chimney on your left, again turn right.

> This large **abandoned chimney** is controversial for being left in situ in such a beautiful location by the electricity board. From here you are looking down the gorge (Tajo de la Encantada) into the El Chorro valley. Cut out of the limestone rock by the Río Guadalhorce, it is 400m deep in places and 4km long.

The road brings you to the huge retaining wall on the east side of the reservoir. From here you can look over to the **Sierra de Huma** with its highest peak of La Huma at 1191m. Do not follow the road along the dam, but go slightly left down a track below the reservoir wall. After 200–300m keep a sharp eye out for a little path down to the left, taking you away from the reservoir. It is soon marked by a post with a black arrow. Follow this path steeply downhill for 3km, with El Chorro clearly visible far below. ▶ When you meet the road at the bottom, turn right, cross the bridge and turn left to climb into **El Chorro** 400m further on.

The path downhill is spectacular and quite untypical of the trail so far, carving a path along and below precipitous cliffs.

87

EL CHORRO 200M POPULATION 250

Accommodation, campsite, restaurant/bar/café, drinking fountain, food shop, telephone, transport.

Accommodation and food

There is a food store by the station and lots of bars and places to stay including:

Albergue-Camping el Chorro (A) is a campsite with cabins set among eucalyptus and pines with a pool, bar/restaurant and *albergue*, 350m towards the gorge out of the village: tel 952 495 244, www.alberguecampingelchorro.es. **Finca la Campaña** (A) is a bunkhouse and camping ground with pool, shop and range of outdoor activities on offer, just outside village on the top road: tel 952 112 019, www.el-chorro.com. **Apartamentos la Garganta** (C) is an old mill building converted into classy colourful rooms and flats round a lovely pool, heating, air conditioning, kitchens, also a pleasant bar/restaurant: Bda el Chorro (on road up to station), tel 952 495 000, www.lagarganta.com.

Transport

There are trains from Málaga and a bus from Álora, which has a more frequent train connection to Malaga.

A rock climbers' paradise of a tiny village dominated by sheer limestone cliffs. Its amazing network of underground caves are also deservedly famous. If you're interested in other outdoor pursuits it's a good place to stop off for a while for climbing, mountain biking, horseriding, canoeing, windsurfing and other activities.

STAGE 9
El Chorro – Valle de Abdalajís

Start	El Chorro railway station
Distance	10km
Time	3h
Highest point	679m
Height gain	590m
Height loss	450m

A long steep climb up an beneath the imposing Sierra del Huma is rewarded by fantastic views before a gentle descent through remote farmland into the Valle de Abdalajís.

From the station at the top of the village, continue uphill on the road leaving the station on your left and after 400m turn left up the minor road signed to Valle de Abdalajís. This takes you onto a gravel track and you join the signposted Haza del Río route. Where the track divides soon after, take a left and begin zigzagging your way up the hill, climbing through pines and eucalyptus. At a T-junction where you join a wider track, take another left and continue uphill with the impressive rock face of the La Huma highest point ot the **Sierra de Huma**, towering above you at nearly 1200m.

After around 2km there are turnings off to the left and right but stick to the main path and another kilometre on near the top of a steep section, where the track divides again, keep on the main track and don't take the right turn (GR7 signposts). Soon afterwards take a right fork, diverging from the Haza del Río footpath and rising to the top of the climb. ▶

At a T junction head downhill to the right and when you meet another track, go through a gate and turn left. Go uphill quite steeply again briefly passing several smaller tracks off to farms but keeping to the main track. The landscape turns from pines to olive groves and becomes more cultivated as you begin to descend.

See map in Stage 8.

At around 700m you have great views down into the Abdalajís valley as the track levels out.

| El Chorro | Turn right onto a track which starts off as concrete and turns to tarmac. Here, 7km from the starting point, you meet with the yellow PR85 route. Ignore a smaller turning down to the right and continue on beneath the rock face of the Tajo del Cuervo. When you meet the main road (MA226) turn left and it takes you down into **Valle de Abdalajís** along the C/Almería. |

VALLE DE ABDALAJÍS 340M POPULATION 2700

Accommodation, restaurant/bar/café, drinking fountain, food shop, cashpoint, telephone, PO, pharmacy, tourist information, transport.

Accommodation and food
A few hostales and hotels to choose from and a reasonable selection of small local bars and restaurants:

Hostal Vista a la Sierra (A/B) has friendly owners and seven pleasant rooms with good views and two flats to let: at top of town, Prolongación C/Viento, tel 952 488 052. **Hostal Refugio de Alamut** (A) has helpful staff with knowledge of local walking. Good restaurant and chalet accommodation: Ctra Antequera K26.9, tel 952 489 064, www.refugioalamut.com.

Further information
Town hall: tel 952 489 100 www.valledeabdalajis.com.

Transport
Taxi: tel 952 488 124.

Quiet village most popular with tourists who like hang-gliding. Its name is thought to have come from that of the Arab who founded it, Abd-el-Aziz.

STAGE 10
Valle de Abdalajís – Antequera

Start	Centre of Valle de Abdalajís
Distance	18.5km
Time	5h30
Highest point	781m
Height gain	560m
Height loss	400m

After some climbing to start, a relatively easy route with small sections of road walking broken up by nice tracks with views of the dramatic rock formations of the Parque Natural El Torcal.

To leave Valle de Abdalajís continue down through the village to join the main road (A343) where it crosses the river. Turn left (do not cross the bridge) and follow the road uphill (signposted Antequera) for 200m to a petrol station. Take a road to the right just before the garage. This takes you down, passing a signboard and across a small ford in the **Arroyo de las Piedras**. Just after you cross, ignore the tarmac road back to the right and then one off to the left. ▶ Start climbing steeply on a concrete track signed to Fuente la Zarza. Pass another track off to the right, with the Cerro de los Perdigones on your left, and pass under 2 sets of electric pylon wires. Then after 2km, passing through cereals fields and almonds, when you reach a crossroads carry straight

There is a potentially confusing marking on a stone on this track.

91

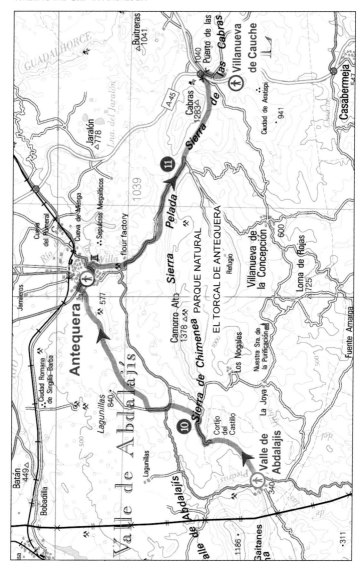

Rooftops of Antequera

on. Around the corner you'll come to a second crossroads, with a post pointing you to the left which takes you downhill between fields to a ford then along the track. Climb towards the very visible farm high on the hill, to the right of a rocky outcrop and below a round silo.

After 2km mainly climbing you come to a T-junction. Turn right and then left, passing the **Cortijo del Castillo**, on a track which curves round the east side of a large rocky outcrop in zig zags before levelling out. ▶

There are open views of the top end of the Valle de Abdalajís and the plains to the north.

After 1.7km leave the main track to the left. Continue on this track, passing a turning to the right after just under 1.5km and 500m come to the main Antequera road, the A343. Turn right along it then immediately left up a wide track heading north initially through olives and then through fields. Climb gently on this, continuing straight on at a junction after 1km, then 500m later you reach a crossroads at Casilla Castro. Turn right here and walk for just over 1.5km, climbing gently to a junction at a building where you turn left on a track which continues gently uphill. When it forks (the track ahead is gated) turn right to walk round the east side of a small hill. ▶

From here it is 7km to Antequera and you soon see it in the distance.

The track heads downhill and east towards **Antequera**. Follow it on, passing a turning to the left, until it becomes a tarmac road and then stay on the tarmac road avoiding all turnings. You pass a 5 star hotel (La Magdalena) and then the Antequera Golf Club before heading steeply downhill, passing a football ground, crossing a river bridge and rising gently to a roundabout by the Antequera Golf Hotel. Go straight ahead and follow the Camino de Gandía and then the Camino de los Capuchinos to reach the town centre.

ANTEQUERA 577M POPULATION 42,000

Accommodation, campsite, restaurant/bar/café, drinking fountain, food shop, cashpoint, telephone, PO, pharmacy, tourist information, transport.

Accommodation and food
Wide range of good value places to stay and eat including Indian, Chinese and Italian cuisine for those who fancy a change:

Pensión Toril (A) is central but a little on the shabby side, with TV and courtyard: C/Toril 3 tel: 952 843 184. **Hospedería Colon** (A) is right in the centre of town and has 25 rooms with cable TV, air conditioning, heating and internet access, set around a pretty courtyard: C/Infante Don Fernando 31, tel 952 840 010, www.castelcolon.com. **Hotel San Sebastián** (B) is good value with central location and smart interior, TV, internet and air conditioning, terrace seating area: Pza de San Sebastián 4, tel 952 844 239, www.hotelplazasansebastian. com. **Camping El Torcal** (A) is a campsite 6km from the centre of town on the GR7 in the El Torcal natural park with restaurant, supermarket and pool: Ctra Comarcal C-3331, Km6, tel 952 111 608, www.campingeltorcal.com.

Further information
Tourist information: Plaza de San Sebastían 7, tel 952 702 505, www.turismoantequera.com.

Transport
Train station: Av. Estación, tel 952 843 226.

Bus station: tel 952 841 957.

This historic town's skyline is dominated by the towers of the Moorish fortress (the Alcazaba) and its many church spires. It has layers of history, having been inhabited since the Bronze Age. If you stay here it is worth visiting the dolmens – some of Europe's oldest and biggest mass tombs made from huge rock slabs, dating from 2500BC to 1800BC, located in the park to the west of town. In the town centre you can also visit the recently excavated Roman baths, Gothic churches, the 19th-century bullring and beautiful Renaissance fountains and climb through the 16th-century Arch of the Giants up to the castle.

STAGE 11

Antequera – Villanueva de Cauche

Start	Centre of Antequera
Distance	14.5km
Time	4h
Highest point	942m
Height gain	520m
Height loss	350m

Small, pretty paths through fields of crops and wildflowers more than make up for an early uphill road walk. Views of the Parque Natural el Torcal accompany you for most of this route into the small village of Villanueva de Cauche.

Head through the historic part of town, passing below and to the north and then east of the Moorish fortress, going down towards the river (Río de la Villa) and along the Bajada del Río. Walk out along the C/Henchidero and then the C/Ribera with the river on your left and after about 1.5km you come to the old La Concepción **flour factory** on your left, the first GR7 marking of the day and a junction with the A7075 road.

See map in Stage 10.

Turn left up the road which runs alongside the beautiful **Parque Natural el Torcal**. After 2km of climbing, where the road bends left before crossing the river take a small road on the right which soon turns left where there is a signpost for a local walk. ▶ Go past the source and a campsite on your left to rejoin the main road a km on. Climb for a further 3km until you come to two tracks on the left on the second of two hairpin bends. From here it is about 2h to Villanueva de Cauche.

This takes you to the source of the river (el Nacimiento del Río de la Villa).

EL TORCAL NATURAL PARK

Possibly Andalucía's strangest natural park, the Parque Natural el Torcal (17km²) contains a myriad of wierd and wonderful rock formations. The whole park is a limestone plateau that originated under the sea millions of years ago. The waters of the Tethys Sea were responsible for carving out shapes in the soft, porous

Villanueva de Cauche

limestone, which was then brought to the surface, over a hundred million years ago, by movements in the Earth's crust. The limestone retained its formation and since that time has continued to be sculpted by wind and rain.

Wildlife

The rocky landscape and height of the park, in which the peak of El Torcal reaches 1336m, limits the type of vegetation and wildlife that can exist within it. However it is known for its wildflowers, especially orchids, with over 30 varieties growing in the park. Unsurprisingly rock plants and flowers are abundant and some trees manage to grow between the rocks.

In terms of wildlife, reptiles are the most numerous with many varieties of lizards and snakes to be found in the rocky crevices, including the two-metre-long Montpellier snake and the spine-footed lizard.

Bird life, too, is rich with the many birds of prey making the park a special protection zone for birds. Look out for griffon vultures, Bonelli's eagles, peregrines and eagle owls.

Lovers' Leap

The highest cliff within in the park, La Peña de los Enamorados (or Lovers' Leap), has been made famous by the legend that is attached to it. It is a Romeo and Juliet-esque tale that tells of a Muslim girl and a Christian boy falling in love but throwing themselves from the cliff when their families refused to accept their love.

Take the second of the tracks and you soon emerge into beautiful open countryside. For most of the way from here to Villanueva de Cauche the steep slopes of the **Sierra de las Cabras** tower up on your left whilst there are extensive views of the valleys and occasional villages to the south. At the next divide, at the brow of the hill, take the more minor track off to the left. After a kilometre this track becomes rougher for a while. It passes an olive grove on the right, and then climbs to reveal the peaks of the Peña Negra (1,337m) and the Morrón de Gragea (1,295m). Follow the track downwards until Villanueva de Cauche comes into sight. ▶ Descend towards the Hotel las Pedrizas, passing through an underpass to reach the hotel. Cross its car park and go through a second underpass beyond. Go up the gravel track to meet a tarmac road.

The view of the ancient hamlet is somewhat marred by the noisy N331 dual carriageway between you and it.

This is **where the GR7 divides**, with one fork heading north towards the province of Córdoba and the other heading south into the Granada province.

From here you can go right, cross straight over a roundabout and down the road crossing the A7204 into the village (1km, 25m) to pick up the Southern Fork of the route or, for the northern route, carry on to Villanueva del Rosario (11km, 3h40) up a marked route to the left before you enter the village.

VILLANUEVA DE CAUCHE 700M POPULATION 298

Accommodation, restaurant/bar/café, drinking fountain, food shop, telephone, transport.

Accommodation and food
Nothing in the village but one hotel on the major road before you enter the village: **Hotel las Pedrizas** (B) is a motel-style hotel on main road, Ctra Madrid-Málaga, Km527, tel 952 730 850.

A tiny white hamlet that is sadly totally overshadowed by the busy dual carriageway. There is not much here except a little plaza with a drinking fountain.

2 NORTHERN FORK – MÁLAGA, CÓRDOBA AND JAÉN

*VILLANUEVA DE CAUCHE
TO PUEBLA DE DON FADRIQUE*

On route to Alcalá La Real (Stage 19A)

MÁLAGA PROVINCE

An overview of the route in Málaga, and practical details such as transport information, are given at the beginning of the section 'Málaga province' in Part 1.

VILLANUEVA DE CAUCHE
TO RUTE (107.4KM)

STAGE 12A
Villanueva de Cauche – Villanueva del Trabuco

Start	Villanueva del Cauche
Distance	15.3km
Time	4h10
Highest point	819m
Height gain	330m
Height loss	340m

A gentle route passing between fields and olive groves with mountains always on the horizon distracting the walker from the busy road that the route shadows for much of the way.

Note: If you arrived at the village on the GR7, come back out on the same road you came in on, but don't turn back down to the underpass, instead head right and follow the road up the hill.

Villanueva de Cauche – Villanueva del Rosario (11.3km, 3h)
Head out of Villanueva de Cauche on the road to the north. Cross straight over a larger road, the A7203, and ignore the underpass down to the left. This takes you onto the old road up the hill, crossing straight over a roundabout and looking down on the busy motorway below.

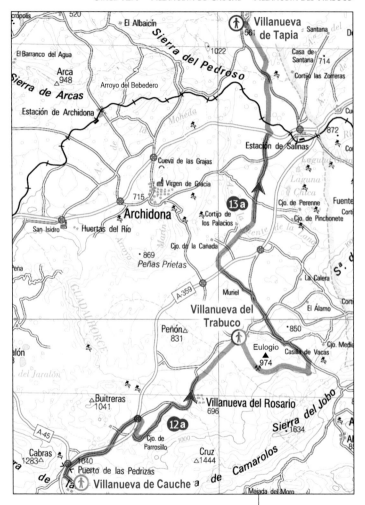

After 2km, avoid turning across a bridge, instead turn right to avoid coming down to the motorway. Carry on up this quiet road through olives, ignoring tracks to either side and a small underpass. The road you are on then goes left

You can see Villanueva del Rosario ahead of you among olives and fields of corn.

under an underpass. Continue along the road until it meets another road and then turn right. ◄ Pass under another underpass and then take the track to the right to avoid walking in on the main road, which you rejoin just before **Villanueva del Rosario**.

VILLANUEVA DEL ROSARIO 670M POPULATION 3600

Accommodation, restaurant/bar/café, drinking fountain, food shop, telephone, pharmacy, transport.

Accommodation and food
A range of places to eat, mainly tapas bars and a couple of hotels on the main road into the village:

Hotel Cerezo (A) is just on the road into Villanueva del Rosario: Huerta del Moruno, tel 952 742 129. **Hotel las Delicias** (B) has 12 rooms with a popular restaurant downstairs: Ctra las Pedrizas, tel 952 742 432.

Further information
Town hall: 952 742 008

Situated at the foot of dramatic rocky mountains, Villanueva del Rosario has a rich cultural history with several archaeological sites, two dating from the Copper Age, in the area. The Romans left much evidence of their presence in the form of Roman roads and artefacts. There is believed to be Roman treasure yet to be discovered beneath the Peñon de Solis, 3km from the centre. It is worth paying a visit to the museum in the Plaza Medieval del Saucedo if you're interested in finding out more.

This river source is a natural spring which provides the drinking water supply for the village and has pools and waterfalls.

Villanueva del Rosario – Villanueva del Trabuco (4km, 1h10)
Pass a sign up to the Nacimiento de la Villa. ◄ Head out of the village on the road then, when it bends to the left after 1km, carry straight on along a dirt track by a faded GR7 sign. Follow this track through olive groves the entire way.

VILLANUEVA DEL TRABUCO 700M POPULATION 5400

Accommodation, restaurant/bar/café, drinking fountain, food shop, cash point, telephone, PO, pharmacy, tourist information, transport.

Accommodation and food
Several bars and restaurants but limited accommodation:

Hotel Paneque (C) is a big establishment on the main road a few kilometres out of the village: Ctra Málaga-Granada, Km50, tel 952 111 479, www.paneque.es.

Further information
Town hall: tel 952 751 021, www.villanuevadeltrabucho.com.

Villanueva del Trabuco is an expanding but still attractive place located at the foot of the Gorda and San Jorge mountains, and providing the start to many walking routes. With water supplied from both the Río Guadalhorce and Río Higueral, the village's Fuente de los Tres Caños ('fountain of the three pipes') is famous for never running dry, even in droughts. It has a large and growing English population, so don't be surprised when you come across the 'Corner Shop'. According to local legend the name *Trabuco* ('Blunderbuss') comes from an innkeeper long ago who grew tired of highway robbers and became infamous for his violent defence of his wares with his large-bore shotgun!

Walking into Villanueva del Trabuco

STAGE 13A

Villanueva del Trabuco – Villanueva de Tapia

Start	Bridge over the Rió Guadalhorce in Villanueva del Trabuco
Distance	30.6km
Time	8h30
Highest point	957m
Height gain	550m
Height loss	600m

A long but beautiful loop on the hillsides around the village can be bypassed by a shortcut following the right branch of the road east out of the village for 2km then rejoining the route as it continues along tracks through wide open farmland and olive groves.

See map in Stage 12A

Come out of town over a bridge over the Rio Guadalhorce, with a play park on your right where there is a signboard with a map and description of the day's route. Take the road up to the left of this (Av. Miguel Indurain), towards the Sierra Gorda, through olives. After 500m the road divides, and you stay on the right, tarmac branch. Climb for just over 2km on this road, entering oak woodland, then take the gravel track up to the left behind the small peak of **Eulogio**.

Here you can look down over the entire village of Villanueva del Trabuco.

Continue on the track past the Cortijo los Canales, ignoring a smaller track downhill, and contour round the hillside passing a track off to the left. ◄ When you meet another track turn right and carry on past two tracks, one on either side. You will come to an intersection of tracks; take the second left and begin heading downhill.

This, just over 10km since the start, is the point you would start if you took the shortcut, saving 8km of walking.

When you reach a tarmac road, turn left and stay on this until you reach the neighbourhood of El Chorrillero. Turn right at a GR7 signpost. Head up the hill past a useful drinking fountain on the right, continuing on through olive groves on a gravel track up to the road (MA225).

◄ Cross over the road (or turn left if you took the shortcut), turning onto the Vereda de Archidona a Alfarnate track.

Pass by the Montes de Guadalhorce Aceite de Oliva Virgen Extra olive oil plant on the left and, 1km on when you meet another road coming out of Villanueva del Trabuco, turn right onto it. After 300m, take a turning on the left at another olive oil plant, then turn immediately right onto the gravel track (rather than the tarmac one). Pass another track on the left and carry on through the olive groves.

You pass two turnings, one on either side, and take the underpass under the **A359**. The track from here takes you across fields before turning right at a crossroads. ▶ Go straight on at two more crossroads, ignoring smaller turnings, to arrive at Fuente de Fresno after 3km (13.8km, 4h35 to Villanueva de Tapia). From here continue along the tarmac road and after 1km carry straight on at a crossroads, with the PRA125 local route which goes round **Archidona**.

The track continues heading north, now through some of the best conserved Mediterranean woodland in the province. It crosses another road after 2km. Continue on the same track. 1.5km on, when you approach a major road, the **A92**, take the underpass beneath it and turn left on the other side to get you to the Bobadilla–Granada **railway line**. Pass underneath the railway to join the Via Pecuaria Cañada Real de

At this point you are almost halfway, having walked almost 15km.

En route to Villanueva de Tapia

Sevilla a Granada, and turn left alongside the railway tracks at a GR7 signpost. After 1km turn right up a marked track and follow this east, passing Finca Sureco.

> If you're in need of somewhere to stay, there is nowhere in Villanueva de Tapia so you might want to try the **Hotel Rural Carlos Astorga** at the Centro de Actividades Cinegéticas signposted off to the right along a minor road just before you reach a GR7 signpost and the main road.

If not, continue down to the road and turn left towards Villanueva de Tapia. Continue along the road, following marks to take short sections away from the traffic (passing a signpost Villanueva de Tapia 5.25km), which brings you back onto the road further up. Turn left along the road and then take the next right off it onto a track signed on a large red board 'Camino del Entredicho' but with no GR7 mark. ◄ Pass two *cortijos* on the left and to come to another sign pointing left for Camino del Entredicho and Mirador, this time with a GR7 post. Turn left to follow these signs and carry on along the well-marked track that will take you all the way to Villanueva de Tapia. 500m from the signs take the left fork when the track divides, then left again another 400m on. You come to a farm and take the track to left of it then carry straight on just beyond it, ignoring a track off to the left. This carries on between olive groves. 1km on from the farm ignore a track off to the right to climb gently to the brow of the hill. ◄ You carry straight on, the track briefly becoming concrete, descending to the village, ignoring a further track off to your right. Stay on this main track all the way into the bottom of the village, entering on C/Nueva, which you can follow uphill to the centre of **Villanueva de Tapia**.

Just beyond this turning is the Hotel Rural Paloma, a good option for somewhere to stay and/or eat – see below.

Tapia is now visible just below and there is a viewpoint just to your left.

VILLANUEVA DE TAPIA 661M POPULATION 1660

Accommodation, restaurant/bar/café, drinking fountain, food shop, telephone, PO, transport.

Accommodation and food
Nowhere to stay in the town but a couple of places on the way in and a couple of bar/restaurants to eat in:

Hotel Rural Paloma (B) is a charming hotel with a good on-site restaurant cooking fresh produce from its own garden, all rooms ensuite with air conditioning and breakfast included: Ctra Salinas a Villanueva de Tapia, tel 657 344 888, www.hotelrurallapaloma.com.

Set within a hunting centre, with a plush country club atmosphere, **Hotel Rural Carlos Astorga** (B) has nice rooms set around swimming pool, breakfast included, restaurant on site, 1km up a turning just before you meet main road to Tapia: Ctra A-333 Salinas a Villanueva de Tapia, tel 608 982 576, www.hotelcarlosastorga.es.

Further information
www.villanuevadetapia.org.

A friendly village with busy little high street with a range of shops and a market with fresh produce. It takes its name from Pedro de Tapia, the member of the Supreme Royal Court who bought the village when King Felipe III decided it was no longer of value around the 17th century.

STAGE 14A
Villanueva de Tapia – Villanueva de Algaidas

Start	Centre of Villanueva de Tapia
Distance	16.9km
Time	4h30
Highest point	900m
Height gain	520m
Height loss	660m

A pretty section of undulating tracks through seemingly endless olive groves, interrupted only occasionally by cornfields and whitewashed *cortijos*.

Head out of the west of the village to reach the main road and pass under an underpass and onto a track marked with a signboard for the Ruta de Algaidas y Feria de Ganado. Climb up through olive groves, sticking to the larger track when it divides and climbing higher.

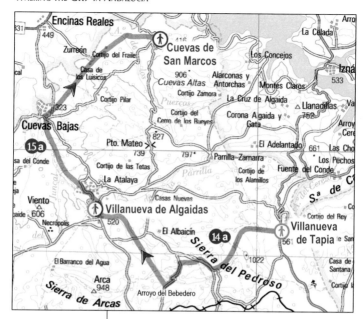

While stopping to catch your breath, look back over the endless stripes of olive groves below you.

◄ As the path levels out, after about 3km, you reach several ruined buildings and the track branches at an old whitewashed farmhouse (Cortijo de la Morena). Turn left downhill here then left again where there is a fork in the route just after a house.

If you want a diversion for more drinking water, turn right at the next fork in the track to a spring (which may be dry in summer), otherwise continue on the main track through more olive trees. Take the next left turn and descend slightly, ignoring the next left and continuing on the same track as it turns to tarmac.

You meet a minor road where a sign tells you it's a further 3h50 and 11km to Villanueva de Algaidas. Turn right along the road and after just over 1km head up a signposted track to the left. Turn right at a building and continue along with great views. When you meet a small tarmac road turn left and follow it downhill. Before climbing the daunting-looking slope on the same road, stop off at the **Arroyo del Bebedero** for more water at a fountain next to the bridge (again seasonal).

After almost 1km of climbing, turn right up the first track opposite a house and when this track splits soon afterwards, take the right fork round the hillside then downhill. Avoid tracks off to the left and pass another sign for a water point before re-crossing the stream. ▶ Carry on along the main track, ignoring tracks off to the left and then right. The track turns to tarmac in places after crossing another river and brings you down into the hamlet of **El Albaicín**. From here it is 3.5km to Villanueva de Algaidas.

Cross straight over the road here and continue on a gravel track. Turn left and head downhill then back up through olive groves, passing a small track off to the right and making a final steep climb up to the road. Turn right down into an industrial estate and on into **Villanueva de Algaidas**.

Farmhouse on the way to Villanueva de Algaidas

Both spring and stream may be dry in summer.

VILLANUEVA DE ALGAIDAS 545M POPULATION 4500

Accommodation, restaurant/bar/café, drinking fountain, food shop, cash point, telephone, PO, pharmacy, tourist information, transport.

Accommodation and food
Several bars and restaurants offer a choice for eating and there are a couple of hotels as well as an upmarket B&B:

Hostal Algaidas (A) is spacious and cheap, with good food, at the south end of village: C/Archidona 75, tel 952 743 308. **Hotel la Rincona** (B) is a nice enough hotel restaurant with pleasant rooms but unappealingly located in the industrial park: Polígono Industrial, Av. del Olivar, tel 952 745 008, www.hotelrestaurante larincona.com. **La Casa de la Fuente** (B) is a British-run, luxury B&B with spacious and distinctive rooms, some with jacuzzi baths, and bar serving breakfast and evening meals: C/Málaga 18, tel 952 745 030, www.lacasadelafuente.com.

Further information
www.villanuevadealgaidas.es.

A large and lively village whose claim to fame is being the birthplace of internationally renowned sculptor Berrocal. There is an exhibition of his work. The church and the 16th-century Los Recoletos de San Francisco de Asís convent are also worth a visit.

STAGE 15A
Villanueva de Algaidas – Cuevas de San Marcos

Start	Centre of Villanueva de Algaidas
Distance	17km
Time	5h
Highest point	540m
Height gain	290m
Height loss	445m

This overgrown route alongside the river bed of the Arroyo de Burriana can be a little like hacking your way through a jungle, but once you've emerged it is an easy walk along wide tracks from one Cuevas to the other.

See map in Stage 14A.

Villanueva de Algaidas – Cuevas Bajas
(8.5km, 3h or 8km, 2h by road)
Walk out of Villanueva de Algaidas, heading downhill along the main street (called Archidona then Granada) and leave on the Cuevas Bajas road (A7201), where there is a huge maroon sign for the route.

The ruined Franciscan convent of Nuestra Señora de la Consolación

After 100m on this road take the first road on the right. ▶ After 200m where the tarmac ends, head left down a dirt track which dwindles into an overgrown path, passing to the left of a white water pump house after a further 200m with the ruined Franciscan convent of Nuestra Señora de la Consolación ('Our Lady of Consolation') coming into view to the right. You then head steeply downhill to meet the A7201 (just before Km17) and turn right along it to come to a large brown GR7 sign and the convent. ▶

Follow the paved path past the convent and it soon turns into a narrow path running up the Arroyo Burriana, a tributary of Río Genil. Don't be put off by the fence posts made from leftover marking posts with yellow and white crosses! The route takes you under fig trees and across a small medieval bridge before zigzaging up the bank of the other side of the river on a small overgrown path. At the time of writing

There's a marker with an old illegible GR7 signpost hidden under a fig tree.

It is worth having a look around and visiting the interesting 9th–10th century Mozarab cave chapels behind it.

111

this was passable, but partially blocked by rubble just before you enter the small hamlet of **La Atalaya**.

Once you come to the cement road go up it, then turn left at the top where you meet the tarmac street and then turn left again at the entrance to the hamlet (where there is a sign for La Atalaya) to descend away from the hamlet down a tarmac road. When you come to a mini roundabout, turn right up the road.

> The **next section to Cuevas Bajas** is not recommended as it becomes extremely eroded and overgrown and very poorly marked so you may prefer to continue along this road (for 6km) into Cuevas Bajas. If you do want to brave the actual GR7 route, turn left onto a marked dirt track into the olive trees (after 400m).

Cuevas Bajas to Cuevas de San Marcos

After 2km the track disappears when it meets the river bed of the Arroyo de Burriana. From here you need to fight your way alongside the river, always staying on the right (east) bank, through fields and some wilder terrain. ▶ There are occasional markings along the way for encouragement and the path gets clearer towards the end. You rejoin a track at some solar panels. Follow this track and take the right fork when it divides. This takes you uphill and to the main road into **Cuevas Bajas**. Cross the main road at this point and walk down the old road into the village.

As long as you stay near the river you can't get lost but it is very rough and frustrating walking and will take some time.

CUEVAS BAJAS 323M POPULATION 1,600

Accommodation, restaurant/bar/café, drinking fountain, food shop, telephone, PO, pharmacy, transport.

Accommodation and food
A couple of bars, a pizza place and very little in the way of accommodation:

The GR7 runs right in front of **Casa Rural Arrebola** (D), a four-person *casa rural*, which is 1km from the village and can be rented by the day if not occupied: Paraje las Canteras, tel 952 729 524. **Casas las Canteras** has four-person log cabins with BBQ and air conditioning on the banks of the river on the outskirts of the village: Camino Cuevas de San Marcos, tel 952 729 588/620 740 462, www.casaslascanteras.com.

Further information
Town hall: tel 952 727 501/02, www.cuevasbajas.com.

Cuevas Bajas sits on the banks of the Río Genil which flows through the village. Thanks to the river, the land around the village is lush with vegetation, even though it is set within an arid area of scrubland. The river is also good for fishing.

Cuevas Bajas – Cuevas de San Marcos (8.5km, 2h)
To leave Cuevas Bajas head east from the main plaza down C/Real. This is the same way as a newly marked pilgrim route to Santiago and you pass an information office for this as you head downhill. It is also the same way as the well-marked Ribera del Genil walking route. A sign for this on the east of the village takes you right on a wide road through the industrial estate, which becomes a track. A GR7 signpost informs you that it is 3h to Cuevas de San Marcos, though in reality it is closer to 2h. Where there is a

You may wish to take a short detour here to the impressive 19th-century irrigation waterwheel, la Noria de la Acena.

divide in the track take the right fork, ignoring the walking route signs pointing left. ◄

Carry on for 3km, steeply uphill at first, passing smaller tracks off to the right, then at the next divide, 4km from the start, take the right fork again (GR7 sign 1h15) to come alongside the Río Genil.

From here there are a few smaller tracks going off on either side but stick to the main track. After just over 6km from the start you come to a clear junction just past a large metal walking signpost. Ignore the right turn here (a small tarmac road) and instead continue straight on. After about 300m you need to leave the main path, taking a less distinct track to the left into the olive groves. There are some GR7 posts here to guide you as you follow this track northeast to meet the road out of Cuevas de San Marcos by some plane trees and just before the bridge over the Río Genil. ◄ You continue left down to the Luis de Armiñán Bridge.

Here a signpost indicates that Cuevas de San Marcos is 20min to the right.

Should you **miss the turning into the olive groves**, continuing along the main track will take you into Cuevas de San Marcos from the west by a roundabout. Continue straight across the roundabout, passing a garage to your left and a tourist information office to your right. Just past this take the main road down to the left and out of town to rejoin the main route just before the river.

CUEVAS DE SAN MARCOS 360M POPULATION 4100

Accommodation, restaurant/bar/café, drinking fountain, food shop, cashpoint, telephone, PO, pharmacy, tourist information.

Accommodation and food

Limited accommodation but plenty of places to eat:

Casa Bob Guest House (B). British-run guesthouse with small but pleasant rooms, bar and good home cooking available: C/Grama 22, tel 690 217 055/952 728 231, www.casa-bob.com; note that this may change hands or close, as the owner is trying to sell. Near the top of town, where ther GR7 enters, **Hostal/Pensión Vista Bella** (A) has seven rooms: Ctra. de Pantano, tel 952 728 123. **Hotel Mi Refugio** (C) is a large hunting and spa hotel on the southern edge of town: Ctra. Villanueva de Algaidas, Km7.2, tel 951 904 906, www.hotelruralmirefugio.com.

Further information
Town hall: tel 952 728 102, www.cuevasdesanmarcos.es.

Situated amidst the Sierra del Camorro mountains and valleys of olive groves, this is a small town with a few sites of interest including: the Belda cave where prehistoric remains were found and which has one of the most important bat populations in Europe; the archaeological site of Belda, a medieval town, on the top of the Sierra del Camorro; the Archaeological Museum with finds from the area; and in the town itself there's the 17th-century Church of San Marcos and the 18th-century Ermita del Carmen.

STAGE 16A
Cuevas de San Marcos – Rute

Start	Luis de Armiñan bridge
Distance	12.3km
Time	3h30
Highest point	679m
Height gain	560m
Height loss	345m

A beautiful section crossing from Málaga into Córdoba province through pines with ancient and dramatic views across the Embalse de Iznájar.

If you went into Cuevas de San Marcos leave town to the northwest on the road which leads to the bridge over the Río Genil. After 1.5km of walking along the road you will cross the Luis de Armiñan bridge, built in 1910.

After you cross the bridge take the track immediately on the right and follow it along the river, ignoring another track off to the left, and into the hamlet of **Vadofresno**. Take the first road on the right as you come in where a GR7 signpost states that it is 2h20 to Rute. ▶ This takes you along a road marked as a dead end that turns into a gravel track. Soon after a sign marks the end of the road, with a steep

From here there are few GR7 marks.

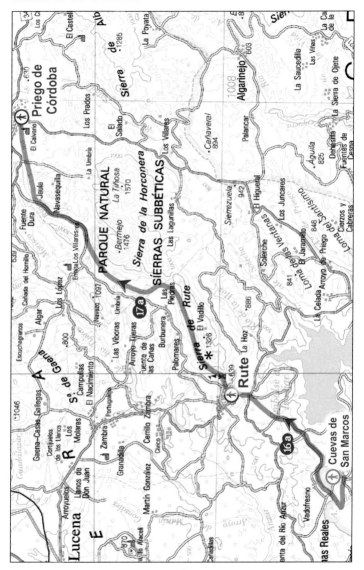

gravel track heading uphill to the right. Ignore this and instead take the track immediately to the left of it, heading through olive trees. This heads uphill to the northeast before dropping down and across the Arroyo de Bujeo, from where you then head southeast down the other side of the Arroyo. Here you are heading for the buildings and palm trees of **Camorro de la Isla**. The track comes down to join a small tarmac road, turn left along this passing a small GR7 marking to come into Camorro de la Isla, where you will find a drinking fountain. Continue straight on from here along the small road which heads uphill, with panoramic views down over the **Embalse de Iznájar**, Andalucía's highest-capacity reservoir.

After 2km, you reach a road and cross straight over. This brings you onto a new section of road next to a large new building. Turn left along it and it soon becomes a track again. When you reach another crossroads a further 2.5km on, again cross straight over to continue up the long but final climb to **Rute**. The track brings you in at the south of the town: to reach the centre turn left when the track meets the road.

Camorro de la Isla

RUTE 637M POPULATION 10,600

Accommodation, restaurant/bar/café, drinking fountain, food shop, cashpoint, telephone, PO, pharmacy, tourist information, transport.

Accommodation and food

There is a big supermarket, a range of grocers and other shops and two hotels as you enter as well as a few restaurants scattered around town including:

Bar-Restaurante Venega is a good option with typical local menu and an *anís* still on the bar: C/Blas Infante, tel 957 539 279. Situated just as the GR7 enters Rute, **Hotel María Luisa** (B) is an upmarket hotel with private balconies, indoor and outdoor swimming pools, air conditioning, bar and restaurant: Crta Lucena-Loja, Km22, tel 957 538 096, www.hotelmarialuisa.es. **Hotel el Mirador** (B) is a smart hotel just around the corner from the María Luisa with balconies, air conditioning and the El Balcón restaurant: Ctra Rute-Encinas Reales, Km0.2, tel 957 539 404, www.miradorderute.com.

Further information

Tourist office, Parque Nuestra Señora del Carmen, tel 957 532 929, www.rute.org.

Transport

Taxis: tel 957 538 368/608 662 351/957 538 698

The whitewashed town overlooks the Iznájar reservoir and is dwarfed by the Sierra de Rute that looms above it. It is best known for its manufacture of *aguardiente de anís*, an aniseed-flavoured liqueur, an industry that has been thriving here since the 19th century. Try it at any of the town's *bodegas* where it is produced, or visit the Museo del Anís on the Paseo del Fresno (tel 957 538 143). Rute is also home to a ham museum (tel 957 539 227) – perhaps not quite as enticing a tourist attraction as the ruined Moorish castle or Baroque church.

CÓRDOBA PROVINCE

Peak of the Sierra Subbética Natural park (Stage 17A)

The route passes into the province of Córdoba from Málaga province, just after the village of Cuevas de San Marcos. On a scenic, winding route through olive groves, the GR7 takes you up to the small town of Rute, famed for its special liqueur, *anís*. From here you take a charming old woodland path with great views across the Subbética mountains, including the highest peak in the province, La Tiñosa, at 1568m. This brings you up to Priego de Córdoba, a striking historic town on a plateau looking down over the dramatic scenery of the park.

Onwards from here you visit the tiny village of La Concepción and pass through more olive groves, with panoramic views of the Sierra de los Judíos mountains and endless patterns of olives below, to reach Almedinilla. The route leaves Córdoba behind here and continues into Jaén province.

TRANSPORT

There are regular bus services linking many of the towns on the route with each other and the cities of Córdoba, Jaen and Granada.

Granada to Priego de Córdoba and Almedinilla run by:

- Alsina Graells: tel 952 841 365, www.alsa.es.
- Autobuses Carrera: 957 50 03 02, www.autocarescarrera.es

In addition to the companies own websites, the site www.autobuses.costasur.com is useful for finding times for buses from all companies.

Numbers for local taxi firms are also listed in the place information boxes.

TOURIST INFORMATION

Andalucía tourist information office in Córdoba: C/Torrijos 10, 14003, Córdoba, tel 957 355 179, www.andalucia.org.

OTHER WALKS

There is a good network of shorter walking routes in the Subbética, including the newly restored 58km route along an old olive oil train route (Via Verde del Tren de Aceite) which links Lucena, Cabra, Doña Mencía, Zuheros and Luque. Its stations have been turned into restaurants and the railway architecture and buildings – bridges, a tunnel, level crossings and the workers' housing – have been restored.

Many of the routes cross over, or link up with, parts of the GR7 and provide interesting extra sections if you want to spend more time in the Córdoba province or create circular routes. For further information it is worth trying to get hold of the walking guide to La Subbética from Mancomunidad de la Subbética, tel 957 704 106, www.subbetica.es.

RUTE TO ALCALÁ LA REAL (55.5KM)

STAGE 17A
Rute – Priego de Córdoba

Start	Centre of Rute
Distance	23.2km
Time	7h20
Highest point	1000m
Height gain	1020m
Height loss	1050m

A route made up mainly of magical woodland paths passing through pine and oak trees with stunning views over Córdoba's highest peaks before it returns to olive groves as it nears Priego de Córdoba.

RUTE 637M POPULATION 10,600

Accommodation, restaurant/bar/café, drinking fountain, food shop, cashpoint, telephone, PO, pharmacy, tourist information, transport.

Accommodation and food
There is a big supermarket, a range of grocers and other shops and two hotels as you enter as well as a few restaurants scattered around town including:

Bar-Restaurante Venega is a good option with typical local menu and an *anís* still on the bar: C/Blas Infante, tel 957 539 279. Situated just as the GR7 enters Rute, **Hotel María Luisa** (B) is an upmarket hotel with private balconies, indoor and outdoor swimming pools, air conditioning, bar and restaurant: Crta Lucena-Loja, Km22, tel 957 538 096, www.hotelmarialuisa.es. **Hotel el Mirador** (B) is a smart hotel just around the corner from the María Luisa with balconies, air conditioning and the El Balcón restaurant: Ctra Rute-Encinas Reales, Km0.2, tel 957 539 404, www.miradorderute.com.

Further information
Tourist office, Parque Nuestra Señora del Carmen, tel 957 532 929, www.rute.org.

Transport
Taxis: tel 957 538 368/608 662 351/957 538 698

The whitewashed town overlooks the Iznájar reservoir and is dwarfed by the Sierra de Rute that looms above it. It is best known for its manufacture of *aguardiente de anís*, an aniseed-flavoured liqueur, an industry that has been thriving here since the 19th century. Try it at any of the town's *bodegas* where it is produced, or visit the Museo del Anís on the Paseo del Fresno (tel 957 538 143). Rute is also home to a ham museum (tel 957 539 227) – perhaps not quite as enticing a tourist attraction as the ruined Moorish castle or Baroque church.

See map in Stage 16A.

To leave Rute head east out of the Paseo del Fresno past the secondary school (*colegio*) and off C/Chacarra, where a small track takes you uphill to the right into pine trees. Follow this, staying close to the right-hand side of a fence until it joins a wider dirt track, which you take to continue on up and around the hillside passing by a sign to the Fuente Alta picnic area.

From here you can see out across the whole valley, down to the ruins of Old Rute which was abandoned in the 15th century, and across the hills and the endless olive-clad ridges.

When the wide track ends, after just over 1.5km, continue uphill in the same direction on a smaller path, again through pine trees. At a clearing in the trees you can see the rocky outcrop of Sierra de la Gallinera (1095m), **Sierra Alcaide**, **Pico Bermejo** (1474m) and **La Tiñosa** (1570m) behind you. After another 500m you come to a **viewpoint**. ◄

From the viewpoint the small, shady path continues picking its way through pine woodland on the side of the Sierra de Rute and you should be able to see the small village of **Palomares** down to your left. When you reach a young olive grove, be careful not to miss the path which goes up to the right (rather than into the olives) and then continues along the edge of the field passing through beautiful woods, this time with some gall oaks.

The path continues, with many small junctions clearly marked, until it reaches a gorge. Here the path divides and you should head down a rocky ridge to the left, across a boulder field heading northeast and into grassy open countryside. When the path almost disappears, follow the edge of the field marked by a broken fence and an old wall. Now, 3h20 and about 10km from the start of the route, you come to a water supply at the Cortijo de Vichira.

Boulder field on the way to Priego de Córdoba

Pass the fountain and come to a signposted track. Turn right and continue along and then through a farmyard, ignoring a track off to the left. When the track divides, take the right fork uphill, passing behind a building to find a small path starting off to the right in the olive field. ▶

When the track meets another, turn right and then, when you enter another olive field, head left and then almost immediately right again. From here a smaller shady track takes you downhill to the road not far from the small village of **Los Villares**. Turn left for Los Villares or right to carry on with the route to Priego de Córdoba.

From here the path is patchy, but good markings take you back onto a track within 15min.

LOS VILLARES 612M POPULATION 5,000

Accommodation, campsite, restaurant/bar/café, drinking fountain, food shop, telephone.

Accommodation and food
A campsite with *casas rurales*:

Cortijo los Villares (A) campsite with has space for 70 people and various flats, swimming pool and restaurant: Ctra Carcabuey-Rute, Km6, tel 957 704 054, www.casasdelasubbetica.com.

Further information
Centro de Visitantes de Santa Rita: Ctra. A-339 Cabra–Priego Km11.2, Cabra, www.subbetica.com.

The village of Los Villares is located deep within the beautiful surroundings of the natural park with great views.

SIERRA SUBBÉTICA NATURAL PARK

The beautiful Parque Natural de la Sierra Subbética (320km²) is famous for its craggy limestone peaks which contrast sharply with the rolling lower hills covered in olive groves and the green woodland in which it sits.

Wildlife
The park is home to many gall and holm oaks, wild olives, maples and hackberries and a wide variety of wildflowers including irises, daffodils, peonies and orchids which bring it its colour in spring.

The area is very rich in bird life including one of the largest breeding colonies of griffon vultures in the south of Spain, and about 70 other bird species, including black wheatear, hoopoe, cuckoos, red-legged partridge, rock buntings, and common and alpine swifts.

Andalucía's largest population of peregrine falcons nest in the limestone crags and are the symbol for the park. It is also home to many other birds of prey – booted, Bonelli's and short-toed eagles, kestrels and several species of owl.

Stay on the small tarmac road for 4km, with great views back to **Pico Bermejo** and the Sierra de Rute, then turn right off onto a gravel track. This crosses a small bridge and then divides. Take the left fork and then the second track off to the right to go up and over a low pass before returning to a road. Turn left along the road and then, after 600m, right onto a gravel track. This is the old Rute road (Camino Viejo de Rute) which takes you all the way into **Priego de Córdoba**. You arrive in the town at a very old and battered looking GR7 display board. To get to the centre from here turn right along Av. de España.

PRIEGO DE CÓRDOBA 649M POPULATION 23,500

Accommodation, campsite, restaurant/bar/café, drinking fountain, food shop, cashpoint, telephone, PO, pharmacy, tourist information, transport.

Accommodation and food
There's a selection of hotels and also some lovely *casas rurales* if you're thinking of staying for a while, some busy tapas bars and a variety of restaurants:

Hotel Río Piscina (B) a large place on the GR7 route out of town with pools, restaurant and café: Ctra de Granada, tel 957 700 186, www.hotelriopiscina. com. **Hostal Rafi** (B) is a central 26-room hostal with restaurant and café below. Nice clean rooms with TV, air conditioning: C/Isabel la Católica 4, tel 957 540 749, www.hostalrafi.net. **La Posada Real** (B) is a traditional Andalucian house in historic area of Priego, available to rent as full house or per room: C/Real, tel 957 541 910, www.laposadareal.com.

Further information
www.aytopriegodecordoba.es.

Transport
Taxis: tel 657 588 059/636 772 487/610 678 641.

Perched on a hill above the Sierra Subbética, this elegant old town is known for its baroque churches, and, unsurprisingly given the number of trees you'll have passed, its olive oil. To get a feel for the architecture of the place visit the Iglesia de la Asunción, the Iglesia de la Aurora and the famous Fuente del Rey, an 139-spout fountain topped by a statue of Neptune. It's also worth strolling up to the 13th-century Islamic castle and to the picturesque Barrio de la Villa, the maze-like centre of the old town with cascades of colourful flowers and bright doors and windows set off by whitewashed walls.

STAGE 18A
Priego de Córdoba – Almedinilla

Start	C/Puerta Granada on eastern edge of Priego
Distance	10,4km
Time	2h40
Highest point	755m
Height gain	290m
Height loss	195m

With great views back over Priego, the route heads up through olive trees to Almedinilla. Markings are sparse for this section.

Leave Priego on C/Puerta Granada on the eastern edge of town. This small road takes you out past a right turn to C/Era, which you ignore: continue keeping to the right to get to the main A339 road. Turn right along this in the direction of Almedinilla for less than 100m before taking the first turning on the left onto a gravel track, signposted La Concepción 55min, Almedinilla 2h55.

As you leave the buildings behind you begin to get a great view back over Priego.

When this track divides take the left fork. ◀ At the next fork turn right as the track climbs uphill through olive trees. Stay on the main track and when it divides again, take a left and continue uphill for about a kilometre to where a signpost directs you right and east along a small path through the olive fields. After another 10min you arrive in **La Concepción** (restaurant/bar/café, drinking fountain), 4.5km and just over an hour from the start.

Turn right into La Concepción and continue down to the bottom of the village, passing the drinking fountain. There are two roads out of the village here; take the one to the left and follow it for a kilometre keeping a close eye out for a track off to the right at a bend in the road before you would pass a house up to the left. Take this unmarked track through olive fields, turning right and then left at the two junctions. When you come to some houses turn right onto a minor

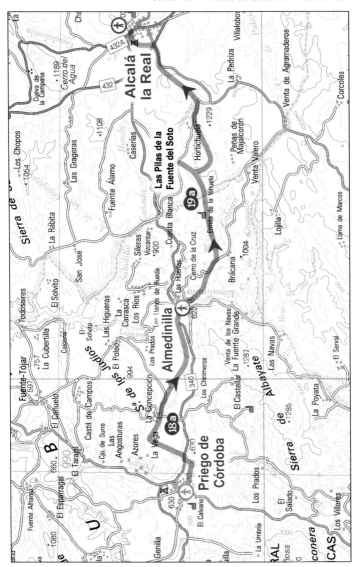

Priego de Córdoba

tarmac road and then, when that road meets another small tarmac road, turn left.

Cross the main road and walk past the football ground to get to the centre of the village.

Walk along the road for 2km and then turn right off it onto a wide gravel track, just before it goes up a small but steep hill. This takes you alongside a stream and then across it when the track divides. Follow this uphill to arrive in **Almedinilla**. ◄

ALMEDINILLA 622M POPULATION 2,500

Accommodation, restaurant/bar/café, drinking fountain, food shop, cashpoint, telephone, PO, pharmacy, tourist information, transport.

Accommodation and food
There are various restaurants and bars to eat in, including Mesón Rural La Era, which is beneath **Posada Venta El Gañán** (B), with large rustic rooms with good views: Plaza de la Era 1, tel 957 703 201. A number of *casas rurales* situated around Almedinilla can be found at: http://almedinilla.turismodelasubbetica.es.

Further information
Tourist office: Ctra A-339, Km37, tel 957 703 317, www.almedinillaturismo.es.

A pretty village with streets lined with orange trees. It was important in Roman times and you can visit the ruins of a large Roman villa. A former watermill in the village has now been turned into a museum and there is also an Iberian necropolis.

STAGE 19A
Almedinilla – Alcalá la Real

Start	Centre of Almedinilla
Distance	21.9km
Time	6h30
Highest point	1109m
Height gain	930m
Height loss	610m

A steady climb through olive groves followed by a scenic descent to the picturesque Alcalá dominated by its impressive castle. Markings are sparse for this section.

Follow road signs to Alcalá la Real out of Almedinilla, passing a junction off to the right with the road to Brácana next to the international school. Take the next right after this, following signs to the Museo Arqueológico. A paved footpath brings you up the impressive gorge on the left-hand side of the river.

See map in Stage 18A.

This path brings you out onto the **Brácana** road at a GR7 signpost (Las Pilas 2h25). Cross over the road here and take a small track up to the right steeply uphill and over the Cerro de la Cruz. ▸

A less steep, but also less attractive, option is to continue on the small local road until just after Km4 where you can take the turning to the left off the road highlighted in the directions below.

If you carry on over the hill, you climb steeply past some ruins and continue on the same path, the ancient Camino de los Caños. Do not turn off onto any smaller paths, and carry on through olive trees with beautiful views down to the village. You come out onto the CO8203 Camino de Almedinilla road and head right down it, passing an abandoned

On route to Alcalá La Real

farmhouse and another signpost (Las Pilas 1h50). After 100m turn left, then left again 500m further on at the next junction leaving the CO8203 onto a smaller tarmac road which you continue to follow downhill, despite the lack of markings.

After 30min and 2km you come to a water storage tank with a white tower at the ruined Cortijo de Santa Teresa. Pass by the tower and take the next dirt track up to the right, ignoring a track off to the left. Keep to the main track here, passing through olives and oaks and when you reach a crossroads after about 2km, continue straight on.

After a house on your right and then a track doubling back to the right just past it, take a right at a fork and continue on, passing a further track to the right. This main track, Camino de la Fuente de Zarza, will bring you to the road where you turn left and, after a few hundred metres, you leave the Córdoba province for Jaén. At a divide in the road 500m further on, take the right fork uphill to continue on the route or the left fork down and round the corner to visit the small village of **Las Pilas de la Fuente del Soto** (860m, restaurant/bar/café, drinking fountain, cashpoint, telephone, transport), 1km and about 15min further on.

If you went into Las Pilas, you can exit on the same road you came in on, taking the signposted turn up to the left in the direction of Alcalá la Real back to the main route. Head uphill on this road from here for about 2.5km (40min), through olive groves. Once you start to go downhill you should come to a signpost beside a house (Alcalá 2h10), after about 300m.

Here leave the road to follow the track passing Cortijillo los Chatis on your right. ▸ At a pylon the route turns up into olives and heads east towards cherry trees and a second pylon, where you meet a clearer track, less than 1km from the road. Turn right up this and after 60m left off it again to carry on another less clear track downhill through olives. ▸ The track seems to stop at the bottom of the field by stone walls and a water pool. Cross a drainage ditch on a small concrete bridge to your right (less than 200m from the track). Stay to the right of the drainage ditch, heading down the edge of another field before bending to the right to cross a second drainage channel 100m on from the first. Then go left to the bottom of the field keeping the ditch to your left for a further 100m to reach a clearer track. Carry on this ignoring a right turn by a large agricultural shed, continuing past a house to your right and through a farm to reach the road, JA5300, at a GR7 signpost (2km from last road).

It joins the road after Km3 at which point you turn right. An easier option is to leave Las Pilas on the same road you came in on, but in the opposite direction and take its right fork when it divides. After about 4km the GR7 joins this road and you can continue along the route from here.

After this point, follow the road as it climbs gently for 1.7km then head down to the left on a signposted smaller tarmac road (signed Alcala 1h25). After 200m take a right fork up a concrete track to climb briefly to over 1000m with a white cross up to your right and your first views of Alcalá dominated by the Arab Castillo de la Mota (300m from last turn). Stay on the track to the left, which is gravel from here, on level terrain for 500m. Here you come to a track off to the right signposted Alcalá 1h10. Head down steeply on little, unclear tracks to reach a main track below by a small breeze block building, 300m from the signpost. Go left along the track and at a junction just over 800m further on go right to continue descending. The track comes down to meet a little tarmac road after 750m signposted Alcalá 30min to the right. Go right up it very briefly then left off along a gravel track to arrive at the main road. Go left along this busy main road

After this house the track becomes much less clear.

This next short bit of route is unmarked and difficult to follow passing through fields without paths.

crossing straight over a large junction. At the roundabout just beyond, take a smaller road off to the left. This takes you up the hill towards and round behind the castle. You come into the town on C/de San Francisco.

ALCALÁ LA REAL 950M POPULATION 21,000

Accommodation, campsite, restaurant/bar/café, drinking fountain, food shop, cashpoint, telephone, PO, pharmacy, tourist information, transport.

Accommodation and food
There are many places to eat, from restaurants to tapas bars, several hotels in the town and lots of *casas rurales*:

Pensión Río de Oro (A) is central, with clean pleasant rooms above a bar: C/Abad Moya 2, tel 953 580 337, www.hostalriodeoro.com. **Hotel Torrepalma** (B) is upmarket, with restaurant, café, free wi-fi, on the way into town: Conde de Torrepalma 2, tel 953 581 800, www.hoteltorrepalma.com. **Hospedería Zacatín** (B) is a friendly guest house down a little side street from Río de Oro with standard rooms and luxury ones with hydro massage in the bath, hairdryers and minibars, busy bar underneath: C/Pradillo 2, tel 953 580 568, www.hospederiazacatin.com.

Further information
Tourist office: Palacio Abacial, Carrera de las Mercedes, tel 953 582 077, www.alcalalareal.es.

Transport
Taxis: tel 687 322 831/953 580 507/653 974 274.

An attractive town with an impressive eighth-century castle, La Mota, which now houses a small museum. Also worth a visit is the imposing abbey church located within the original city walls on the site of the original Alcalá Abbey. Built in a combination of various architectural styles, including Gothic and Renaissance, it has a tower which is over 40m high. It is also lovely to go for a stroll along the exterior walkway, used for markets, fairs and evening *paseos*.

JAÉN PROVINCE

The endless olives on route to Quesada (Stage 26A)

HIGHLIGHTS OF THE ROUTE IN JAÉN PROVINCE

- castles – Jaén province is home to the most castles per km² in Europe
- lofty peaks and stunning views of the Parque Natural de la Sierra Mágina
- the tree-covered slopes of the remote and wild Parque Natural de las Sierras de Cazorla, Segura y las Villas

Over 300km of route take you through Jaén province's most important mountain ranges: the Sierra Sur, the Sierra Mágina and the Sierras de Cazorla, Segura y las Villas. Jaén is full of wild spaces and is the province with the highest number of protected areas in Spain. Its protected parks and reserves cover 304,000 hectares in total, almost a third of the province.

The route crosses into Jaén from the Córdoba province at Alcalá la Real,

which is the biggest place on the route in Jaén, dominated by an impressive eighth-century castle, La Mota. From there, the route passes over the imposing Sierra de Alta Coloma and down through the pretty white villages of Carchelejo and Cambil before crossing into the Parque Natural de la Sierra Mágina, home to Pico Mágina, the highest peak in the province at 2167m.

From there, the route takes you through a sea of olive groves between

Bedmar, Jódar and Quesada before arriving back at the foothills of large peaks in the vibrant and beautiful Cazorla, the gateway to the largest natural park in Andalucía, the Parque Natural de Cazorla, Segura y las Villas. You get a magnificent feeling of freedom as the route winds its way around and over the pine-clad lofty peaks of the park and emerges at the source of the Río Guadalquivir.

Here the valleys and countryside have great grandeur and natural beauty and you pass through a few final villages on your way to Santiago de la Espada, the last destination of the GR7 in the Jaén province. The route then crosses over into Granada province to rejoin the Southern Fork of the GR7 in Puebla de Don Fadrique. From this point onwards, the route goes out of Andalucía and into the Murcia region of Spain.

TRANSPORT

Alcalá la Real and the city of Jaén itself offer the best transport options to and from places along the route of the GR7 in Jaén province, with regular buses running from both to most villages on the route. The buses are run by several companies and it is best to get in touch with them to check out up-to-date timetables. The two main companies are:

- Alsina Graells, which runs buses to/from Alcalá la Real, Carchelejo, Cazorla, Frailes, Jódar and Torres: tel 952 841 365, www.alsa.es
- Muñoz Amezcua, which runs buses from Jaén bus station to Quesada, Jódar, Albanchez de Mágina and Bedmar, stopping at many of the small places en route: tel 953 222 883, www.munozamezcua.es

Local taxi firms are listed under the information box for each place.

FURTHER INFORMATION

- Alcalá la Real bus station: tel 953 583 000
- Jaén train station: tel 953 270 202
- Jaén bus station: tel 953 254 442
- Andalucía tourist office: C/Maestra 13, Bajo, 23007, Jaén, tel 953 242 624

OTHER WALKS

There is a range of walking and cycling routes in the Sierra Mágina, taking in some amazing scenery. They are not very well marked, but a couple of little 'Magica Mágina' guides with descriptions and sketch maps are available from the Asociación para el Desarrollo Rural de la Sierra Mágina (www.magina. org) which has an office in Cambil (on C/Posada above the health centre).

In the Sierras de Cazorla, Segura y las Villas natural park there is a huge network of paths and tracks but most of them are unmarked. You can get hold of maps and route descriptions from the Cazorla tourist office or the visitor centres (see Stage 27A). The Sendero Río Borosa (19km, 7h round trip) is one of the park's better known routes, starting at the Torre de Vinagre visitor centre and taking you through a spectacular gorge hewn out by the Borosa river, past waterfalls to the beautiful Laguna de Aguas Negras and the Laguna de Valdeazores. There are also shorter walks such as the 2km Sendero Cerrada de Utrero to the Linarejos waterfall.

ALCALÁ LA REAL TO PUEBLA DE DON FADRIQUE (285.4KM)

STAGE 20A
Alcalá la Real – Frailes

Start	C/Utrilla, near Consolación church, Alcalá la Real
Distance	9km
Time	1h50
Highest point	1010m
Height gain	235m
Height loss	240m

Climb out of Alcalá and look back on great views of the town. Pass through nearby Santa Ana and head into more open countryside, looking out on olive-covered slopes, holm oaks, walnut, cherry and almond trees and the distant Sierra Nevada as you approach Frailes.

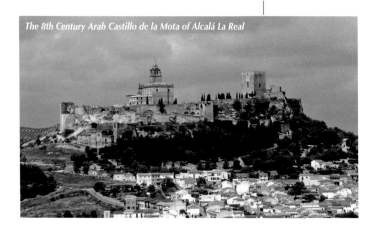
The 8th Century Arab Castillo de la Mota of Alcalá La Real

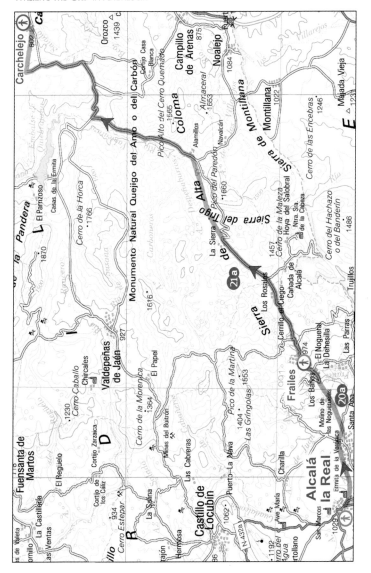

ALCALÁ LA REAL 950M POPULATION 21,000

Accommodation, campsite, restaurant/bar/café, drinking fountain, food shop, cashpoint, telephone, PO, pharmacy, tourist information, transport.

Accommodation and food
There are many places to eat, from restaurants to tapas bars, several hotels in the town and lots of *casas rurales*:

Pensión Río de Oro (A) is central, with clean pleasant rooms above a bar: C/Abad Moya 2, tel 953 580 337, www.hostalriodeoro.com. **Hotel Torrepalma** (B) is upmarket, with restaurant, café, free wi-fi, on the way into town: Conde de Torrepalma 2, tel 953 581 800, www.hoteltorrepalma.com. **Hospedería Zacatín** (B) is a friendly guest house down a little side street from Río de Oro with standard rooms and luxury ones with hydro massage in the bath, hairdryers and minibars, busy bar underneath: C/Pradillo 2, tel 953 580 568, www.hospederiazacatin.com.

Further information
Tourist office: Palacio Abacial, Carrera de las Mercedes, tel 953 582 077, www.alcalalareal.es.

Transport
Taxis: tel 687 322 831/953 580 507/653 974 274.

An attractive town with an impressive eighth-century castle, La Mota, which now houses a small museum. Also worth a visit is the imposing abbey church located within the original city walls on the site of the original Alcalá Abbey. Built in a combination of various architectural styles, including Gothic and Renaissance, it has a tower which is over 40m high. It is also lovely to go for a stroll along the exterior walkway, used for markets, fairs and evening *paseos*.

To leave Alcalá head uphill on C/Utrilla near the Consolación church and climb to the top of the hill, marked by a cross. From here take the right track signposted as the Ruta del Califato. ▸

There's no GR7 marking to begin with.

The small track meets a larger dirt track after 600m. Follow this round to the left along the fence line with the village of Santa Ana visible in front of you. There are some GR7 marks here as well as some blue marks which the local walking club also use to mark the route.

Turn left at the crossroads on the edge of **Santa Ana** to leave the Ruta del Califato, which goes right and come round the side of an orchard. Then follow red wooden arrows between buildings to come up to the tarmac road. You then

137

come to a tarmac road, Camino de Frailes, which you cross straight over to ascend C/Fuente Somera and come into the suburbs of Santa Ana (shop, pharmacy). At the Club Fuente del Rey (on your left) turn right down the road then carry straight on.

The tarmac road passes through housing then turns into a dirt track which you continue to follow, ignoring tracks back to the left and forward to right. When you meet another tarmac road after 400m, continue on in the same direction briefly and then back on a gravel track straight on. Keep right at two forks to keep going in the same direction until you reach the edge of Santa Ana at a tarmac road. Turning right brings you to the main road, JA4302, where you turn left out of the village, an hour from Alcalá.

After 500m, by a white cross, you leave the main road to the left on a signed track (Frailes 1h) which takes you out into the countryside and through fields. Keep on the main track, passing straight over a crossroads and ignoring smaller tracks off into fields. At an equal divide take the left fork down to a small stream, the Arroyo del Salograr, and a stone wall. Ignore the track to left and head uphill on a *cañada real*.

Pass another white cross at the top of the hill, where you get your first view of **Frailes**, and start back downwards turning right when you meet a small tarmac road, which you follow into the village, entering on C/Camino de la Cuesta (9km, 1h50).

FRAILES 780M POPULATION 1,730

Accommodation, restaurant/bar/café, drinking fountain, food shop, cashpoint, telephone, PO, pharmacy, transport.

Accommodation and food
A couple of small bars, several restaurants and a couple of good value places to stay:

Mesón Hostal la Posá (A) bar and restaurant has spacious, bright rooms above: C/Tejar 3, tel 953 593 218. **Pensión/Hostal Ardales** (A) has five recently renovated rooms above a café-bar: C/Avenida 18, tel 953 593 508, www.hostalardales.webcindario.com.

Further information
Taxi: tel 953 594 138.

The village of Frailes is built around the church of Santa Lucía and has been the site for a number of important archaeological finds. Nestled into the surrounding rock faces, it is made more picturesque by the Río Vellilos, which runs through the village. You can read more about the village in the novel *The Factory of Light: Tales from My Andalucian Village* by Michal Jacobs, who lives here.

STAGE 21A
Frailes – Carchelejo

Start	Beside the Río Vellilos in Frailes
Distance	35.5km
Time	9h30
Highest point	1497m
Height gain	1755m
Height loss	1870m
Note	A tent is essential if you want to break the journey

Leave behind olive trees and fields to climb into wild hills where you'll have the views all to yourself, apart from the goats and the sheep. Descend through the rocky Valdearazo gorge, with impressive views of the Embalse de Quiebrajano, return to cultivated land and on into Carchelejo. Markings are sparse and some sections are slippery and potentially dangerous if wet.

You leave Frailes on the same road you came in on beside the Río Vellilos. Follow the road through the village and out, passing by a park on the right with a GR7 display board. Passing a right turn just as you leave the village (this is an alternative route on a *cañada real*, which rejoins the road after the Hoya de Salobral turning), after 600m take the next right fork in the road signed to **Hoya de Salobral**. This small road takes you 3km uphill to **Los Rosales**, walking next to olives then hazels and poplars (4km, 1h).

To leave Los Rosales continue upwards along the road past the drinking fountain. After 500m the road forks and

See map in Stage 20A.

This begins to take you into much wilder countryside, looking ahead to the Sierra del Trigo.

you take the gravel track to the left (GR7 signpost Carchelejo 8h30 and to Cerezo Gordo). ◄

One kilometre further on, ignore a track to the right signposted to Las Lomillas. When you come to a divide where the left fork is signposted to Cueva la Yedra, head right. The road becomes much more track-like and takes you gently uphill through beautiful woodland into hillier territory.

Ignore a track back to the left and then a second one up to Cerezo Gordo as you begin to climb. Stay on the main track, past two cortijos, one in ruins, and head towards a hill with prominent wind turbines (*paredón*). Climb up the first zigzag on this hill and then turn left when it divides (signpost Carchelejo 6h40), now some 6km from Los Rosales. The right turn would take you to the village of **Noalejo** in 2h30.

After climbing gently you reach a crossroads where you turn right to curve round the side of **Pico del Paredón**, now up to your right. Pass through three gates on the same track then after the third, with ruined buildings on your left, take a smaller track up to your right, passing a small spring.

After just less than 1km (just after the wind turbines go out of sight), the track bends sharply into a valley. Keep a close eye out here for a very small path heading steeply uphill to the right. The path is not clear on the ground but is well marked and takes you up the **Sierra del Trigo** heading southeast until you reach a pass at 1500m. ◄

Here you are rewarded with panoramic views of all the surrounding mountains.

From the pass, head back downhill on a small track slightly to your right into trees and stay on it until you go through a gate (made of bedsprings at time of writing). After another 50m, head left down off the track again on a steep, unclear but well-marked path.

The path now follows the valley. Keep slightly to the right and you'll come out of the trees near a large track. Don't take the track, but instead take a path down to the left of it towards the Cortijo los **Alamillos**. This brings you back to the track at the farmhouse on a shorter route.

From here continue along the main track for almost 8km, descending alongside the route of the **Río Valdearazo**, ignoring one track off to the left. At a crossroads at the Cortijo Prados continue down and across a stone bridge. At the next divide take the left fork across a low bridge/ford.

The track continues on but you leave it at the first big hairpin bend after it starts to go up. Here a small path, with its signpost missing, heads off to the right. Follow this into the

Quiebrajano reservoir

Valdearazo gorge where it clings, in places precariously, to the rocky sides. The path then crosses the river by means of a small footbridge before beginning the long climb on a steep zigzagging rocky path to the Cerro de la Piedra de Palo, a climb of around 300m with great views into the gorge and over the green water of the **Embalse de Quiebrajano** far below.

▶ Follow the path down to the farmhouse and then right along a track from it onto a tarmac road. Turn left along the road and carry on for 2.5km until a sign directs you right through olive groves onto a dirt track. Keep on the main track, ignoring two smaller ones off to either side. The track then becomes a smaller path making its way between two stone walls. Keep going downhill all the way now to **Carchelejo**, only turning off to the right onto a smaller path just before you reach the village. This brings you into the centre.

When you reach the top, a signpost indicates that it is 2h to Carchelejo, most of which is mercifully downhill.

141

CARCHELEJO 820M POPULATION 1480

Accommodation, restaurant/bar/café, drinking fountain, food shop, cashpoint, telephone, PO, pharmacy, transport.

Accommodation and food
There are a couple of restaurants and some lovely *casas rurales*, flats and a hotel out of the village.

Mezquita de Mágina Rural Apartments (A). Newly refurbished, high-quality, self-contained flats/houses set around a pleasant courtyard: C/Jesús 14, tel 953 302 482, www.carcheles.es/turismo/apartamentos-mezquita-de-magina.html.
Hotel-Restaurante Oasis (B). At a busy road junction next to a petrol station several kilometres from the village, reached by continuing along the road out of Carchelejo instead of going under the underpass: Ctra Bailén-Motril, Km59, tel 953 302 083, www.hotel-oasis.es.

A number of *casas rurales* are available to let by the room or as whole houses: 953 302 389/953 302 204/953 275 402/953 302 455. www.carcheles.es/turismo/casas-rurales.html.

Further information
Town hall: tel 953 309 004, www.carcheles.es.

Carchelejo, with neighbouring Cárchel, makes up the municipality of Cárcheles. Its economic mainstays of olives and livestock are evident from the groves and pasture around. Sites to visit in the town include the 18th-century church, Nuestra Señora de los Angeles, and the Ermita de San Marcos.

STAGE 22A
Carchelejo – Cambil

Start	Av. de España, Carchelejo
Distance	11.8km
Time	3h30
Highest point	834m
Height gain	420m
Height loss	470m

Pleasant track and path walking through farmland, olives, fields and orchards and alongside the river into Cambil. The path is occasionally overgrown with poor marking and there is one river crossing on a rickety bridge.

Leave Carchelejo on Av. de España to join and turn left up the the road to Cárchel. 500m from Carchelejo, just after a large sausage factory (*Fábrica de Embutidos*) on the right of the road, leave the road to the right on a narrow concrete track (signed Cambil 3h10). Descend, sticking to the main track which becomes gravel taking a right fork after 350m to descend into a small fertile valley with big solar panels above you to the left. After a further 500m on the track with a ruined building on your left a GR7 'X' marks the track ahead and another post sends you up the hillside to the right. This takes you along a very eroded and overgrown path – you can either fight your way along this, contouring just above the track, or just continue along the track for 400m to a chain across a track at a farm entrance, where the little path rejoins it anyway.

At this point the little path leaves the track again up to the right. Follow it up the valley, contouring around the hillside for about 600m to where the path is interrupted by a small channel caused by water erosion. This is easily crossed and immediately after this the path splits. You take the less clear path downhill just above the olive trees. Then at a post head down into the olives towards a stream to meet a track that crosses the stream. Climb, staying on this main track which then takes you up the other side of the valley

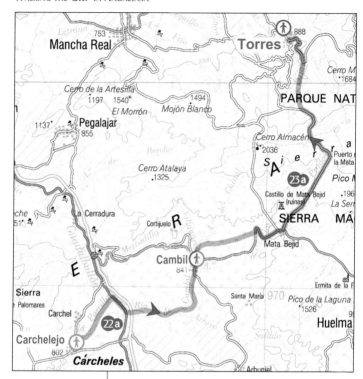

to come to a signpost (Cambil 2h25) and head down to the right: straight on would take you to **Cárchel** (25min). Stay on this main track, passing two tracks off to the right soon after to descend through olives. 700m from the signpost the track peters out but continue in the same direction which is northeast, through the olive grove and you'll soon find it again albeit a bit more rough and overgrown. At a split in the track soon after take the more minor track down to the right which turns into a path down through olives again in the same direction parallel to the stream. ◄ The path then turns into a track that you follow down to the road (3.5km from leaving the Carchelejo to Cárchel road, 1h). Go right along the road for just under 1.5km then turn left under an underpass just before a small layby. It is about 7km to Cambil from here.

At this point dramatic rocky outcrops known as 'el Diente de la Vieja' the 'old woman's tooth' come into view to your right.

The track bends round to the left next to the **Rio Guadabullón**, then right across a bridge over the river. Marking is pretty absent from here for a couple of km, but continue, passing some ruins on your left and climbing gently to a junction after about 600m. Go right here. After about 70m there is a chain to block vehicle access but you continue on this same track. After 300m pass a track on the right which leads to a small building and about 200m further on you will come to a large new cortijo on your right.

On route between Carchelejo and Cambil

Stay on the same track, climbing gently, ignoring two tracks to the right down to houses and a further track into olives. You are now above the river, looking down on olives and vegetable patches below. The track crosses a bridge and then cuts through the hillside to come to a ruined *cortijo* (now nearly 2km from the road). Here you leave the track and head up to the left towards a post above an olive field. Go right from here along a very overgrown path. The path is hard to follow but you just need to keep to the top edge of the olive groves, crossing two gullies to come round the hillside and down into a flat field of olives by the river, with poplars ahead and another ruined *cortijo* after about 700m.

From here you climb on a track, passing another ruined *cortijo* on your left after 100m and climbing for a futher 200m to reach a junction. Go right to continue in the same direction but now downhill passing another ruin to come to another olive grove. Again, go along the top edge of the field to come to the river and a missing bridge! Follow the river upstream to come to a makeshift and slightly precarious bridge after about 100m. Cross this and go straight ahead up a track which zigzags up to meet another track which you turn left along. ◄ Stay on the main track couring around the hillside then dropping to pass through a farmyard and around a house. It then takes you on bridges over the Rio Arbuniel and **Rio Cambil**, and then alongside the left of the river all the way into **Cambil**, passing vegetable plots and occasional houses.

There are great views of the Sierra Mágina ahead.

CAMBIL 780M POPULATION 3300

Accommodation, restaurant/bar/café, drinking fountain, food shop, cashpoint, telephone, PO, pharmacy, tourist information, transport.

Accommodation and food
There are a couple of options for accommodation and a few restaurants:

Los Castillos Hostal Restaurant (A) is a good café-bar popular with locals, friendly owners with a few modest clean rooms, C/Huerta de Leonor, tel 627 281 404.
Hostal Monzón (B), despite the name, no longer has rooms but has a good restaurant with local specialities and pleasant terrace: Paseo del Señor del Mármol, tel 953 300 578, www.restaurantehostalmonzon.com. **Casa Rural El Mirador** (B) has pleasant flats available to let by the night if not booked, some with roof terraces: Posadas 11, tel 953 300 029.

Further information
Town hall: tel 953 300 002, www.cambil.es.

In a valley between the Engeño and Achuelo hills, Cambil is one of the villages richest in water in the area. The source of Río Arbuniel next to the village is now a picnic area. Olive cultivation is a key part of the local economy and there is a focus on using methods that avoid chemicals and minimize damage to the environment. It is also home to an ecological co-operative that produces high quality organic olive oil. Buildings of interest include the castle and the 16th-century church.

STAGE 23A
Cambil – Torres

Start	Cambil, on the road to Huelma
Distance	26.7km
Time	8h
Highest point	1655m
Height gain	1155m
Height loss	995m

A beautiful stretch in the heart of the Parque Natural de la Sierra Mágina, passing the ruined castle of Mata Bejid, and enjoying excellent views of the mountains including Jaén's highest peak, Pico Mágina, and El Almadén (recognisable by the communications tower on its top). There are options to climb both these peaks on routes that leave from the GR7.

Leave Cambil on the main Jaén to Huelma road. Take a small road heading off to the north signposted to Vuelta al Almadén, Bornos and Bercho Nacimiento. This leaves the village on C/Camino de la Loma and climbs uphill. After 1.5km (around 25min) take a right fork in the road, signposted for Bornos and Almadén.

See map in Stage 22A.

Climb more gently through olive groves staying on the main track until you reach a Sierra Mágina signpost, another 1.5km on. Here take a right turn signed to N324 Almadén, again staying on the main track through olive groves. ▶ Carry on straight heading east (ignoring a small track off to the left) until you reach an intersection of a few tracks, where you take the one forward to the right (oddly signposted to Cambil N323). When you meet another track turn left to come down to the road (5km, 1h10).

The mountains of the Sierra Mágina dominate the horizon to your northwards to your left.

Turn left along the road and stay on it for just under 1.5km before turning left again up a signposted gravel track just before the old settlement of **Mata Bejid**. Continue on this track heading uphill into wilder countryside.

The countryside changes here as a result of the much more **humid climate in the valley** – lots of streams from hillsides descend to fill the Río de Cambil. The vegetation becomes oaks and gall oaks with green slopes used to pasture sheep and goats.

After 2km you come to the ruins of the **Castillo de Mata Bejid** on your left. Stay on the right-hand track, passing two smaller ones off to the left. It continues uphill and you can enjoy beautiful views back over the mountains through which the route has already passed – feeling satisfied at how far you have come. The path then climbs to an area called Cortijo de los Prados where a signpost points you off the path to the left to a nearby fountain, 4km after the ruins (although it does not always have water).

Enjoy the amazing views as far as the Sierra Nevada to the southeast and over the rest of Jaén province to the north.

A kilometre further on, ignore a right fork, which is a route up **Pico Mágina**, and stay on the main track which heads ever upwards towards the crags, passing ancient, thick-trunked oaks, and then, finally, reaching the top of the pass, **Puerto de la Mata**, at 1650m. ◄

In the Sierra Mágina natural park

SIERRA MÁGINA NATURAL PARK

The Parque Natural de la Sierra Mágina (199km²) is a huge mountain massif rising out of a sea of olive groves. Although small, it has some of the highest mountains of the province. The mountains act as a barrier to the Atlantic winds and as a result produce strong climatic contrasts and varied landscapes. In the westernmost part, where the clouds break, the vegetation is lush woodland with pines and oaks. In contrast, the eastern part, which suffers from a lack of rain, has a landscape of dry white clay. This semi-desert area extends from the right bank of the Río Jandulilla to the valley of the Guadiana Menor.

During the winter months snow covers the highest peaks of the Sierra Mágina, including Pico Mágina, which is the highest in Jaén at 2164m. The limestone rocks which make up the mountains of the Sierra Mágina act as porous sponges, absorbing the water from snow melt and rain through plentiful caves and potholes. Most of the sub-soil is full of subterranean aquifers which come to the surface as springs. The water from all these springs turns into streams and rivers which run into the Jandulilla and Guadalbullón valleys and feed the Río Guadalquivir.

The area has been populated since prehistoric times and has been of great strategic importance through the ages as a route for transport and communication to the interior of the country.

Wildlife

The park has a great botanical diversity, with over 1290 known plant species, some of them endemic, spread across a range of altitudes, including 300 species of wild mushroom and 20 species of orchid.

It is also home to 240 known species of vertebrates, the majority of them protected by regional, national, or European environmental legislation and some of them, like the Iberian lynx, in danger of extinction. Only about 100 live in the wild, all of them in Andalucía. Other mammals found in the park include ibex, wildcats, foxes and wild boar. The hocicuda viper is the rarest of the snakes in the park.

There are 185 species of bird which either live permanently in the park or migrate there for a period of the year, including large raptors such as the peregrine falcon and two types of eagle.

Further information

Park visitor centre: in the castle in Jódar, tel 953 787 656, open Thursday–Friday 10am–2pm, weekends and public holidays 4–6pm (October to March) and 6–8pm (April to September), www.magina.org.

The track descends through pines and you can see Torres down in the distance. Don't take the right turn at the bend 2km from the top, but take the next right almost 1.5km

If you want to continue on to Albánchez (1h20), take the signed track off to the right at the edge of Torres.

further down when you meet another track. Now 19km from the start, you zigzag down the hillside. Ignore a track down to the left just after passing another fountain then take the one to the right marked with a wooden post.

When you come to the small Camping Hondacabra (only open in high season) and another fountain, take the track to the right which takes you to the road into **Torres**. Continue down the road for just less than 2km to enter Torres. ◄

TORRES 900M POPULATION 1,650

Accommodation, campsite, restaurant/bar/café, drinking fountain, food shop, cashpoint, telephone, PO, pharmacy, transport.

Accommodation and food
Torres offers three fairly grand hotels, the first of which is less likely to have coach parties staying:

Hotel-Restaurante Jurinea (B) is a smart, friendly place which you pass on the way in, organising outdoor and cultural activities, with good restaurant serving local dishes, a lively bar, air conditioning and TV: Camino de la Ladera, tel 953 363 021, www.hoteljurinea.com. **Puerto Mágina Hotel** (B) is an upmarket hotel on edge of the village which prides itself on its restaurant, swimming pool and air conditioning: Ctra Torres-Albánchez, Km3, tel 953 363 192, www.puertomagina. com. **Hotel Almoratín** (C) is a very smart new spa hotel on the outskirts next to the Puerto Mágina with 61 rooms, bar, restaurant, free wi-fi and air conditioning: Ctra Torres-Albánchez de Mágina, Km2.8, tel 953 363 100, www.almoratin.com.

Further information
Town hall: Plaza de la Constitución 2, tel 953 494 005, www.aytorres.es.

At the foot of Cerro de la Vieja, Torres is rich in water from various different fountains and is known for its production of barley wine as well as olives. There is an open-air museum of the old rough millstones used in olive oil production and the 200-year-old large earthenware jars which were used to contain the oil. If you are staying in the village you can also visit the nearby paleolithic cave paintings at la Cueva del Morrón.

Some other good walking routes leave from here including circular routes to Aznaitín. It is worth going to the town hall to pick up information on routes.

STAGE 24A

Torres – Bedmar

Start	Park at the entrance to Torres
Distance	15.3km
Time	4h50
Highest point	1162m
Height gain	570m
Height loss	875m

A climb through almond and cherry orchards and fields to the Albánchez pass then on along a route which contours around the very edge of the Sierra Mágina foothills, looking out across the flat expanse to Bedmar. The route is somewhat circuitous in order to take in an ancient fountain and watchtower.

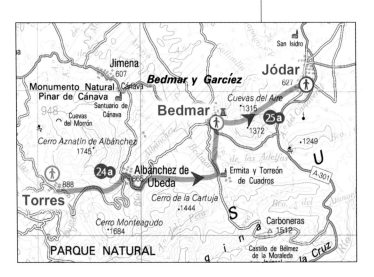

Torres – Albánchez de Úbeda (4.6km, 1h20)

The route to Albánchez leaves the park at the entrance to the village on a track up to the left signed Albánchez 1h20. The track climbs steeply and where it splits take the path to the left. This soon turns into a track, stay left along paths and tracks close to the gorge, marked in places. After 800m where you turn up into a cherry field head right along the track to zigzag up above the cherries and climb to the road (1.2km, 30min) at 1090m, (signed Albánchez 35min).

Continue left along the road, climbing gently over the Albánchez pass at 1250m and then leaving the road again

The route down into Albánchez de Úbeda with the cliff face on your left

after 1.3km, just after the Km5 road marking. Take a small path down to the left passing between fields of almond trees. Then take a tiny, and in places extremely overgrown, but well-marked path zigzagging down the hillside to avoid the large loops in the road.

You emerge onto a small tarmac road less than 2km later. Turn left to rejoin the main road, and then left again to enter the village of **Albánchez de Úbeda**, passing a viewpoint over the craggy rocks of El Torcal and Alto de la Serrezuela (1272m), the mountain behind Bedmar.

ALBÁNCHEZ DE ÚBEDA 860M POPULATION 1,350

Accommodation, campsite, restaurant/bar/café, drinking fountain, food shop, cashpoint, telephone, PO, pharmacy, tourist information, transport.

Accommodation and food
There are a few options for accommodation and food:

2km from the village, **Camping el Ayozar** (A) is a large campsite with a variety of options for accommodation and lots of facilities including a swimming pool and restaurant: on the road into Jimena, Km2.5, tel 953 35 74 63, www.ociomagina. com/camping.php. **Casa Cati** (A) is a *casa rural* with kitchen and terrace in the centre of the village: C/Juan XXIII 25, tel 953 358 431. **San José de Hútar** (B) is a smart hotel with spacious rooms, air conditioning, restaurant and swimming pool on road to Jimena, tel 953 357 474, www.hotelhutar.com.

Further information
Town hall: tel 953 358 339, www.albanchezdemagina.es.

The village sits in the foothills of Aznaitín, its white buildings crowned by an Arab fortress which was once, due to its strategic position, one of the most important in the region. You can visit it by climbing 300 narrow steps, but it is perhaps more spectacular from a distance. Also worth seeing are the Renaissance church, some Iberian and Roman remains, and numerous natural springs.

The village has only been called Albánchez de Úbeda since 1917, when it was bought by the Duchy of Úbeda, and many locals do not like the name and prefer Albánchez, or Albánchez de Santiago or de Mágina.

Albánchez de Úbeda – Bedmar (10.7km, 3h30)
Leave Albánchez on C/Eras, heading down out of the village and passing Fuente de la Seda on your left on a small potholed tarmac road. Follow this for just over 2km from

153

the edge of the village and then take a right turn up a small road, concrete at the junction then briefly tarmac. Here you turn left almost straight away signposted Bedmar. The road becomes a dirt track after 900m.

Stay on the main track, ignoring small tracks off into fields and one larger one off to the left just over 1.5km after leaving the road.

A kilometre on, you come to a sign for the Abrevadero de la Fresneda, a brief detour to a fountain up to the right. The route continues straight on, ignoring a track to the left following a white arrow on the wall. Continue on, ignoring little paths (feeling almost as if you're going to pass Bedmar by). When you come to a crossroads a kilometre later carry straight on, following another walking route's wooden signposts. Another 200m from here is the path to the **Torreón de Cuadros**, a 12m-high Arab watchtower.

After 700m, you come down to a small car park on a road and turn left (signpost Bedmar 1h55). Turn right just over 1.5km further on after passing over a small bridge into a field of olive trees. Take the left of the two tracks heading up towards a building. As you approach the building take a small path round the right of it and follow it along the edge of the field and then along a fence. You reach a viewpoint and **Bedmar** is 10min along the main road to the left.

BEDMAR 650M POPULATION 3,100

Accommodation, restaurant/bar/café, drinking fountain, food shop, cashpoint, telephone, PO, pharmacy, tourist information, transport.

Accommodation and food

There is a handful of bars and restaurants and some accommodation: **El Paraíso de Magína** (B) is the only hotel in the centre of town. It has a good bar/restaurant beneath: Av. Virgen de Cuadros 58, tel 953 760 010, www.paraisomagina.com.

There are a number of *casas rurales* available to let as whole houses (often with minimum two night stay) including: www.elcercadillo.com (a number of properties), www.casadelatercia.com, and www.riocuadros.com (on the GR7 route) and www.lachopera.es

Further information

Town hall: Plaza de la Constitución, tel 953 760 002, www.bedmargarciez.es.

Bedmar is dominated by the ruined castle on the hill above it, which you can walk up to for a good view down over the town. Its main economic activity is still agriculture carried out using very traditional techniques (principally olives and more recently white asparagus).

STAGE 25A
Bedmar – Jódar

Start	Centre of Bedmar
Distance	7.8km
Time	2h20
Highest point	1125m
Height gain	500m
Height loss	470m

One of the steepest climbs in the Andalucian section of the GR7 takes you up over the Serrezuela de Bedmar and then you descend more gently through olives to Jódar.

Head out of town on the high road to the east – with globe street lamps – and after just less than 1km turn up to the left onto a track (marked by a broken signpost at the time of writing) which immediately splits into two. Take the right fork and then continue straight on, following the path up by the edge of an apricot orchard and then round to the left.

Head up the steep scree slope for about 1.5km: the path is a bit difficult to spot in places, but it zigzags upwards. ▶ Keep heading upwards and you should reach the grassy top after about an hour of walking. The path becomes a wider track and you curve down the other side of the hill towards **Jódar**, which is clearly visible below.

Stick to the main track until you reach a divide at the outskirts of town about 4km from the pass; here you take the left fork. Then, just before you meet the road, take the right fork and head down into town.

See map in Stage 24A.

Take care not to stray too far off it onto the scree, which can be very slippery and dangerous, especially after heavy rains.

Bedmar Castle

JÓDAR 627M POPULATION 12,230

Accommodation, restaurant/bar/café, drinking fountain, food shop, cashpoint, telephone, PO, pharmacy, tourist information, transport.

Accommodation and food
A couple of hotels and plenty of choice of places to eat:

Hotel Ciudad de Jódar (B) has 20 ensuite rooms with air conditioning, free wi-fi and balcony, housed in mock mansion with pool: Jose Gallego Montiel, tel 953 785 051, www.hotelciudaddejodar.com. **Hotel los Molinos** (B) is a central hotel with its own restaurant, TV and air conditioning: C/Sanabria 47, tel 953 787 732, www.hotelrestaurantelosmolinos.com.

Further information
Town hall: tel 953 785 086, www.jodar.es.

Castle visitor centre: C/Alhorí, tel 953 785 086.

Museo de Jódar (and tourist information point): Casa Municipal de la Cultura, C/Juan de Mata Carriazo 4, tel 953 78 40 12, www.saudar.com.

Transport
Taxis: 670 883 578/953 786 917/680 522 825/637 837 298/953 785 364.

Jódar was in its prime in Muslim times when it was the political, cultural and administrative capital of the area on one of the most important communication routes. It was famed for its production of high quality olive oil and also red dye. Today it remains the largest town in the *comarca* and a key commercial and administrative centre. Its castle, which houses an information centre on the natural park, is worth a visit in itself and for the views.

STAGE 26A
Jódar – Quesada

Start	Av. Andalucía in Jódar
Distance	34.4km
Time	9h30
Highest point	665m
Height gain	670m
Height loss	630m
Note	Camping possible en route at Hornos de Peal

The first stretch takes you though endless olive groves, mainly on roads then on tracks to Hornos de Peal – a route that may well leave you dreaming of olive trees and with sore feet from tarmac walking. This is followed by an easy stretch though grassland and rolling hills, passing the Arab castle La Toya and making a final steep ascent to Quesada, prominent on its hilltop.

This section can be split by camping, which is allowed beside the sports ground in Hornos de Peal (ask locally).

Leave Jódar on Av. Andalucía and continue bending round to the left to reach a roundabout on the A401 road on the east of the village. A footbridge to the right of the roundabout takes you across the road, then you head north following road signs for Úbeda. Just after – and before you reach a large warehouse, Riegos – turn right off the road onto a gravel road signed Camino de Cortijo de Palomares. Follow this long straight road through olive trees and continue over

En route to Quesada | at a crossroads after 1km, from where it becomes a dirt track. 600m on, where the track divides by a GR7 signpost (Quesada

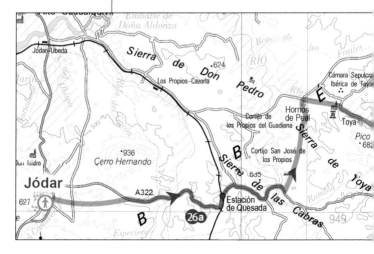

7h10), take the left fork. After 2.5km, this brings you to the **A322** road. Turn right along the road for about 5.8km.

> The **landscape you pass through** is still dominated by olive trees with rows and rows of them on either side of the road. The mountains of Cazorla are ahead and, looking back, is the Macizo de Sierra Mágina and the Serrezuela de Bedmar, which the route crossed over to Jódar. Towards the west is the unmistakable point of Cerro Jabalcón, which the GR7 passes in Granada province.

After 5.8km the road crosses a railway line and turns turn left to pass the old **Estación de Quesada**. Just over a kilometre beyond the station, the road splits and you take the right fork which is the A322 road to Larva, leaving it just over 2km further on when it itself divides.

At this point you take the left fork signed to Huesa and still the A322 (signed Quesada 4h30) for 1.3km to arrive at, and cross, the Río Guadiana Menor. Just after the bridge across the river, you leave the road for a dirt track to the left heading northeast (signed 4h15). ▶ The track takes you through more olive plantations with the Alto de la Colmena up to your right. Stay on the main track ignoring a track

From here it is just under 6km to Hornos de Peal.

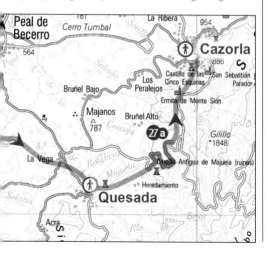

to the right after 900m then go left when you join another track 200m later. Climb past agricultural buildings and continue uphill on the main track heading for Cortijo Mansute up to your right. When you reach a junction of many tracks just below the ruined buildings of the *cortijo* about 1km on from the bridge, ignore the track back to the left but take the next left. After this you stick to the main track passing a turning to the right (after almost 1km and one to the left soon after. Climb steeply to pass another large track off to the left after a further km and one to the right signed to Masuti. Ascend briefly and stay on main track to descend into the small hamlet of **Hornos de Peal** (440m, population 445, campsite, restaurant/bar/café, drinking fountain, food shop, telephone). ◄

> Camping is allowed beside the village sports ground (ask locally).

Leave the village heading downhill from the plaza in front of the church (with drinking fountain) towards olive fields, then, at a signpost which over-optimistically tells you that it is 2h30 to Quesada, turn right along a gravel track that runs along the edge of a field.

OLIVES AND JAÉN PROVINCE

The landscape of this area of Jaén province is dominated by olive oil production. In the Sierra Mágina alone 180,000 tonnes of olives are grown each year, producing around 40,000 tonnes of oil.

Not only are there the rows upon rows of trees, but the beautiful white *cortijos* set among the olive groves have also been built especially for the olive oil industry. They are usually made up of one big house for the plantation owner and several more humble dwellings for the workers. Some still have old oil processing mills, although now most processing is done in larger, modern plants.

There are hundreds of different varieties of olive oil and the quality of each is determined by its acidity. The highest quality is extra virgin olive oil, which is not allowed to go above 0.8 per cent acidity. Virgin olive oil has to be below two per cent acidity.

Olives have a long history in the area, first introduced by the Greeks and Phoenicians thousands of years ago. The Romans cultivated olives but it was the Muslims who perfected oil extraction techniques and, as a result, started planting more trees across the Sierra Mágina and especially around Jódar and Garcíez. Christian conquerors paid little attention to the cultivation of the trees until the 19th century, when the fall in cereal prices led to a huge expansion in olive cultivation and oil production as their income earning potential was realised.

When the track divides about 200m further along, stick to the wider right-hand branch and then continue on the main track, avoiding smaller tracks off to the left into the fields, including a large one after another 500m.

The track comes up to meet a bigger one and you turn onto it heading left (ignoring a smaller left just before it). **Castillo de Toya** is on the hill up above you and you climb towards it, crossing a small stream and then, at a bend just after it, ignoring a track off to right and heading uphill. At the fork shortly afterwards, take the left track which bends around the side of the hill.

> If you want a short detour to **climb to the castle**, take the right fork. The castle has a long history of destruction and reconstruction in battles between Christians and Muslims and the faint terraces still visible on the hill are thought to be man-made. Fragments of Roman and Medieval pottery have been found on the hillside.

You continue on walking through grassland and pines with olive groves below you and at the next fork stay right, continuing round the hill until you come to the Ermita de San Marcos. ▶

This chapel was built at the beginning of the 20th century.

Cross the bridge next to the chapel and just round the corner the track meets a small tarmac road which you follow to the right into the tiny hamlet of **La Toya** (about 3.5km and 1h10 from setting off). Continue between the houses till you come to a small square with a fountain. Then turn left across the bridge to reach a signpost (Quesada 1h55).

Stay on the main track, bending round to the right and passing two left turns, then, when you reach some pine trees visible up to your left, stay right at the junction heading for olive groves. About 10min from leaving the village when you meet another track, turn right and continue straight on on the same track, passing another fountain on the left 1.5km and about 30min out of the village.

The track then heads uphill and you stay on it ignoring turnings to the left into olive groves and a fork to the right doubling back the way you've come. Turn right just before you reach the building that is visible ahead of you.

The left fork just heads up to an abandoned house, Cortijo Cerrillo.

At a T-junction, turn right again then stay right at a fork soon after. ▶ When you meet a bigger road after a total of about 1h40min and 8km from La Toya, cross over it onto a track almost directly opposite with large agricultural hoppers (signpost Quesada 25min).

Follow this same track up to **Quesada**, whose pretty white houses and church spire are visible in the distance perched on the hillside at the foot of the Cerro de la Magdalena.

After 1.5km take the left fork and then turn right just after it at a signpost to cross over a little stone bridge. At the next fork 500m further on, continue up the right fork then turn right again at the T-junction which brings you steeply uphill into the village.

QUESADA 728M POPULATION 5,850

Accommodation, restaurant/bar/café, drinking fountain, food shop, cashpoint, telephone, PO, pharmacy, tourist information, transport.

Accommodation and food
There are a few eating options in and around the main plaza, some offering good tapas.

Hotel Sierra de Quesada (B) ia a good, straight forward family-run hotel with 28 air conditioned rooms: Av. de Úbeda 37, tel 953 733 277, www.hotelsierradequesada.com. Ask in the bar at **Hotel Restaurante Capri** (B) to rent rooms or flats with wood fires, TV and kitchens (some also have air conditioning and washing machine): Pza Santa Catalina 2, tel 953 733 128/953 733 650.

There are lots of *casas rurales*, most are listed on the town hall website: www.quesada.es/turismo.html.

Further information
Town hall, Pl. Constitución s/n, tel 953 733 025, www.quesada.es.

Transport
Taxi: tel 635 204 888.

A bustling large village with pleasant shady tree-lined plaza. There are some exciting caves to explore in the surrounding area including some of Andalucía's most important prehistoric cave paintings, in the Abrigo del Cerro de Vitar, in the Sierra de Quesada south of the town.

STAGE 27A
Quesada – Cazorla

Start	Plaza in Quesada
Distance	17.4km
Time	4h30
Highest point	1199m
Height gain	930m
Height loss	760m

Leaving the neat cultivated land and olives behind you, enter the wild woodland and exhilarating rugged mountains of the Cazorla natural park and descend into Cazorla, after passing the Monasterio de Monte Sión with a stunning panorama of hills behind.

Set off from the plaza past Bar-Restaurante Capri and head east downhill on C/de los Espinillos. At the first junction you'll come to a sign directing you right (Cazorla 4h25).

See map in Stage 26A.

Take a second right turn, then a left turn down to and across the Río de Quesada and then climb along the road, ignoring two tracks off to the right. Turn left when the road divides (signpost Cazorla 4h) and continue on the tarmac road, passing several dirt tracks off to either side. When the tarmac road itself divides, 1.75km out of the village, go right.

Follow this road up through terraced olive groves and reach a few pines after another 1.25km. ▶ At a crossroads shortly afterwards, you are directed to turn left through a large metal gate and pass round a house to climb over a mound of earth back onto the track. The alternative is to just continue straight on and this brings you up the same track, passing the house on your left.

Here the tarmac gets a bit rougher and turns into a track with great views back over Quesada.

The route is sparsely marked from here but stay on the track, curving into a gorge and crossing over a crossroads at the edge of pine forest. The track contours round the hillside then meets a tarmac road about 40min from Quesada (signpost Quesada 1h30, Cazorla 3h30).

The Monasterio de Monte Sión in the Sierra de Cazorla, Segura y Las Villas natural park

Turn right up the road and pass a couple of *casas rurales* (Alojamiento Rural Casa María and Majuela Casa Rural, www.welcometospain.net/rural/cortijomajuela). Cross a little bridge and follow the road for almost 5km to the top of the hill where you enter the Sierras de Cazorla, Segura y las Villas natural park, Spain's biggest natural park covering almost a fifth of Jaén province.

Here the tarmac ends and the road divides. You take the main left fork signposted Cazorla 2h45 (ignoring a smaller left track). The right fork (the continuation of the road) heads up to the Casa Forestal el Chorro (50min walk away). Now high up with great views, you follow the same track, ignoring another track to the left. The balcony track contours around

SIERRAS DE CAZORLA, SEGURA Y LAS VILLAS NATURAL PARK

This 2143km² area was made a natural park in 1989 after being designated a Unesco biosphere reserve in 1983. It is hugely important from an ecological point of view, housing some of the country's wildest areas and largest forests, and is extremely rich in animal and plant life. It is also home to a multitude of water sources, including two important rivers: the Guadalquivir – which carries its water 700km from the mountains to the Atlantic – and the Segura. The whole park is over 600m above sea level with its highest peak, Pico Empanadas, reaching 2107m.

Wildlife
Roughly 70 per cent of the forestry in the park is pine, including some laricio pines that are estimated to be over 1300 years old. The park contains around 1300 species of plants, including fragrant herbs, beautiful wildflowers and two endemic species of daffodil.

Although one of the park's major attractions is its abundant and varied wildlife, human intervention has meant that some of the mammals that used to roam these mountains, including bears and wolves, have disappeared from the region. Wild boar, deer and mouflon – a wild sheep with distinctive large horns – have all been reintroduced, following their extinction in the 1950s. Together with the Spanish ibex, stone marten, wild cat, badger, polecat, weasel and others, they make up some of the park's 51 mammal species.

Bird life is also rich, with 185 species including 29 different raptors such as griffon vultures, Bonelli's eagles and the famous and rare Lammergeier, with its immense wingspan, which can still be sighted occasionally, although it no longer breeds in the park. There are 21 species of reptile (including an the endemic Valverde lizard), 12 amphibians, 11 fish and 112 butterfly species.

Further information
Cazorla tourist information office: Paseo del Santo Cristo 17, tel 953 710 102, www.cazorla.es.

Museo de Caza Centro de Interpretación de Torre del Vinagre: Ctra del Tranco, Km48.8, tel 953 713 017.

Turisnat, a tour company that provides excursions into the park also gives out information and sells maps and guides: Paseo del Cristo 17, tel 953 721 351, www.turisnat.org.

the hillside with vistas through the pines all the way back to Jódar.

Stay on the main track. Around the corner from a signpost (Cazorla 1h45), turn left onto a smaller track which takes you down the stream bed of the Arroyo del Chorro towards

The striking Castillo de las Cinco Esquinas up on the hill above you adds to the beautiful panoramic views.

the monastery and **Ermita de Monte Sión**. Then, just before the monastery, take a left turn to pass by it. ◄

You get your first view down onto Cazorla as you walk along the shoulder of the hill. The track then heads downhill and you keep following it until it turns to concrete and brings you down to a fountain and a turning off to Ermita de San Isicio to the left (a 500m each way detour). Otherwise take the right fork down into **Cazorla**, emerging into the bustling old square the Plaza de Santa Maria at the bottom of town.

CAZORLA 836M POPULATION 8,000

Accommodation, restaurant/bar/café, drinking fountain, food shop, cashpoint, telephone, PO, pharmacy, tourist information, transport.

Accommodation and food
Cazorla's popularity as the gateway to the natural park means that it has a good range of places to sleep and eat. There's a great atmosphere in the evenings in some of the restaurants on the Plaza de Santa María.

Hotel Guadalquivir (B) has smart, modern rooms with air conditioning: in the centre, C/Nueva 6, tel 953 720 268, www.hguadalquivir.com. **Hotel Parque** (B) has clean ensuite rooms with air conditioning and wi-fi: Hilaro Marco 62, tel 953 721 806, www.hotelparque.net. **Villa Turística de Cazorla** (C), just beneath the castle, is made up of nice small flats with a shared swimming pool: Ladera San Isicio, tel 953 710 100, www.villacazorla.com.

Further information
Tourist office: Paseo de Santo Cristo 17, Bajo, tel 953 720 102, www.cazorala.es. www.turismoencazorla.com.

Transport
Taxis: tel 608 854 701/953 720 582/953 721 511.

A busy little town with a dramatic setting, beneath the sheer rock faces of the hills of the natural park. Its two castles and five convents demonstrate its religious and strategic importance throughout its history under both Christian and Islamic control. It is now an important centre for trade and services for the surrounding area. The Moorish Castillo de la Yedra ('ivy castle') was built on the remains of a Roman fortress and now houses El Museo del Alto Guadalquivir – a collection of local art and artefacts.

STAGE 28A
Cazorla – Vadillo de Castril

Start	C/Herrón in Cazorla
Distance	15km
Time	5h30
Highest point	1394m
Height gain	1080m
Height loss	960m

This highly recommended section is a great way to get a taste of the vast pine forests and dramatic rocky crags of the Sierras de Cazorla, Segura y las Villas natural park. Most of the route follows an ancient path, looking down on views of the Guadalquivir valley, the villages of La Iruela and Cazorla.

Climbing to the Ermita Virgen de la Cabeza

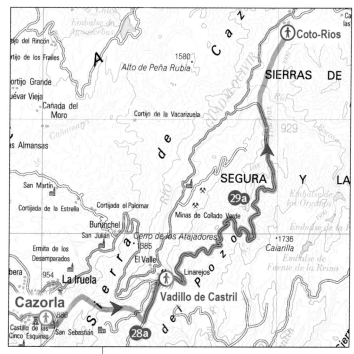

It's worth taking a breather here to take in the panorama of contrasts – the straight neat patterns of olive groves and jagged mountains of the park, including the Cinco Esquinas castle again from the other side.

Leave by C/Herrón, continuing up a steep concrete slope out of the houses to come to a GR7 signpost (El Vadillo 5h20) and park information board which marks the GR7 and other walking routes. Take a small steep footpath uphill and continue up to the left at a junction after 350m (but ignore smaller track marked as private down to left).

This path picks its way uphill, zigzagging through lush green undergrowth and pines, and, after about 20min, brings you up to a viewpoint. ◄

From the viewpoint, a wide track takes you uphill heading northeast and left towards the chapel, the Ermita de la Virgen de la Cabeza, situated high on the hill 150m above Cazorla.

At the divide, take the paved path on the left, with commanding views down over the village, towards the *ermita*. Pass the chapel (which has a fountain) and head up the little path into the pines which forks off to the right of the main wide track (signpost Vadillo 5h).

Once in the trees, curve round to the left following the edge of the woodland onto a stony path which takes you uphill before contouring round the left side of the hill. ▸

Continue on the same undulating path, now going east through beautiful pine woodland and across meadows.

> There's a good chance here of seeing some **exciting wildlife** around here. It's not uncommon to see deer or mountain goats and, although sightings of wild boar are less common, there are often traces of them having been around.

About 2km from the chapel, now at over 1200m, turn left towards a ruined *cortijo* sitting in its own meadow. Then, beyond it, cross a small stream (which may be dry depending on the season) and turn left.

The path then heads out of the trees and zigzags downhill. Stay on the same path and pass a fountain, the Fuente de Rechita, surrounded by poplars, following an old path built into the hillside. A signpost points you uphill (Vadillo 3h20) and you continue on the same path.

It follows the contours of the hill and then climbs again. About 3km on from the signpost you take the left fork and after 500m (now about 10km and 3h45 from Cazorla) you reach the pass at 1369m with great views of the rocky range of Loma de los Castellones to the south with its highest peak of Gilillo at 1848m. ▸

From here you turn right along the ridge following the well-conserved ancient path, which was built up with stones to form an even path for horses to use. It takes you down through trees and across clearings. After 2km, turn right just after a clearing, going around the side of it rather than immediately into the woods. This path brings you down to meet a road in another 15min and you turn right to the Fuente del Oso (sometimes dry).

After the fountain you take a left off the road again onto a small path, signposted Sendero de la Fuente del Oso. You quickly take another left just after the fence ends, heading down to the left. Continue on this path downhill, ignoring a path doubling back on the right and one to the left and keep descending to the Puente de las Herrerías.

You are heading north with views down over the ruined Castillo de la Iruela strategically positioned on top of a rocky pinnacle.

You can also see back to the Sierra Mágina.

This **15th-century bridge** is said to have been built in one night, thanks to divine intervention, so that the Catholic Queen Isabel could cross the river. There is a picnic area here and a fountain and the **Río Guadalquivir** provides a great spot for swimming in crystal-clear, turquoise waters.

Cross the little wooden bridge onto a small path up to the road and follow it along to the left past the campsite and round a bend to the right. Another 20min (2km) on from the campsite pass Fuente de Perdy and come to a big signboard welcoming you to the Comarca Sierra Cazorla. If you want to go into the hamlet of **Vadillo de Castril** turn left onto a little path just before it, down to the left doubling back on the road. Walk along with the river on your right and cross the bridge towards the houses.

VADILLO DE CASTRIL 960M POPULATION 60

Accommodation, campsite, restaurant/bar/café, drinking fountain, food shop.

Accommodation and food
There is nowhere to stay in El Vadillo itself but there is a campsite with a hostal on the route a couple of kilometres before you reach it and a bar/restaurant in the village itself:

Campsite Puente las Herrerías (camping (A), room in hostal (B) is a leafy campsite next to river with bar/restaurant, swimming pool, wooden cabins and hostal: Ctra Nacimiento Río Guadalquivir, Km2, tel 953 727 090, www.puentedelasherrerias.com.

A tiny peaceful place dominated by a forestry centre and government buildings.

STAGE 29A
Vadillo de Castril – Coto-Ríos

Start	Centre of Vadillo de Castril
Distance	34.5km
Time	8h
Highest point	1446m
Height gain	1675m
Height loss	1975m

Forest tracks with glimpses of beautiful views bring you out next to the crystal clear Río Guadalquivir and onto a hidden tiny footpath for the final stretch to Coto-Ríos.

Head back to the road to continue on the route and at the junction just after the big signboard turn right uphill on road marked to Linarejos (signpost Coto-Ríos 8h). Just after this, turn off to the left up a steep little path signposted with a GR7 signpost to Linarejos. After 700m this path brings you out onto an old tarmac road, along which you turn left.

See map in Stage 28A.

Take another left when the road divides about 500m further on. This brings you to a bridge which you cross, ignoring tracks off to the sides, and you continue climbing on the same forestry track. This brings you to **Linarejos** with its natural swimming pool built into the river, fountain, picnic ground and bar/restaurant (only open in high season). ▶

It is worth a short detour here to the famous and beautiful waterfall the Cascada de Linarejos.

From here, continue uphill on the same track. You don't have to worry about finding the way and you can relax into appreciating the dramatic scenery through gaps in the trees. The track brings you up to a pass at 1443m and 7km from Linarejos, and you come down to a fountain just before a building on the right-hand side of the track, around the corner.

After the building (Refugio Roblehondo) there's a signpost (4h45) and you continue downhill, still on the same track (the track off to the left would take you to Cantalar). Stay on it, crossing several old stone bridges and, at a split in the track nearly 7km further on, stick to the main left fork which brings you down, after a further 8km, to the beautiful **Río Borosa**, which feeds the **Río Guadalquivir**.

You cross it at a sign directing you downhill (1h30) past a fountain. Continue down to beautiful bathing pools and when you reach the fish farm head straight up the hill to Loma de Maria Angela.

If you have time for a detour, the fork up to the left takes you to the **Centro de Interpretación de Torre del Vinagre**, the park's main information centre in an old hunting lodge which has information on the park's plant and animal life as well as routes within the park.

Next to it is a **botanical garden** with a good collection of over 300 types of plants including many endemic ones, grouped according to the altitude at which they are found. The **Museo de Caza** is also here, a museum about hunting, with stuffed wildlife from the park and an antler collection.

Loma de Maria Angela is a small hamlet with another fountain.

The path to Coto-Ríos

◀ Keep on the same road through the houses, not turning off until you reach the last buildings and the fountain (Fuente Puchardo) where you take the road up out of the hamlet. The road quickly becomes a path and you pass through a bed-spring gate and follow the same winding path through olives, cork oaks, orchards and meadows until you reach denser pine woodland where you take the left path into the trees. Keep following it through the pines and **Coto-Ríos** will come into view.

COTO-RÍOS 640M POPULATION 340

Accommodation, campsite, restaurant/bar/café, drinking fountain, food shop, cashpoint, telephone, transport.

Accommodation and food

A few well-placed campsites, lots of *casas rurales* and a hotel-restaurant 2.5km away:

Camping Chopera de Coto-Ríos (A) is a pleasant, shady campsite just on the edge of the village beside the river with swimming pool, bar and shop: Ctra del Tranco A-319, Km53, tel 953 713 005/953 713 074, www.campingchopera.es. **Camping Llanos de Arance** (Camping (A), cabin (B)) is right on the route of the GR7 just on the outskirts in the forest, with swimming pool and lovely wooden cabins: Ctra A319, Km 53.8, tel 953 713 139, www.llanosdearance.com. **Los Villares Apartamentos** (B) has well-equipped flats in the village with own terraces and outdoor seating, tel 606 986 757, www.sierracazorla.es/villares.htm. **Hotel Mirasierra** (B). 33 air-conditioned ensuite rooms, pool and restaurant, about 2.5km out of town on Ctra. de la Sierra – A-319, Km 51, tel 953 713 044, www.hotelmirasierracazorla.es.

Because of its location on the edge of the natural park, Coto-Ríos is a popular destination for walkers and adventure sport lovers. It is a slightly strange place which was built to house the residents of the national park and has the feeling of an outpost.

STAGE 30A

Coto-Ríos – Pontones

Start	Plaza in Coto-Ríos
Distance	30.3km
Time	7h30
Highest point	1733m
Height gain	1710m
Height loss	1060m

Another beautiful section of natural park that leads through peaceful pinewoods (where there is a good chance of seeing Spanish ibex), past abandoned *cortijos* and between dramatic rock faces to descend into pasture land.

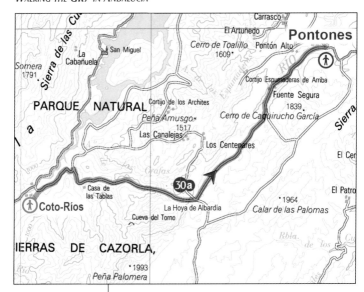

From the plaza, head east past a GR7 signboard and a church up a gravel track to the right (signposted to Pontones). Stay on the gravel track and turn left at the fork 200m on, following it down over a little bridge and through pines (ignoring smaller tracks to both sides). Pass the cemetery on your right. After 1.5km the track meets a small gravel road (signpost Pontones 7h); turn right along it, walking past the Camping Los Llanos de Arance and over another bridge.

The track bends round to the left before curling uphill and you ignore a fork off to the left (sign Pontones 6h30) and then a second left fork a kilometre on. 500m later, after passing two buildings you come to a fountain. The same track continues past the fountain running alongside a scenic gorge.

From here the track climbs steadily for almost 10km and as it does you'll be able to catch glimpses through the trees of forested hills and bare rocky outcrops. After almost 10km it arrives at a lofty viewpoint with wooden rails. ◄

From the viewpoint a small path continues uphill (signposted Pontones 4h) past the ruins of Cortijo de la Fresnedilla, once a fertile productive *cortijo*, with green meadows and fruit trees surrounded by pines.

From here you get a breathtaking, 360° panoramic view of the rocky peaks around you, with eagles often circling overhead.

At this point, there is a sign marking the route as hazardous. The path is fine but do take care. Follow the small, well-marked path up through pines and rosemary bushes to a 1400m pass with views down to the other valley – the Arroyo del Hombre – and up to the peak of Castellón de los Torros and, below in valley, the abandoned Cortijo de Cuvero. Keep right along the ridge following a little path as it contours around the hillside. At 500m from the pass, as you're following a small dry stream bed, you meet another little path. Turn left along this to head east.

After another 500m, the path ends in an open valley beside a semi-ruined goat shed surrounded by once-cultivated land. Keep the building on your right and cross straight over the valley floor heading north towards the poplar trees where there is a GR7 post. Follow the line of the poplars on a faint path until you reach some ruined houses at **La Hoya de Albardía**, and then carry straight on through the field on an unmarked section staying by a small stream bed. After 200m it becomes a clearer path going in the same direction gently uphill to a signpost (Pontones 3h15) which directs you right on a path which heads south. You double back on yourself briefly as you pass above the farmhouses higher on the hillside before contouring round to the east. There is a small

On route to Pontones

divide in the path after a kilometre, but both forks bring you to a flat open area of grassland with a signpost (Pontones 3h).

There are two paths heading off from here; take the left one going northeast which becomes a track taking you through rocky, well-grazed landscapes with far fewer trees at over 1700m.

The track comes to another signpost after 2km with a 20min detour to the Mirador de Juan León straight on and the route heading downhill to the right. ◄ To stick to the route, continue downhill for about 4km, ignoring a track off to the left halfway down, and you arrive at another track and an intersection with the GR144. Turn left along this track and after 1km it will bring you to the road on the way into Fuente Segura (café, drinking fountain) at a picnic area.

Turn left along the road. After 750m you pass by the village itself but stay on the bottom road. 500m further on, turn off at a bend in the road to the right onto a rough track with some farm buildings on your left. This turns into a little path running along the base of some huge sloping slabs of rock before rejoining a very small road at some houses after 500m.

Follow the small tarmac road heading uphill, passing a signpost to Pontones (30min). Once up the hill and past the buildings take a gravel track to the left. This rejoins the road after 400m, but just before it does, you take a very small path off to the left passing a farm building and heading in the same direction as the road.

Ignore smaller paths through fields back to the road and when it divides take the right fork. Carry on along the little path which goes gently downhill with fields to the right and rock outcrops to the left. Where the track divides by a dry stone wall and dry stream bed carry on in the same direction keeping to the left of the stream bed on barely trodden path for 300m, at which point it divides again. Take the right fork down and across the stream bed and then up a short, steep path to meet the road, and a well-hidden post, 400m from the village. Go left along the road until you come to a signpost directing you left into **Pontones**.

If you fancy a detour to the viewpoint it offers excellent views of the whole of the Valle del Guadalquivir, the Sierra de las Cuatro Villas and the Sierra de Albacete.

PONTONES 1350M POPULATION 5021

Accommodation, restaurant/bar/café, drinking fountain, food shop, telephone, PO, pharmacy, tourist information, transport.

Accommodation and food

One hotel and a couple of casas rurales with a renowned restaurant in the centre:

Hotel-Restaurante Ruta del Segura (B) is a handy hotel as you enter the village of Pontones de Abajo, with tasty food in the restaurant below, air conditioning, TV: Av. Democracia, tel 953 438 287. **Refugio del Segura** (B) has stylish flats on the road heading north out of Pontones de Abajo: Av. Sierra de Segura 17, tel 953 438 107, www.refugiodelsegura.es. **Casa Rural Alta Segura** (B) has comfortable rooms in peaceful house with friendly and helpful owner: in the upper part of the village (Pontón Alto) about a kilometre up the road, tel 953 438 328.

Further information

Town hall: Av. Sierra de Segura, tel 953 438 088, www.santiagopontones.es

Pontones is almost two villages. The lower of its two neighbourhoods (Pontones de Abajo) is situated on the banks of the Río Segura. The lushness of the gardens and fields surrounding the village provide a pretty contrast to the rocky hills that enclose it.

STAGE 31A
Pontones – Santiago de la Espada

Start	Church in Pontones
Distance	13.5km
Time	3h15
Highest point	1632m
Height gain	490m
Height loss	485m

A gentle, scenic route following tiny (sometimes hard to find) paths and streams across rolling open farmland.

From the church, cross the bridge over La Rambla and turn right then left through a break in the buildings along a little path which brings you out onto the road by a GR7 display and signpost to Santiago de la Espada. If you miss this path you can just go past the church and southeast out on the road to the same point.

Walk along the road for 500m/10min, then turn off to the left onto a dirt track (signposted Santiago 3h) and follow it through green pastures. As you near a goat shed, head off to your right to reach a GR7 post (with the goat shed just up on your left). From this point there is only a faint unmarked path which is easily confused with goat tracks but if you keep heading northeast on the right-hand side of the valley following the

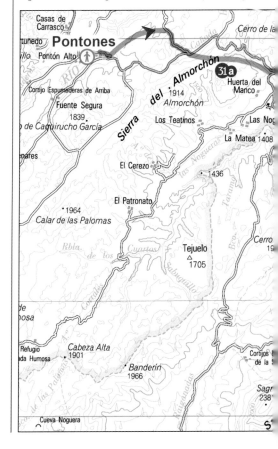

edge of the trees and the line of the pylons you will arrive back on a small path with some markings after 500m.

You arrive at a small v-shaped dry stone wall by two pylons 100m further on, with the small hamlet of **Poyotello** directly ahead. ▸ Head down the right side of the dry stone wall onto a path going south leaving the line of the pylons behind. The path curves southeast between hills before doubling back up to the left (and north) to come to the farm of Los Cerezos and a clear gravel track. Follow the track to the

Here the path seems to disappear again.

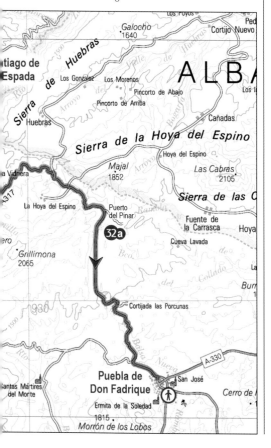

right, away from the farmhouse, and onto the Poyotello road. Turn right along the road and after 700m you will come to a signpost (Santiago de la Espada 1h45). Stay on the road going in the same direction until you come to the main, but still small, road between Pontones and Santiago de la Espada, 1.5km on.

Cross over the road diagonally to the left, into a field with poplar trees. A very faint track and GR7 posts direct you across a small stream and through a gap in the poplar trees heading east-northeast. Staying roughly parallel with the road and leaving the poplars down to your left, you climb very gently uphill to a wider track which you cross over before heading downhill again on small path. When you reach another track, cross over it, still following GR7 posts, along a small path heading east.

From here the path follows the stream bed of the Arroyo Zumeta almost the entire way to Santiago de la Espada, making navigation easy.

◄ A further 500m after entering the valley, keep to the left and higher of two tracks heading into pine trees but still following the stream. After another 1km you come down and cross the stream into a clearing in the trees with the road just in front of you and a signpost (Santiago de la Espada 1h), directing you right and along the stream on its right-hand side. Pass a small dam and follow the line of the road on the other side of the gorge.

Another 3km on from the signpost, the track divides. You take the left fork, doubling back briefly downhill through a stone archway to cross over to the other side of the gorge before following a track, running beneath the road, around the hillside to the right by the edge of the trees and arriving into **Santiago de la Espada** at a roundabout and garage.

SANTIAGO DE LA ESPADA 1,340M POPULATION 1500

Accommodation, restaurant/bar/café, drinking fountain, food shop, cashpoint, telephone, PO, pharmacy, tourist information, transport.

Accommodation and food
There is just one hotel in Santiago itself:

Hotel San Francisco (B) is reasonable and central with spacious double or twin rooms and bar/restaurant serving traditional dishes: Av. de Andalucía 25, tel 953 438 072, www.hotelsan-francisco.com. **Apartahotel Don Ramón** has flats just opposite Hotel San Francisco: tel 667 631 050, www.apartahoteldonramon.com.

Further information
Town hall: Plaza de la Constitución 1, tel 953 438 002/953 438 003, www.
santiagopontones.es

Transport
Taxis: tel 608 259 795/953 438 312/953 433 754/953 438 499.

The last destination of the GR7 in Jaén, Santiago de la Espada is set in rocky countryside to the south of the Sierra de Segura. Its high altitude makes its climate colder and harsher than that of nearby villages and prevents the cultivation of olive trees. Instead the people of Santiago make a living from cattle and forestry.

STAGE 32A
Santiago de la Espada – Puebla de Don Fadrique

Start	C/Hondo del Pecho in Santiago de la Espada
Distance	34.2km
Time	8h
Highest point	1662m
Height gain	980m
Height loss	1100m

The charming route to the intriguing Cortijo de las Cuevas is overshadowed by the final long road walk which is a bit of an anti-climax to the whole Northern Fork of the GR7 in Andalucía. While the road is small and picturesque, it is a long walk on tarmac and not recommended.

Leave the village heading south on C/Hondo del Pecho. Cross the bypass and continue in an almost straight line on a dirt track. After 300m come to a junction with a pool on your left. Continue straight on ignoring a route off to the right and one off to the left just afterwards. A few metres further on, at the next divide, take the right fork.

See map in Stage 31A.

Leaving Santiago de la Espada

Cross the Arroyo Zumeta and then keep it on your left. About 600m further on, ignore a track which joins you from the right. Then, 50m after this, leave the track on a path to the right which keeps climbing.

Once you reach the top, head down on a small rocky path passing above and around the settlement of Cortijo de las Cuevas, which is mainly cave-houses, many now abandoned, set into the hillside. Come down to the river and cross over a wider track onto a very overgrown path which takes you around a field before rejoining a wide track.

Here you come across the last GR7 sign before Puebla de Don Fadrique and the end of the Northern Fork of the GR7 in Andalucía, which it states is 6h away.

The sign directs you along the track which crosses the Río Zumeta and then heads uphill to the road and into the Granada province. Turn left along the road (A317) for the long unmarked road walk to Puebla de Don Fadrique. After the first 3.5km along the road you come to a junction and take the left turn signposted to Puebla de Don Fadrique, 28km away.

After a further 3km, you pass by an impressive hotel complex with helipad at the **Pinar de la Vidriera** (Ctra

Comarcal C-32, Kilómetro 25, Huéscar). A track off to the right here looks tempting but unfortunately the route sticks to the road. From here it climbs steadily up through beautiful pines to a high point of 1664m at the **Puerto del Pinar**, 14km from your destination. While in the pines you can only catch an occasional glimpse of a view but from here the scenery starts to open out a bit as you start the long downhill into Puebla de Don Fadrique.

As you head downwards into the valley basin in which Puebla sits, the landscape becomes **drier and harsher**, with scrub vegetation rather than trees. Here rivers that are near-torrents in the winter dry up almost entirely in the summer months.

Continue down the road passing several small tracks off to isolated farmhouses. With the end now clearly in view, you take the left fork when you arrive at another junction (less than 2km from Puebla) to enter the **Puebla de Don Fadrique** from the northwest at the Ermita Nueva and the graveyard.

Cuevas del Engarbo

PUEBLA DE DON FADRIQUE 1164M POPULATION 2,400

Accommodation, restaurant/bar/café, drinking fountain, food shop, cashpoint, telephone, PO, pharmacy, tourist information, transport.

Accommodation and food
The hotel is the main place to stay and eat, although there are a few bars.

Hotel Puerta de Andalucía (B) has spacious, bright but characterless rooms, with bar and restaurant downstairs: Ctra Granada-Valencia 1, tel 958 721 340/958 721 076. **Apartamentos Don Fadrique** (B) has well-equipped tourist flats with kitchens, heating and TV: Ctra Granada, behind petrol station, tel 958 721 116.

Lots of *casas rurales* – information available on the town hall website: www.puebladedonfadrique.com/turismo/alojamientos-rurales

Further information
Town hall: Av. Duque de Alba, tel 958 721 011, www.puebladedonfadrique.com

From Puebla there are two buses a day (one at weekends) to Granada (3h45) and very regular connections to Málaga from there.

A pleasant little town with white houses and its 16th-century church of Santa María surrounded by fields of cereals and almonds. It has a rich past, first as a Muslim settlement and later a Christian one.

3 SOUTHERN FORK –
MÁLAGA AND GRANADA
VILLANUEVA DE CAUCHE
TO PUEBLA DE DON FADRIQUE

Walking on route between Juviles and Timar (Stage 23B)

MÁLAGA PROVINCE

An overview of the route in Málaga, and practical details such as transport information, are given at the beginning of the section 'Málaga province' in Part 1.

VILLANUEVA DE CAUCHE TO VENTAS DE ZAFARRAYA (46KM)

STAGE 12B
Villanueva de Cauche – Riogordo

Start	Centre of Villanueva de Cauche
Distance	20.8km
Time	5h
Highest point	936m
Height gain	670m
Height loss	820m
Note	No accommodation in Riogordo: see below

This stage is mostly a long slog up tarmac but with good views of Peña Negra and Morrón de Gragea. Note: there is nowhere to stay in Riogordo itself, but you pass Hospedería Retamar on the way or you can take a short taxi ride to Colmenar from Riogordo.

The first 17km of this section is all on tarmac, but not too busy, roads. The scenery is impressive but if you want to avoid a long road walk, you might prefer to get a taxi to the turn-off to Hospedería Retamar at Km519.

If you want to walk, head out of the village to the north (the same way you came in if you arrived from Antequera on the GR7), passing a GR7 signpost which only indicates the start of the Northern Fork. Instead of following this, turn right up

*Descending to
Hospedería Retamar*

the first road you come to, the A7204 and continue straight
on at the next junction. 2km from the junction at the edge of
the village, pass a fountain which is often dry and continue
uphill, with Peña Negra on your right and passing through
cereal crops. Soon you see the village of **Casabermeja** to
the south. You enter the Comarca de Axaquia and soon after
join the A4152 road between Alfarnate and Colmenar, 9km
from the start. You turn left uphill towards **Alfarnate** and
climb steeply on the quiet tarmac road through almonds and
olives, heading towards the Sierra Prieta. You reach a *mirador*
on your right after 6km. ▶

The bright building-
wagons of the
Fantasia circus school
are below you and
the sea is visible in
the distance beyond
the Montes de
Málaga.

Continue up the road for a further 2km until you
reach Km519, just over 8km since you joined the A4152.
Here there is a marked track down to the right signposted
to Hospedería Retamar. Take this track downhill, sticking
to the main track through almond groves interspersed with
occasional holm oaks, broom and scrub with the distinctive rocky outcrop of the Sierra de Santa Ana up to your left.
After 1.7km meet another track and go right downhill to pass
another track back to the right and ascend to **Hospedería
Retamar** ((C) 11 airconditioned rooms and a great restaurant
with a lovely patio for outside dining, tel 952 031 225, www.
hospederiaretamar.com) just over 2km after leaving the road.

Turn right at the hospedería to continue down the broad
gravel track and arrive at a signed junction (Riogordo 45min
and Zafarraya 6h). To descend into **Riogordo** continue downhill on the gravel track to reach the road after 1km. Follow
this road down for a further 1km to reach the village by a
GR7 signboard just before a bridge over the Río de la Cueva.

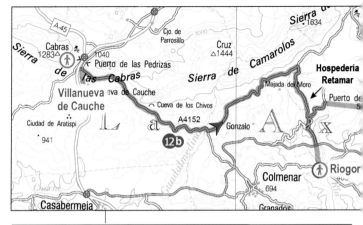

RIOGORDO 400M POPULATION 2800

Campsite, restaurant/bar/café, drinking fountain, food shop, cashpoint, telephone, PO, pharmacy, tourist information, transport.

Accommodation and food
There are a couple of bars serving tapas and food shops but nowhere to stay in the village itself. There is a **wild camping area** 1.5km away on the route and a hotel/restaurant in nearby Colmenar (6km away) which can be reached by a regular bus service from the main square: **Hotel-Restaurante Belén** (B) has comfortable rooms with a popular bar/restaurant below serving traditional dishes and bar food/tapas: Urb Chorropinos, Colmenar, tel 952 730 031, www.hotelrestaurantebelen.com

Further information
Town hall: Pza de la Constitución 14, tel 952 732 154, www.riogordo.es
www.riogordo.com

Museum of Popular Arts: tel 952 732 154, open 5pm–9pm and mornings at weekends.

Transport
Taxis: tel 952 732 005/952 732 211/659 156 847.

Riogordo, which means 'wide river', has a colourful history. After being established by the Phoenicians and Romans, it was taken over by the Moors and the village is still laid out in an Arabic style. In the 19th century, it was best known as a haven for bandits because of its proximity to the mountains.

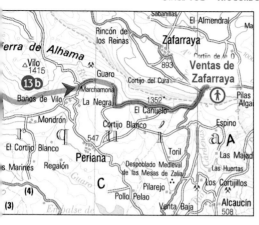

STAGE 13B
Riogordo – Ventas de Zafarraya

Start	Hospedería Retamar
Distance	25.2km
Time	6h30
Highest point	946m
Height gain	1000m
Height loss	630m

Mostly track walking through beautiful scenery dotted with hamlets and then along an old railway line to reach your destination.

Riogordo – Guaro (17.5km, 4h)

If you stayed at the Hospedería Retamar, continue the walk from here. If you detoured to Riogordo, return to the junction near the hospedería and turn right. Follow the main track round ignoring all turnings (including one off to the left after just over 1.5km).

189

The peak of Doña Ana

As you continue downhill, the ruined **Cortijo de Auta** and the caves underneath it come in to view below you. This is said to have been the birthplace of Andalucía's famous 9th-century Robin Hood character Omar Ibn Hafsun who managed to hold a huge stretch of territory from his rebel army stronghold at Bobastro castle.

You arrive at the farm where an X marks the track uphill with an information board about the farm. The route continues down as if to enter the farmyard, but instead you pass in front of it, keeping it on your right to cross the Río de la Cueva on a little hidden bridge. You then climb on a dirt track which levels out bringing you towards the distinctive outcrop of Doña Ana and then round beneath it to the right on a pretty track through grass and crops. Continue on this same track, as it crosses the Arroyo de Auta after 1.5km and bends sharply to the south. Descend to a junction where you turn left onto a road and you continue along it. After just under a km, pass a track steeply up to the left at a sign for the Tajo del Gomer. Just over 600m after this take a marked track off to the left. This soon brings you down the road at a pass, the **Puerto del Sabar** (598m), with a nice viewpoint. Turn left down the road (C-340) for 2.6km. At KM40.8 of the road you come to a big panel of mailboxes and take a dirt track up to the left that provides access to several farms and buildings.

Follow this track for just under 1.5km and at the top of the track you reach the Cortijo de la Molina, with several signs for the route up the Tajo del Gomer. Turn right down MA157 road and follow it for just over half a km. Then, just after passing a bar on your right, the Venta la Fuente, turn off onto a track to the left signposted Cortijada Pulgarín. ▶

It is 17km and 4h from here to Ventas de Zafarraya.

A GR7 mark takes you onto a dirt track and past the *cortijada*. You come to a junction after 250m and take the left up a briefly concrete track and then almost immediately turn left again (not right across bridge decorated with old cartwheels). Climb for 300m, getting increasingly good views back to the peak of Doña Ana, then at a divide take the right fork. From here you can see all the way back to Colmenar. As the track heads southeast around the hillside the **Embalse de la Viñuela** comes into view with more panoramic views over the hills to the left and down to the hamlet of **Mondrón** below.

1.5km after you left the road, the track arrives at Cortijo de la Cueva and meets another track at a T-junction. Here you come across a GR7 signpost indicating it is 5h back to Riogordo and 3h30 to Zafarraya. Go left up the track between the buildings. At a divide 200m on take the right fork and then stay on this track, for about 2km coming around the hillside and over a small rise to get your first view of the hamlet of **Guaro**. Go straight over the little crossroads at the top of the rise and continue downhill passing a farm on the right and crossing a small stream by way of two makeshift bridges to the left of the track. This then brings you to the road, where again you go straight over to enter the hamlet on a little tarmac road, passing a fountain on the way in.

Guaro – Ventas de Zafarraya (7.7km, 2h30)
Walk straight through Guaro, staying on the same road. ▶ The road passes through the bottom of a little plaza then carries straight on becoming gravel as it leaves. Climb nearly to the top of the hill to meet another track (with a falling down signpost at the time of writing). Left is to **Marchamona**, you go right to continue on the route to Ventas. After 600m you arrive at a crossroads where you turn left, signposted to

On your left you will pass the restaurant Caserón de Guaro (952 033 600) and the source of the Río Guaro.

Carrión, joining a track which was once a railway line and which will take you all the way to Ventas, along the way passing into Granada province.

Another 1km from the crossroads, pass by a farmhouse to your left, carrying straight on with the reservoir coming into view again, passing by lots of broom interspersed with olives on the hillside. From here you can see ahead a now oddly placed bridge over the old railway line you are following. Pass under this before carrying on through a short tunnel 3km further on. You reach the road and the village of **Ventas de Zafarraya** 300m after you leave the tunnel arriving by a viewpoint and car park. A bridge crosses the road to your right with a miniature railway line on it. You, however, head left down to the road entering the village on C/Delicias.

VENTAS DE ZAFARRAYA 920M POPULATION 1340

Accommodation, restaurant/bar/café, drinking fountain, food shop, telephone, PO, transport.

Accommodation and food
A couple of basic places to stay both with restaurants and a handful of bars, including a traditional one in the old railway station hotel which also houses a small antiques museum:

Aquí Te Quiero Ver (A) is a budget, friendly hostal on the main road as you enter the town, with restaurant and bar: C/Delicias 21, tel 958 362 001. **Casa Bartolo** (A) is a pensión with bar/restaurant: Buenos Aires 12, tel 958 362 012.

Further information
Town hall: Pza de Santo Domingo de Guzmán 1, tel 958 362 000, www.ventasdezafarraya.es.

As its name implies, the town started life as a *venta*, an inn, on the ancient route between Málaga and Granada. Thanks to its location on a fertile plain it has recently experienced a revival and population growth as a result of large-scale intensive agricultural production for national and international markets.

GRANADA PROVINCE (AND ALMERÍA)

On the ridge between Arenas del Rey and La Resinera

HIGHLIGHTS OF THE ROUTE IN GRANADA PROVINCE

- getting lost among the narrow car-free streets of the traditional villages of the Alpujarras with whitewashed houses and colourful flowers pouring from balconies
- soaking tired muscles in numerous thermal spas and Arab baths including in Alhama, Baños de Zújar and Lanjarón
- the novelty of staying in a cooling cave house
- archaeological sites of the Hoya de Baza area, especially the museum at Orce

The 419.5km of the GR7 in Granada province are some of the most varied and beautiful in the whole route. The section has everything: from breathtaking views of snowy peaks to pretty winding ancient paths joining the dots between tiny villages; and from the wild green spaces of three natural parks to the immense sun-baked desert landscapes of the *altiplano*.

Leaving Málaga province in the fertile plains around Ventas de Zafarraya, you come to the beautiful town of Alhama de Granada with its dramatic gorge and wonderfully relaxing *balneario* (spa bath). From here you pass into the green valley of Lecrín and walk beside babbling *acequias* (ancient irrigation channels) and between lush orange and lemon groves.

The route then winds its way into the Alpujarras. Passing through the villages of Albuñuelas and Nigüelas you come to Lanjarón with its famous spring water. The section that leaves here is perhaps the best-known and most-walked part of the route. It takes you right into the Alpujarras, an area known for its timeless whitewashed villages clinging to the steep hillsides.

Entering the Parque Natural de Sierra Nevada (see Stage 18B), you walk through some genuinely wild landscapes with stunning views of the Sierra Nevada mountains and plenty of opportunities to climb them, including Mulhacén, the highest peak in the park, and in mainland Spain.

The GR7 then crosses briefly into the Almería province, through Bayárcal, the province's highest village at 1255m, and then climbs further to pass over the pine-forested pass of Puerto de la Ragua (2000m).

Back in Granada province, you head for the arid semi-desert plains landscape of the west of the province which contrasts sharply with the lush greenery that you have already come through. Note that after La Calahorra, the waymarking is very old and sparse and has not been maintained for many years. Many other sections of the GR7 in

Granada province have been well maintained and re-marked in recent years, but the Provincial authority does not actively promote the final section from Puerto de la Ragua to Puebla de Don Fadrique. FAM is considering rerouting some of this section of the route but has no fixed plans at the time of writing. It would be worth checking their website www.fedamon.com and the Cicerone website (www.cicerone.co.uk) for any changes and updates we were aware of.

The route goes through Zújar to its thermal spring baths on the shores of a beautiful reservoir and into Orce, one of the most important prehistoric sites in Europe. The final stretch is a beautiful forested walk, past the peak of La Sagra with breathtaking views all the way to Puebla de Don Fadrique, the end of the route in Andalucía.

OTHER WALKS

Granada province is a popular area for walking and there are lots of options for creating circular routes from the GR7 and diversions up to peaks, especially in the three natural parks. The Alpujarras is also a particularly beautiful area to explore on foot and there are lots of marked routes linking its villages.

There are also many marked routes in the parks, although marking is not always totally reliable or consistent and it is advisable to take good maps. A popular and beautiful route in the Parque Natural de Sierra Nevada, which works as a nice diversion from the Alpujarran section of the GR7, is the Sendero Siete Lagunas, an 8km route which starts in Trevélez and takes you up to seven lakes in a glacial valley at over 3000m, between the peaks of Mulhacén and Alcazaba. You can camp here and continue up to the top of Mulhacén peak the next day, or do the whole thing in one challenging day trip. In poor weather or winter this becomes a major mountaineering challenge.

There are also opportunities to link up with other long-distance routes, including the GR142 which interconnects with the GR7 in Lanjarón and goes from Lanjarón to Fiñana on the northern side of the Sierra Nevada in Almería. Further on, at Puerto de la Ragua, the route also meets the GR140, which forks off to go south to Cabo de Gata where it meets the GR92 which runs right along the south coast of Andalucía.

TRANSPORT

There are fairly regular buses between Granada and the bigger towns of the province including Lanjarón, Antequera, Cazorla and Baza. There are also connections from Málaga and Jaén. Many of them will stop at some of the smaller villages they pass through.

The buses are run by several companies and it is best to get in touch with them to check the latest timetables or search www.autobuses.costasur.com which is useful for finding times for buses from all companies.

The main company which has a useful website is **Alsina Graells**, tel 952 841 365, www.alsa.es: Granada–Lanjarón frequent services (every 1–2 hours weekdays and slightly reduced services at weekends and bank holidays, 1h30); Granada–Cazorla (twice daily via Jaén, 4h); Granada–Antequera (5 daily, 1h50); Granada–Baza (nine daily, 1h45). At the end of the route at Puebla de Don Fadrique, there are twice daily buses (weekdays) and daily buses at the weekend to Granada.

Numbers for local taxi firms are also listed in the place information boxes.

TOURIST INFORMATION

Granada tourist office: Pza Mariana Pineda 10, Granada, tel 958 247 146, www.turismodegranada.org.

VENTAS DE ZAFARRAYA TO PUEBLA DE DON FADRIQUE 419.5KM

STAGE 14B
Ventas de Zafarraya – Alhama de Granada

Start	Old railway line in Ventas de Zafarraya
Distance	19.5km
Time	5h30
Highest point	1100m
Height gain	440m
Height loss	460m

Pass through fertile agricultural land and enter the Parque Natural de las Sierras de Tejada, Almijara y Alhama then follow an ancient droving track through woodland to Alhama in its striking location below the Sierra Tejada and above a dramatic gorge.

VENTAS DE ZAFARRAYA 920M POPULATION 1340

Accommodation, restaurant/bar/café, drinking fountain, food shop, telephone, PO, transport.

Accommodation and food
A couple of basic places to stay both with restaurants and a handful of bars, including a traditional one in the old railway station hotel which also houses a small antiques museum:

Aquí Te Quiero Ver (A) is a budget, friendly hostal on the main road as you enter the town, with restaurant and bar: C/Delicias 21, tel 958 362 001. **Casa Bartolo** (A) is a pensión with bar/restaurant: Buenos Aires 12, tel 958 362 012.

Further information
Town hall: Pza de Santo Domingo de Guzmán 1, tel 958 362 000, www.ventasdezafarraya.es.

As its name implies, the town started life as a *venta*, an inn, on the ancient route between Málaga and Granada. Thanks to its location on a fertile plain it has recently experienced a revival and population growth as a result of large-scale intensive agricultural production for national and international markets.

To leave the village return to the former railway line at the point you arrived, cross the bridge and follow the mini railway track through the southern edge of the village and out on C/Estación. When you come to the school, go round it keeping it on your right and then head out along a small tarmac road which takes you straight through the Hortoventas yard and out on a track which runs through vegetable fields and parallel to the road into **Pilas de Algaida**. Join the tarmac road after less than 1.5km at a GR7 signpost at the edge of Pilas de Alguida (Ventas de Zafarraya 2km, Alhama de Granada 19km; accommodation, restaurant/bar/café). Turn right along the road for 700m, passing through the hamlet to come to a marked track on the right that leaves the road diagonally just after the Horticolas SER building, 30min from the start.

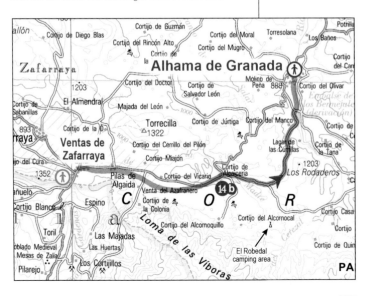

You can see the Lorna de las Viboras, Peñon del Romero and Los Barracones. The highest peak, Pico La Maroma, is further south.

Climb a small hill, and where the track divides, turn left and follow the well signed track along a low ridge then up through farm buildings. To your right are some of the hills of the **Parque Natural de las Sierras de Tejada, Almijara y Alhama**, whose northern border you are walking parallel to. ◄

Stay on the main track until you come down to meet a tarmac road at some warehouses. Ignore the track off to the right and the road to the left and head up round to the right of the warehouses on tarmac, following a signpost to the Alcauca camping area.

The camping area – a nice spot surrounded by oaks and elms 3km from here – is up to the right.

This brings you out on a wide gravel track climbing though oaks. At the next divide, 750 metres further on take the left fork. ◄

The track continues between houses and at the next divide you also stay left continuing though flat fields. When you come to a slightly confusing intersection of five tracks, 500m further on, the route is uphill on the second track on your right towards the white houses. Walk up close in front of the house, taking a track to the left heading east through gorse and oaks. This meets a small road after 400m and you turn downhill to the left. Soon afterwards, take the first track on the right which also splits very quickly and this time take the left hand option. ◄

The marking from here is much more sparse and occasional.

This track passes in front of a building and you ignore the track to the right immediately after the building, but take the next right fork. Then, when you meet another track, turn left down it to come to the main road, now almost 7km and 1h30 from the start. Cross straight over the road, taking the gravel track directly opposite and then the right fork which passes through a field. This meets another track on the other side of the field and you turn right and go back up to the road which you follow for 1.5km/2km to the Bar San Marco and the hotel restaurant Los Caños de la Alcaicería, just over 9km from the start ((A), Ctra Alhama Vélez, Km10; tel 958 350 325).

The route crosses the road and continues along the right hand side of the hotel passing an information board for other walking routes and continues on a very wide well signed cattle droving track. This takes you almost all the way to Alhama, re-entering the natural park. Ignore all smaller tracks and stay on this main one passing through cork oaks and almonds and into pines. ◄

There is a good chance of seeing eagles here and deer and mountain goats are also common.

When this main track divides after 2.5km the route goes left. If you head right, it is 3km to El Robedal camping area,

on the mountain El Robedal, and this is also the way to follow the marked route to the top of La Maroma (the tourist
office in Alhama has information about doing this as an
8–10h, 25km route.)

After this junction the track climbs gently and then goes
down a long valley, passing occasional houses on both sides.
It passes through pines, oaks and gorse and then poplars,
olive and almond groves and some vineyards. Ignore all
smaller turn offs. After another 3.5km (16km from start) you
pass a drinking fountain (not always switched on in the low
season) and soon afterwards a small reservoir, **Embalse de los
Bermejales**, on your right.

Just after this you reach the road into **Alhama de
Granada**. Turn right along this road and cross over the
river below the reservoir dam. You come to GR7 signpost
(Ventas de Zafarraya 19km, Arenas de Rey 21km, Alhama de
Granada 2km). Turn left to follow the lovely route down the
(Los Tajos gorge towards Alhama next to the river. After 500m
cross the river on a wooden footbridge. You then pass the
Ermita de Los Ángeles and reach a GR7 sign to Arenas del
Rey (22.5km). Head down the marked route to the right to
come to a rocky and uneven but pretty path along the river,
past stone washing basins which were used by local women
even up until the 1980s (19km, 2h10). After 100m you come
to a cobbled road and turn left uphill along it to zigzag
steeply up to arrive into town on C/Cuesta de los Molinos.

SIERRAS DE TEJEDA, ALMIJARA Y ALHAMA NATURAL PARK

This relatively new park (407km^2, designated in 1999) protects an impressive
mountain massif between the provinces of Málaga and Granada. Its landscape
is rocky and rugged, with limestone cliffs and ravines in the Sierra Tejeda,
and some of the country's most important dolomite marble sites in the Sierra
Almijara. Its territory is split half and half between Málaga and Granada. Its
highest peak is La Maroma at 2069m. There are many caves in the park, some
with prehistoric remains.

Wildlife
There is a wide diversity of plant life across the altitude range of the park, much of
it endemic. Species of note include the yew (*tejo*), which gives the park its name,
and used to be much more widespread until most of the trees were destroyed
because yew is poisonous to livestock. You will also see pines, including Corsican

and maritime pines; boxwood; juniper; holm, cork and gall oaks; maples and rowans. In the scrub you will find broom, milk vetch and mountain cherries and there are also plentiful aromatic herbs.

The animal you are most likely to come across is the endemic mountain goat, which was once endangered but whose populations are now recovering well. The bird life is impressive and, depending on the time of year, you may also spot eagles (golden, hawk, short-toed snake and booted), peregrine falcons, goshawks, woodpeckers and rock thrushes.

Camping
You are not allowed to camp in the park except in designated areas. The only one of these that the route passes near is El Robedal. This is a good base for a detour to climb La Maroma.

Further information
Consejería de Medio Ambiente, Delegación de Medio Ambiente in Málaga, Edificio Eurocom, Bloque Sur, 29071, tel 951 040 05, www.juntadeandalucia. es/medioambiente.

ALHAMA DE GRANADA 850M POPULATION 6,200

Accommodation, restaurant/bar/café, drinking fountain, food shop, cashpoint, telephone, PO, pharmacy, tourist information, transport.

Accommodation and food
Plenty of nice places to eat with outside seating in the buzzing plaza and a few options for rooms:

Pensión San José (A) has straightforward central accommodation with very friendly owner and little restaurant downstairs offering local fare and pizzas: Pza Constitución 27, tel 958 350 156, www.hostalalhamadegranada.com. **La Seguiriya** (B inc breakfast) has beautifully decorated rooms, a terrace with a view over the gorge and a friendly owner, making this a really special place to stay, with lower prices for longer stays: C/Las Peñas 12, tel 958 360 801, www. laseguiriya.com. **Hotel Balneario** (C) is 3km out of Alhama at the baths with access to massage, physio and pool, with comfortable rooms and a health club atmosphere, the pricier ones with a living room or private terrace: Ctra Balneario, tel 958 350 011/958 350 366, www.balnearioalhamadegranada.com.

Further information
Town hall: tel 958 350 161, www.ayuntamientodealhama.com.

Tourist office: Promenade Montes Jovellar 10, tel 958 360 686, www.turismodealhama.com.

A picturesque little place in an impressive setting, Alhama is famous for the relaxing Arab thermal baths from which it gets its name (*Al-Hamma*, the Arabic for hot spring). The town itself is Arabic in layout with a well-preserved old quarter, including the remains of a defensive wall and watchtower.

STAGE 15B
Alhama de Granada – Arenas del Rey

Start	Centre of Alhama de Granada
Distance	22km
Time	6h
Highest point	1138m
Height gain	535m
Height loss	555m

Leaving Alhama through the dramatic gorge carved out by the Río Alhama, you follow tracks through a mix of orchards, arable land and beautiful oak woodland with panoramic views of the Sierras de Játar and de Almijara to descend into Arenas del Rey.

Retrace the 2km route up the gorge to the sign and road near the dam. Turn left onto the road, passing by the reservoir and the bird observatory on your right and El Ventorro (B, once an inn for horsemen, now a comfortable hotel with spa and cave rooms: tel 958 350 438) on your left.

Around 300m further on, turn right over a little bridge up a smaller road signposted with a GR7 sign (Arenas del Rey 20.5km). Stay on this main track, passing through poplar plantations with the Río Alhama alongside you on your right. Ignore all turnings, including a wide one after about 4km at a building with a tennis court on your right with signs on

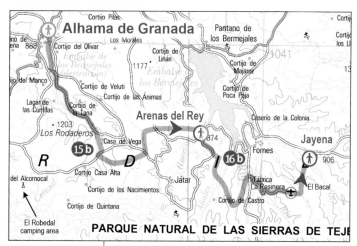

Looking down on the route through the gorge from Alhama

the gate to Fuente Tanguillo, Fuente El Arragonés and Puerta Cuberos. About 700m after this house (and nearly 5km after you join this track) take a little path down to the right.

Follow this path to a stream (which is sometimes a dry bed) and follow the stream for about 100m before crossing it and starting to climb diagonally up the slope on a wider gravel path through holm oaks and rosemary. ▶

You meet another track on the brow of the hill and turn left down it to pass the green roofed warehouse and then continue uphill staying on the main wide dirt track through oaks and gorse until you meet a tarmac road, 700m later. Turn right up the road for about 250m then take a small marked path to the left just before you reach a quarry off to the right of the road. Ignore a steep track up to the left just after you leave the road to cross a small stream bed and climb through oaks and scrub. Join another track back to the right and continue, sticking to this main track with stunning views of the Sierra Nevada to the east and the Sierra de Jatar and the Sierra de Almijara to the south.

When you come to a house and field after 2km keep it on your left and continue on the track through the few houses of Cortijo de Navazo and onwards through a patchwork of arable fields, olives and almond orchards and oak woodlands. At a junction of tracks less than a km later carry straight on to come to a small tarmac road at GR7 signposts (Arenas Del Rey 11km, Alhama de Granada 12km). Turn right up the road and after 200m turn left onto a wide gravel track which you follow through mixed oak woodland and fields for 4km. Then turn right down another dirt track. As it descends, the **Los Bermejales reservoir** comes in to view and you continue down until the track forks 3.5km later and take the marked right fork downhill. Turn right soon after when you meet another track to cross a river bed and pass a shady bench and stools at Los Fuentes/El Cañuelo. The track brings you round on to a wide gravel track that contours round the hillside with great views down to the resevoir. Stay on the main track for the final 2.5km ignoring tracks off the the sides including one back to the left and two tracks that join you from the right soon after. You soon round a corner to see **Arenas Del Rey** and enter at a GR7 signpost (Alhama de Granada 23km).

As you come towards the top of the hill you look down on intensive horticulture to the left and increasingly impressive views of the Sierra de Jatar and the Sierra de Almijara to your right.

ARENAS DEL REY 875M POPULATION 2100

Campsite, restaurant/bar/café, drinking fountain, food shop, telephone, transport.

Accommodation and food
A couple of bars that serve the usual fare but there is no accommodation in the village itself. You can either continue to Jayena or head round the reservoir for about 7km to the northern edge where there is a campsite, **Los Bermejales** (A), tel 958 359 190, www.losbermejales.com; and **Apartamentos Rurales Encanto del Poniente**, nice rustic comfortable tourist flats with additional services including massage available: Camino de Moreta 16, Los Bermejales, tel 687 535 144, www.apartamentosencantorural.com.

Further information
Town hall: Pza Alfonso X, tel 958 359 103, www.arenasdelrey.org.

Transport
Taxi: ask in shop for a local family who will drive walkers to Jayena or the campsite, or contact Jayena taxi firm (see below). The only bus goes very early in the morning.

A little village with a pleasant plaza and a church surrounded by leafy gardens. It retains some traces of Roman settlement but, like many villages in the area, Arenas was almost completely destroyed in an earthquake on Christmas Day in 1884. It was reconstructed by Alfonso XII and changed its name from Arenas de Alhama to Arenas del Rey ('of the King') in his honour.

STAGE 16B

Arenas del Rey – Jayena

Start	Plaza in Arenas del Rey
Distance	16.6km
Time	6h
Highest point	1080m
Height gain	1550m
Height loss	640m

See map in
Stage 15B.

A beautiful climb over the hill with stunning views of the Sierra Nevada takes you down to La Resinera and through mixed pine woodland until Jayena. There are lots of options for other routes in the natural park that leave from La Resinera.

From the plaza, leave the village heading downhill and east on the road out of the village in the direction of Jayena. Pass another drinking fountain and when you come to the bridge at the end of the village, cross it and turn right. ▶

A signpost here states that it is 16km to Jayena.

On the ridge between Arenas del Rey and La Resinera

You soon come to a signboard for the Colada de Camino de Fornes – which is an old agricultural path to Fornes. Pass by this sign and climb on the quiet tarmac road passing agricultural buildings and a small quarry before turning on to a road to the left (1.5km from the edge of the village).

Follow this round the hillside, looking out across lower olive-covered hills, ignoring a large track off to the left near the top of the hill. After 1km on this road, turn down to the right onto a gravel track heading south between polytunnels. Then take a sharp left off the track to double back on yourself and come down to and across a ford. Continue on the gravel track on the other side to start the ascent to the ridge between here and La Resinera. ◄ When the track splits after 200m take the right fork to contour round the hill before climbing again. At the next divide go right again, now passing by wild rosemary and thyme bushes with pine trees on the slopes around you. The track climbs steeply then contours round in a large 'U'-shape to look back over the polytunnels again. Here, just over 2km from the ford, you meet and take a track off to the left to continue the ascent to the ridge (ignoring the track that carries on at the same contour). The final gentle climb is up through a field of almond trees bringing you to the ridge at over 1000m and stunning views of the Sierra Nevada. Here you meet a large level track running along the top of the ridge and there is a chain across the track you've just ascended. Go right along the large track. It drops down slightly, bending to the left to meet another wider track after 200m which you can see running all the way along the top of the ridge. You however turn left to descend on a good track all the way to the valley floor. Once at the bottom, turn left to arrive at the La Resinera – once a **fábrica** ('factory') for processing pine resin.

This section is without any GR7 markings.

The old factory is now an **information centre** with displays about the forest fires in 1975 and 1983 which devastated the resin-processing industry in the area and forced the closure of the plant and an accompanying sawmill.

A 375m signposted detour takes you to a viewpoint, and a fork off to the right from in front of the building takes you on other routes to Puerto de Cómpeta (16km) and Puerto de Frigiliana (11km). You can get information about these and other routes in the centre.

The GR7 continues downhill on a track with the information centre on the left. The track divides again shortly afterwards and you turn left down to the small **Río Cebollón** on a track signposted to the airstrip (*Pista de Aterrizaje*). Cross the little bridge and then stay on the main track, taking a left 100m on, walking through pines. ▸ After a while cross another stream (no bridge) and then begin to zigzag uphill.

The pines are all quite young due to replanting after the fires in the 1970s and 1980s.

Where the track divides just over 1km after the information centre, take the fork to the left. An information board here tells you about the process of extracting resin from the pines. Then ignore a smaller track off to the right. Shortly after this take a left at large junction and ignore a left just after it

Stay on the main track which climbs, more steeply now, zigzagging up to a junction almost at the top of the hill, now 3km from the information centre and almost 12km from the start. The left fork goes up to the airstrip and the right fork, which you take, follows the south edge of it for a while before joining a firebreak between the trees. About 150m later, take the left turn into another firebreak, then 300m further on take a smaller left. After a while you see the airstrip again on your left with a steep valley between it and your track. As the track comes into more open ground the village becomes visible down below towards your right.

From here take a path down to the right which you can see curving ahead of you towards **Jayena**. Ignore a left turn and keep heading downhill for 2km on this winding footpath. The path turns into a track and then meets another track. Follow this across a stream and turn left to head up into the village.

JAYENA 912M POPULATION 1,200

Accommodation, campsite, restaurant/bar/café, drinking fountain, food shop, cashpoint, telephone, PO, pharmacy, tourist information, transport.

Accommodation and food
There is one place to stay in town or you can continue along the route to a campsite. For food there are also a couple of bars with standard fare:

El Bacal Camping Area is a permitted camping area on La Resinera mountain, surrounded by pines, with 50-person capacity, showers, toilets and non-drinking water, 4km beyond Jayena (signposted off the GR7). Contact the Town hall below for availability. **Hospedería la Almijara** (B) is a bar/restaurant with a few rooms upstairs, somewhat chaotically run: Av. del Mediterráneo 37, tel 958 364 157.

Further information
Town hall: tel 958 364 079, www.jayena.es.

Transport
Taxi: tel 958 364 140.

Like many of the towns and villages in the area, archaeological finds suggest that there was a settlement here in Neolithic times. It was also inhabited in Roman times but the Islamic period was definitive in creating the town then known as Chayyana. You can see the Muslim watchtower, and the parish church is also worth a visit.

STAGE 17B
Jayena – Albuñuelas

Start	Plaza Constitución in Jayena
Distance	31.1km
Time	8h30
Highest point	1331m
Height gain	980m
Height loss	1150m

A peaceful pine forest track takes you up into hills with beautiful panoramic views across to the Sierra Nevada, and then down a river bed into the pretty village of Albuñuelas.

Head out of Jayena along Plaza Constitución which leaves the small plaza in front of the church (the Iglesia del Santísimo Sacramento) and continues down to the right. Look out for a GR7 sign (Prados de Lopera 17km) as you stay on this road, crossing a bridge, and carry on climbing gently at times through almonds and olives along the valley towards the wooded hills ahead.

After about 40min (2.5km), pass a turning off to the right signposted to **El Bacal** camping area which is 2km down this

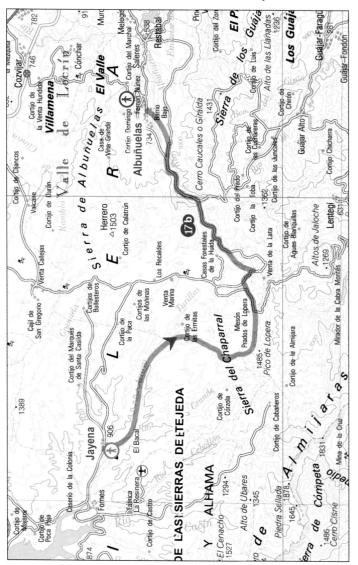

209

Pine nut tree at viewpoint

turning. Continue climbing on the road and after 600m cross the Arroyo Turillas just before the road turns from tarmac into a forestry track. Here there is a sign for 'Senda de los arrieros' and you follow this track to enter the **Parque Natural de las Sierras de Tejada, Almijara y Alhama**.

Follow the track up climbing steadily into the trees, ignoring tracks off to either side. Stay on this main track as it takes you up through shady pines and ignore a track off to the right 1km after entering the woods. You curve round the hill to the left on the main track. For the whole of this section in the woods there are sparse paint markings on trees and occasional faded posts. After about 1h in the woods (4km) you come out of the trees briefly for great views back across green hills to Jayena in the distance.

There are glimpses out now and again to the Sierra Nevada mountains to the east.

At a split about 300m after this clearing, stay right and keep climbing gently, the track passes through scattered low pine forest and scrubland back in the shady pines. ◀

After climbing a further km you arrive on a plateau and walk across scrubland and dotted small pines, climbing occasionally. A further 2.5km on the track passes through a wide firebreak. Shortly after this ignore another turning doubling back to the right. Keep ascending gently to reach a good viewpoint, 12.5km from the start.

Just after the viewpoint the scenery changes dramatically to undulating arable fields. You come to a fork where you stay left. Pass a right turn and after 20min come to the first building of the Cortijo los Prados, which you pass on your left, to climb the track and pass through the farm. Leave through its large green metal gate and turn right onto another track which soon brings you to the A4050 tarmac road at the bar/restaurant **Mesón Prados de Lopera**.

A GR7 signpost here directs you left along the road known as the Ctra de la Cabra to Albuñelas. After about 250m on the road you come to a signboard for the 5km Cardel de la **Venta de la Lata** walk. Continue past this and walk another 500m up the road to a gravelly car park on the right hand side with a small GR7 sign marking a path leading off it. Take this, climbing through young pines, and after 500m reach another wider gravel track down which you turn right.

▸ After just over 1km, turn left onto a smaller path running alongside the streambed of the Barranco del Cañuelo, passing between huge fragrant rosemary bushes. When the track bends up to the right leave it to continue along the streambed on a little-walked overgrown small path which, after 800m, emerges onto the *camino forestal* again. Beware as erosion has made crossing the stream difficult at one point.

This is the camino forestal which will take you down the long descent to Albuñelas with occasional views to the Sierra Nevada in the distance.

Walking the route between Jayena and Albuñelas

Follow the track for just over 1km to arrive at El Cañuelo picnic area.

> At the **picnic area** there are two houses available to rent by contacting the town hall in advance, and you can camp for free. There are also pleasant shady picnic tables to eat at and barbecues (although at the time of writing all fires had been banned in the spring and summer months due to the risk of forest fires). Water should be available here too although it is not chlorinated, so will need to be treated.

The river is bordered by azaleas and pines, and the rocky crags of the Cerro la Buitrera and Cerro Pintado tower above you.

Leave the picnic area on the main track, heading left down the valley around the hillside and down to the stream which feeds the Río Albuñuelas. You then follow the dry river bed (the water has been diverted into concrete tubes) for about 7.5km, starting with it on your left-hand side, but crossing over it several times on bridges. ◄

After about 3.5km, the track takes you up above the river and then you descend down to another dry river-bed at a junction. Here turn left and go more steeply downhill for a short distance with the river-bed on the right hand side. After a while the river you were following earlier comes in from the left at a point where it has washed away a bridge. Stay on the same track and climb gently and above some ruined buildings.

Some 6km after leaving the picnic area, as the track descends you turn right onto a smaller track that doubles back to the right taking you down to the river bed again to cross the river and climb up the track on the other side.

Albuñuelas comes into view after another 1km and you can see the two parts of the village, the higher part (Barrio Alto) at 738m and the lower neighbourhood (Barrio Bajo) below it. Turn down a track to the left towards it, leaving the pines behind and passing between almond trees and cultivated land. Pass a small track off to the left heading into fields and after 10min take the track heading downhill at a junction. Continue straight on where the path divides, walking between two metal fences as the path becomes steep and more overgrown and picks its way downhill into the valley. Cross the narrow valley which is lush with green vegetable patches, orchards and fig trees, and climb the other side on the Camino de los Molinos – a steep cobbled path that quickly brings you up onto a narrow concrete street in **Albuñuelas**, passing between gardens full of orange trees.

ALBUÑUELAS 750M POPULATION 1,000

Accommodation, restaurant/bar/café, drinking fountain, food shop, telephone, PO, pharmacy, transport.

Accommodation and food
The village has a couple of B&Bs and a casa rural plus several bars which do food:

La Casa Azul (B) is an English-run B&B with rooms and flat and a lovely roof terrace, meals available: C/Horno 8, 958 776 366, www.fishinginspain. co.uk. **El Cortijo del Pino** (C) is a small *casa rural* with four doubles and a single and a patio with beautiful views: Fernan Núñez 2, tel 958 776 257, www.elcortijodelpinolecrin.com.

Further information
Town hall: tel 958 776 031, www.ayuntamiento.es/albunuelas.

A charming, historic village. Buildings of note include the 16th-century watchtower, the parish church, the Ermita de San Antonio, and the old archbishop's palace (17th and 18th centuries). There have been human settlements in the area since prehistoric times and you can visit caves just outside the village where archaeological remains have been discovered.

STAGE 18B
Albuñuelas – Nigüelas

Start	Plaza in Albuñuelas
Distance	15.1km
Time	4h30
Highest point	938m
Height gain	575m
Height loss	400m

A day dominated by orange groves and the sound of water bubbling along the ancient irrigation channels. The route joins the dots between several of the small villages of the Lecrín valley before arriving at the foot of the mountains via a section of steep climbing to reach Nigüelas.

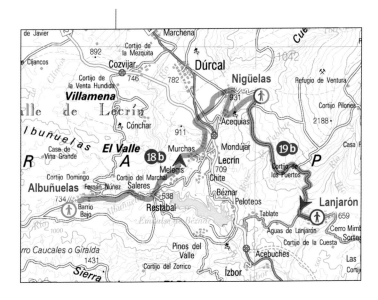

Albuñuelas – Restábal (5.1km, 1h15)
Head east from the plaza, past a bank in the Barrio Alto and along C/de la Estación, pass a *panadería* on the right and go down the Camino Bajo, steeply at first and then contouring on a concrete track below the village with orange groves on your right. Arrive in the Barrio Bajo area of the village on the C/Ramal, following markers. At a point where there is a red and white marker on a stone on a corner at ground level turn right and follow the street down, around to the left passing the old laundry and up (a few 100 metres) to take the next right along C/Mojón to come to a small dirt path and a GR7 sign (Saleres 3km).

> This **lush landscape** is typical of the fertile Lecrín valley, also called the 'Valley of Happiness' (Valle de la Alegría) thanks to its temperate microclimate. The small very narrow path is well marked and takes you straight into the groves of oranges, lemons, almonds, olives and grenadines, alive with the colours and smells of fruits or blossoms depending on the time of year.
> The path follows the routes of the *acequias*, the ancient irrigation channels built by the Moors.

Stay on this small path heading east, ignoring paths off into fields. At a split in the path after 1.8km, take the left (marked) fork up to pass through an orange grove and onto a wider track which becomes concrete. Remain on this, avoiding turns, and heading downhill. Detour steeply up to your left to visit the small village of Saleres (560m, population 300, restaurant/bar/café, drinking fountain) whose winding streets still retain their medieval layout (3.6km, 55min). ▸

If you are not visiting **Saleres**, stay on the track below the village, keeping to the right until you reach a low concrete bridge over the river. Cross the bridge and climb the broad concrete track for about 500m. On your right is a building and on your left is a low battered GR7 post and a narrower track going down to the left. Take this track which is concrete in sections. Follow this through orange groves, passing a few houses and then descending to cross a small stream before climbing up and in to the centre of the village of **Restábal**.

For a short detour, visit the *atalaya*, the village watchtower, which has excellent views out across the valley.

RESTÁBAL 538M POPULATION 600

Accommodation, campsite, restaurant/bar/café, drinking fountain, food shop, telephone, pharmacy, transport.

Accommodation and food
A choice of places to eat including a **Thai restaurant** and **Mesón Despensa del Valle/Bar Jovi**, a good restaurant serving local dishes which rents out rooms and flats (B/C): C/Santa Ana 5, tel 958 793 598/958 793 531, www.despensadelvalle. com. **Camping El Valle** (A) is a campsite with basic dorm beds available if not booked by a group; call to confirm. Pool, shop, bar: Monte de Restábal, tel 634 849 633, www.campingelvalle.com.

Further information
Town hall: Av. Andalucía 34, tel 958 793 181, www.elvalle.es.

Transport
Taxi: tel 958 793 218.

This quiet little whitewashed village surrounded by fruit orchards is the administrative centre for El Valle area (the villages of Melegis, Restábal and Saleres). The sights of the village are the remains of a Moorish castle from the Nasrid period (13th to 15th century), the C/Real market and the 16th-century San Cristóbal church.

Looking back on Restábal

Restábal – Nigüelas (10km, 3h15)

To leave Restábal turn left along the main GR3204 (C/de Llano). After 150m turn left onto a shortcut path that takes you down crossing and cutting two corners off the road. When you rejoin the road, turn right downhill past a GR7 display board and across a bridge over the Río Izbor. Immediately on the other side of the bridge turn off the road to the left. ▶ Then head right along a smaller track through orange trees. Soon afterwards, take another right between some old stone walls.

This is signed to Melegis and Murchas.

Just round the bend from this divide the GR7 leaves the track for a small path on the left, across an *acequia*. This is a little overgrown in places, but well marked, and brings you back to a wider track after a few hundred metres. Stay on this wider track. Descend to, but do not cross, the stream, and follow it upstream. Turn right on the track heading uphill as it becomes concrete. When it splits take the left fork and carry on to arrive at a GR7 sign for **Melegís** (553m, population 450, accommodation, restaurant/bar/café, drinking fountain, telephone), which is a 10min diversion to the right.

On the outskirts of the village and just before a ford/bridge at a sign Restábal 2km take a track to the left (not signed initially). Follow this with the stream on your right. At a crossroads take a signed left turn and continue uphill along a concrete track through orange groves to enter the village of **Murchas** (660m, population 300, restaurant/bar/café, drinking fountain, telephone).

To leave Murchas, carry on through the village following signs for the cemetery ('el cementerio') and passing the church and the fountain. ▶

This is a new section of the GR7 (the old section took you up the far side of the Río Torrente so don't be confused by any old markings).

Where you see a sign on a road to the left (Nigüelas 5.5km), follow this road up steeply, looking back to see the village below you where it levels off. Continue to climb heading north as the road becomes a track. About 15 minutes from Murchas look for a sign to go up a very steep narrow path towards the wind turbines on the hilltop. Climb steeply for 15-20min before joining a track just below the wind turbines. Turn right and climb more gently before joining a wider track from the turbines. Turn right, go downhill a little and follow the track around to the left alongside the motorway, passing an electricity substation and heading northwest. After 500m the track crosses the motorway on a

From here you could make a 2km detour into Dúrcal for supplies or accommodation on foot or by bus.

bridge. Follow this and carry on through almond trees. You soon meet the road to **Dúrcal**. ◀

To continue, cross over the road and carry on in the same direction next to a house and left of the bus stop. After 650m you will come to the Nigüelas road but the GR7 heads left away from the road along a track. At the next crossroad in the track after 250m continue straight on then turn right at the next crossroads next to a water building 250m after that. You should now see the church ahead of you. After a further 500m turn right again next to a concrete wall then turn left to enter **Nigüelas** .

NIGÜELAS 950M POPULATION 1,200

Accommodation, restaurant/bar/café, drinking fountain, food shop, telephone, pharmacy, transport.

Accommodation and food
The range of options for accommodation include a small hostel, B&Bs and a handful of *casas rurales*, which are usually only available for a minimum of two nights, plus some luxury accommodation on the outskirts:

Alquería de los Lentos (C) has beautiful luxurious accommodation situated in a converted mill on the outskirts of the village – rooms have private entrances, open fires, sitting area and air conditioning and it boasts a swimming pool, garden and bar/restaurant: Camino de los Molinos, tel 958 777 850, www. alqueriadeloslentos.com. **Casa de Lino** (B) has 10 rooms in an attractive 16th-century building with indoor courtyard, outdoor terrace and restaurant: C/del Agua 2, tel 617 207 469, www.casadelino.es. **Hostel Almora** (A) has a six bed dorm and a double room: Solanilla 7, tel 677 685 800. **La Huerta del Cura** (B) has rooms and flats with a shared pool: C/Alta 16, tel 958 953 045, www.lahuertadelcura.com.

A number of *casas rurales* – only open in peak season and best booked ahead: www.niguelas.org/turismo/alojamientos.

Further information
Town hall: C/Angustias 6, tel 958 777 607, www.niguelas.org.

Nigüelas is a charming place with an attractive tree-lined square. It has some grand 17th and 18th-century houses and also a number of inhabited cave houses.

SIERRA NEVADA NATURAL PARK

The Sierra Nevada is a walkers' paradise. It is the second highest mountain range in Europe with over 20 peaks at more than 3000m. Its highest peak, Mulhacén (3481m), is the highest on the Iberian peninsula.

The 1718km^2 area has various protected statuses. It contains a national park, one of only two in Andalucía, which has the highest level of protection, and is a Unesco biosphere reserve.

The Sierra Nevada is home to exceptionally diverse plant, bird and animal species at a range of bioclimatic levels from lush green valleys to bleak wind-swept mountain tops. It also has a rich cultural and historical heritage dating back to the Tartessians, Visigoths, Romans and the Moors.

Wildlife

The park boasts the highest number of endemic plant species in Europe and also many North African species. In the spring and early summer the range of wild-flowers is remarkable. The vegetation you are likely to see varies hugely according to the altitude you are at, from gall oaks, maples, wild olives, and shrubs such as prickly junipers lower down, to pines, junipers, bushy thyme, rosemary and broom higher up, and lichens and grass species at the highest altitudes. Near to streams and rivers you'll find poplar, alder, ash, elm and willow.

The park is known for its population of Spanish ibex, a type of native mountain goat, and these are the mammals you are most likely to spot (often posing silhouetted on hilltops!). If you're lucky, you may also see foxes, badgers, wild boars, wildcats, beech martens and genets. On higher slopes you may come across Mediterranean pine voles and weasels. The park also has a huge variety of insect life, and is particularly interesting for its butterflies, with 120 catalogued species.

The bird life in the park is impressive, with over 60 species including important colonies of birds of prey such as golden eagles, Bonelli's eagles, peregrine falcons, griffon vultures and kestrels. In wooded areas you may see or hear hoopoes, short-toed treecreepers, green woodpeckers, great tits, goldfinches and golden orioles. And, in the highest areas, there are Alpine accentors, black redstarts, skylarks, northern wheatears, rock thrushes, rock buntings and red-billed choughs.

Further information

Park information office: Ctra de la Sierra, Km 7, 18191-Pinos Genil, Granada, tel 958 026 300/958 026 303, On the route there are also limited information points at Puerto de la Ragua and Pampaneira.

STAGE 19B
Nigüelas – Lanjarón

Start	Plaza in Nigüelas
Distance	18.5km
Time	5h
Highest point	1282m
Height gain	840m
Height loss	1060m

Small paths and forest tracks take you high up through pines and almonds with expansive views over the Lecrín valley, before a long descent brings you to the spa town of Lanjarón and the start of the Alpujurras.

See map in
Stage 18B.

To leave Nigüelas, head northeast out of the plaza in front of the church. You pass a sign (Acequias 2km) and the street takes you down and out of the buildings. Cross the bridge over the Río Torrente. Ignore the first track immediately to the left, but take the second one which is roughly cobbled in places. When this divides, turn right up a concrete track leaving the village behind you and walking between almonds.

This is now an
interesting small
museum open on
Thurs, Sat and Sun.

Follow this track all the way to Acequias (869m, pop.110) with the broad gorge of the Río Torrente on your right. Shortly before entering the hamlet pass a water mill. ◄ Head up and left just as you enter the plaza in the north of the hamlet passing a sign (Lanjarón 17km). Climb steeply up a concrete track and after 10min bear left at a small white water building. Continue to climb with a stone wall on your left. Just before the concrete track ends at a gate and a yellow house turn right up a steep slope and continue straight ahead into pines, following the signs.

Turning around gives
you increasingly
good views back
over Nigüelas and
neighbouring Dúrcal
and Padul spread out
on the valley floor.

Climb steadily in a northerly direction for 25min and then the path begins to zigzag ever upwards before arriving at a main forestry track, about 2km from **Acequias**. ◄ Go straight on up the main track, ignoring a smaller one heading backwards to the right, and then keep right, passing a turning to the left after 5min. Keep climbing through pines with bare rock faces and water eroded slopes above, and contrastingly neatly ordered olive groves below. Follow the track around to the east passing through an almond plantation.

After a further 1.5km of climbing, at the next divide in the track, take the right fork. The track levels out and you walk round an open hillside getting views down over the villages of the Lecrín valley through which you have passed. ▶

You can also see the sea here on clear days and, on very clear days, all the way across to Africa.

After 2km, going steadily downhill and passing through further almond groves as well as open scrub, walk straight over a crossroads where there is a noticeable change in rock colour from red to grey. Around another 500m on you pass the Icona drinking fountain and from there continue on the main track ignoring small ones off to various farms. The track climbs again until 2km after the fountain where there is a divide in the main track. You head right, going uphill past the Albergue de Lecrín. 100m on the track divides and the left fork is signposted 'Tello' and leads up to the mountains on the GR240, your route continues to the right.

The town of Lanjarón soon comes into view far below you and the track begins to descend in large zigzags to meet it. ▶ After 30 minutes you reach a *mirador* (viewpoint) with a sign-board. As you descend, you will pass several tracks off the main one signposted to 'cortijos'. 30min beyond the mirador you pass a stone sign to Albercón but continue downhill, keeping to the main track all the time. You eventually arrive at a T-junction in among the trees. You head left and from here keep heading downhill, ignoring smaller tracks and keeping to the left side of a small stream. This brings you to the main road (A348) into **Lanjarón**. Turn left along it and where it turns sharp right continue straight on to enter the village on its main street (Av Alpujarra).

From here it is almost all downhill.

ALPUJARRAS

The Alpujarras is an area of valleys between the Sierra Nevada and the Sierras of Almijara, Contraviesa and Gádor to the south. The GR7 crosses the western part of the region, which is in the province of Granada, and a small section of the eastern part in the province of Almería. The walking on this section of the route is typically on smaller steeper mountain paths with less road walking and track walking than other sections.

The name Alpujarras comes from the Arabic *abuxarrat* meaning 'land of silk', and the area, which was the last refuge of the Moors in Spain, still retains a distinctive

Arab influence, evident in the cuisine, arts and crafts, sophisticated irrigation systems and Arabic place names. It is known for its Berber architecture: whitewashed flat-roofed houses with distinctive chimneys packed into steep narrow streets.

In the fertile valleys of the western Alpujarras, the main economic activity (apart from tourism) is still agriculture. The land is still farmed using traditional methods as the steep terrain makes many modern agricultural techniques impractical. You'll pass through cereal crops, olives, vines, oranges and lemons, almonds, walnuts, apples and cherries.

LANJARÓN 650M, POPULATION 4000

Accommodation, restaurant/bar/café, drinking fountain, food shop, telephone, PO, pharmacy, tourist information, transport.

Accommodation and food
A number of good hotels in various price categories, including:

Hotel Alcadima (C) is luxurious with swimming pool, solarium and pretty courtyard full of geraniums with views of the castle. C/Francisco Tarrega 3, tel 958 770 809/958 770 279, www.alcadima.com. **Hotel Miramar** (B) has a swimming pool, large rooms some with their own lounge, air conditioning and balconies: Av. de las Alpujarras 10, tel 958 770 161. **Hotel Central** (A) is a straightforward hotel with clean rooms and free wi-fi opposite Hotel Miramar: Av de la Alpujarra 21, 18420 Lanjaron, tel 958 770 108, www.hotelcentral-lanjaron.es. **Hotel Balneario de Lanjarón** (C) is a giant new grand hotel next to the baths whose waters here have been renowned for their health-giving properties since 1770. You can have all manner of massages, baths, facials and health consultations: Av. de Madrid 2, tel 958 770 137, www.balneariodelanjaron.com.

Further information
Town hall: Plaza de la Constitución 29, Lanjaron, 958 770 002, www.lanjanet.com.
Tourist Office: Av. de Madrid, tel 958 770 462.

Transport
Taxi: tel 958 770 097.

Made famous by its natural spring, Lanjarón is still dominated by water, with many making the trip to visit its spa. This, combined with its billing as the 'gateway to the Alpujarras', makes it a busy place to visit with plenty of hotels and restaurants to choose from and lots of craft shops. If you have time, treat your aching muscles to a massage at the spa.

STAGE 20B

Lanjarón – Soportújar

Start	Main road east from Lanjarón
Distance	12.4km
Time	4h50
Highest point	1128m
Height gain	700m
Height loss	400m

A pretty climb out of Lanjarón takes you up to a path that zigzags round ravines passing Cáñar and crossing an impressive dam, Dique 24, to reach Soportújar.

Lanjarón – Cáñar (7.8km, 2h50)

Head out of Lanjarón east along the main road. You pass the Ermita de San Sebastián, and cross the Río Lanjarón at the east edge of town, heading towards the rock face of the **Cerro Mimbre**. After passing a GR7 signboard and a fountain, continue 250m to a left turn by a white house signposted to Cáñar. Go up past this house then follow the concrete track that turns rapidly into a little cobbled path passing up behind a house and onto another concrete track

Climbing up out of Lanjarón

behind it. You continue up this and then take another steep little path on the right, soon reaching a wide track above. The route then crosses two tarmac roads (turn briefly left and then right), following signposted shortcuts off it to cut off some of the track's loops and come to yet another concrete track.

There are good views back down over the town and you can see the **ruined Moorish castle** down by the river, built to control access to the town. Its tower was used as part of the communication line between the watchtowers throughout the Alpujarras and the coast. When Christians took the town after an epic battle in 1490, Captain Negro, who was defending the town, is said to have jumped to his death from the tower rather than live to see the town fall into enemy hands.

When you reach another concrete track near the top go straight along it for 600m then turn off again onto a little cobbled path that follows a fast-flowing *acequia* after a little while to come out onto a track at a farmhouse where you turn right to come to onto a concrete track again. Turn right along it and follow it downhill through almond and olive trees for about 600m before coming to a junction where you turn left (signposted to Caballo Blanco). ▶

The GR142 is signed to the right, but you do not go this way.

Follow the track, passing a GR142 signpost to Órgiva, ignore the left to Caballo Blanco and take the wider right track. Another 800m on pass a track to the right, continuing on the main track. At the next fork go left (the right is clearly signposted as private land) and continue uphill until the next divide where you go left, then left again almost immediately onto a little path.

This takes you on a narrow and in places eroded path around a ravine. This hugs steep slopes and is and exposed in some sections. ▶ At the divide in the path nearly 1km on take the left fork. The path becomes a little overgrown and difficult to follow but there are marks and you should keep heading north and uphill, passing between oaks and brambles. The path then becomes clearer and you descend to the pretty Barranco de Cañuelo, a pleasant and shady place to rest.

Marking is less evident here than on previous days.

Cross the stream and climb up the other side of the gorge with **Cáñar** coming into view ahead of you. The path then takes in a loop into and out of the next gorge 1km to the north, crossing the Barranco de las Peñas (which is often dry) and onto the Camino de las Viñas, which takes you into the village. Where it splits by a concrete bunker, you can take either the right or the left fork to bring you out at the road which you cross to enter the village.

CÁÑAR 1014M POPULATION 500

Accommodation, restaurant/bar/café, drinking fountain, food shop, telephone, transport.

Accommodation and food
Some bars with food and a couple of options for accommodation:

El Cielo de Cáñar (C) is a stylish hotel housed in a beautiful stone *cortijo*: Granada 18418, tel 958 953 015, www.elcielodecanar.com. **Casa Rural Cáñar Fernando**

(B) has two charming houses available for rental, available by room when not full: tel 696 894 799, www.lamua.com.

Further information
www.cañar.es.

Quiet with leafy plazas, Cáñar, like other villages in the area, owes its layout and architecture to Arabic times with Berber-influenced flat-roofed whitewashed houses. In Arab times its economy was based around the production of silk. It boasts a viewpoint to Africa which is worth a detour on a clear day.

This route is also signposted to the cemetery and Dique 24 which you pass by along with a GR7 information board.

You can see Soportújar straight ahead across the ravine that you are about to walk round.

Cáñar – Soportújar (4.6km, 2h)

Leave Cáñar, passing the church on your left and going down to the right on unmarked streets. You exit on the east side of the village at the Fuente de Ya Bajos and a GR7 sign pointing you northeast along a concrete track with wooden handrails (Soportújar 2h). ◄

Follow the concrete track with great views down to the valley and Órgiva. After 300m, you come to a *mirador*. Here follow the path that contours at this level, despite a GR7 cross, and **do not** take a rough track on the left going uphill. Instead stay under the cemetery wall, and take the marked path diagonally down the hill. This section also has posts with white arrows pointing back the way you have come. The track becomes a smaller path and you turn right at the next small divide. ◄

After 1km on the small path, you come to a divide and take the right lower fork that drops steeply and then climbs again and keep heading into the ravine. After 800m, ignore a path off to the left and stay on the lower path. At the next split both forks take you to the same place.

Just over 2.5km from the start you arrive at Dique 24, so-called because it is the 24th in a series of dams built to reduce erosion from the **Río Chico**. Cross the river behind the dam (you may need to wade) and go down the stone steps on the other side where the small path zigzags upwards briefly through pines before levelling out and passing a building, and dropping again.

The path then follows along the side of the pretty Acequia de la Vega, passing above the ruined hamlet of Varjal. You then cross the *acequia* at a divide in the path and head right downhill through a lush valley with lots of camomile and fig trees. Go left when the path divides and carry on steeply downwards (possibly muddy after rain), coming out onto a concrete track into the village. Turn left then down steeply, initially slightly right, into **Soportújar**.

SOPORTÚJAR 975M POPULATION 300

Accommodation, restaurant/bar/café, drinking fountain, food shop, telephone.

Accommodation and food
There are only a couple of bars that serve food, a small food shop and one place to stay:

La Huerta (B), two well-equipped, self-catering flats with pool for up to four people: Camino de Carataunas, tel 625 811 929, www.soportujar.com.

Further information
Town hall: Pza 1, tel 958 787 531, www.soportujar.blogspot.co.uk.

A sleepy village perched above the valley floor looking down on Órgiva. Have a look into the 16th-century parish church, Santa María la Mayor, on your way past. It was built in the Mudéjar style on top of the site of an old mosque and has a gilded wooden 18th-century altarpiece.

STAGE 21B
Soportújar – Pitres

Start	Main road heading east out of Soportújar
Distance	11.9km
Time	3h45
Highest point	1531m
Height gain	955m
Height loss	635m

A great day starting with a winding path into Pampaneira at the bottom of the beautiful Poquiera valley, then a climb up through Bubión over a pass with incredible views back across the valley and up to the peaks of the Sierra Nevada, before descending to Pitres.

See map in
Stage 20B.

Soportújar – Pampaneira (6km, 2h)

Head east out of Soportújar on the main road, crossing the bridge then heading south and passing a fountain on the left with a GR7 signboard opposite. For 750m continue along the road, then turn off to the left on a right hand bend in the road up a signed concrete track towards a cemetery. Where the concrete ends by the wall of the cemetery, descend to the right onto the GR7 track and turn left along the lower track. When it divides almost immediately, take the bottom right track along a stone wall.

Come round the hill on a small dirt path through broom with amazing views. Climb up to a track along which you turn right for 400m before taking a gravel track to the left. Follow this for 10min looking out for a small sign-posted path off it to the right which you take and carry along past ruined buildings, passing between a house and a wall. Just after these turn right when the path divides.

From here the path enters the Poqueira valley and you can see Pampaneira and Bubión ahead.

◀ Continue on round and into the valley now heading north. The path comes to a wider track after a further 10min and you turn right along it, then immediately left up a concrete track, which looks like a driveway with a gate at the end but actually has a small path running off to the left just before the gates. You take this overgrown path up and behind the building and carry on.

At the next building stay on the small path which then crosses over another track and continues. Again, at a third house, make sure you stay on the small path, ignoring its driveway. Shortly after this you reach a wide track which you follow round to the right.

Turn right at the next divide in the track and then go straight on when another track goes off sharp right with views of Pampaneira now ahead. Just after this split, cross a small stream and then immediately afterwards, take a path off and up to the left. Follow this well-marked little path until you come to another track which you then follow downhill through berries and under cherry, walnut and chestnut trees.

When you come to another little path off to the right, descend on it all the way to the road, which you come out onto just before the bridge over the **Río Poqueira**.

Turn left along the road and across the bridge heading up into the village. A small track off to the left after 200m takes you off the road and zigzags uphill under the electricity pylons. When it meets the road again cross over it and up a narrow village road into **Pampaneira**.

PAMPANEIRA 1050M POPULATION 370

Accommodation, restaurant/bar/café, drinking fountain, food shop, cashpoint, telephone, PO, pharmacy, tourist information, transport.

Accommodation and food
A good selection of restaurants and places to stay, many of the best are around the pretty main plaza:

Hostal Pampaneira (B), pleasant rooms and a terrace looking down on the bustling street life and the popular good value restaurant below, at the bottom of the village: Av. Alpujarra 1, tel 958 763 002, www.hostalpampaneira.com. Hostal Ruta del Mulhacén (B) is oppostite Hostal Pampaneira; this has cosy rooms with a bath, many with balconies or terraces looking down into the valley: tel 958 763 010, www.rutadelmulhacen.com.

Further information
Town hall: Pza Mirador de Poquiera, 958 763 001, www.pampaneira.es.

Transport
Taxi: 958 763 002

Pampaneira is a perfect example of the picturesque, clean, white villages for which the Alpujarras are famous. Its traditional architecture is well conserved including many tinaos (covered streets). It is packed with craft workshops and shops which risk tempting walkers into adding weight to their rucksacks by buying textiles, ceramics, shoes and leatherwork, and ham.

Pampaneira – Bubión (1.4km, 20min)
From the plaza head northeast out of the village, passing the *lavadero*, following some marking on the ground and arriving at signs to the Camino de Bubión which leaves the village from halfway up C/Castillo on a small path to the left. At a T-junction 400m on, turn left and then right at a divide 50m further on at a big dead tree. The path from here goes up among holm oaks, chestnuts and hawthorn before arriving in **Bubión**, passing a fountain at the entrance to the village.

BUBIÓN 1300M POPULATION 350

Accommodation, restaurant/bar/café, drinking fountain, food shop, cashpoint, telephone, PO, pharmacy, tourist information, transport.

Accommodation and food
Accommodation and bars/restaurants are plentiful here:

Hostal las Terrazas (A) has comfortable hotel rooms or (B) self-catering flats with terraces down the hill, just off the main road: Pza del Sol, tel 958 763 034, www.terrazasalpujarra.com. **La Sevillana** (B) is a B&B in an attractive old house with seven light rooms: Ctra de la Sierra 3, tel 958 763 153/628 132 357, www.casala-sevillana.es. **Los Tinaos** (B) has pleasant terraced flats with beautiful views down to Pampaneira: C/Parras, tel 958 763 217/660 515 333, www.lostinaos.com.

Further information
Town hall: C/Haza de los Huertos: tel 958 763 370, www.bubion.es.

Transport
Taxi: tel 958 763 148.

A lively village with a thriving handicrafts industry with little art galleries, hand-weaving workshops and souvenir shops selling traditional Alpujarran products including cheeses, ceramics and the ubiquitous legs of ham which are cured in the high mountain villages. There's also a museum, La Casa Alpujarrena, a traditional house displaying crafts, traditional life and folklore.

Capileira, the village to the north of Bubión, provides the start to many routes in the Sierra Nevada, including to the summit of Veleta. Throughout the summer there is also a bus service to within three hours' walk of the summit of Mulhacén.

Bubión – Pitres (4.5km, 1h25)

Leave Bubión by the A4129 road which connects Pampaneira, Bubión and Capileira on the east side of the village (C/de la Ctra). A GR7 sign 'Capilerilla 3.5km' (not to be confused with Capileira) directs you off the road up C/Ermita past a house and a horse corral, staying on the wider track and starting to climb with chestnuts on both sides. Another 700m on, turn right at a junction and then, very soon after, leave the wide track for a little path up to the right which continues to climb.

After 500m, the path divides and you go left to carry on zigzagging up the hill until you reach the ridge at over 1500m. ◄

There are great views of the three villages of the Poqueira valley and the top of Veleta, at 3394m.

From the ridge, you start the descent to **Capilerilla** and Pitres. Just after the ridge, the path crosses a wide track. Continue on the path downhill southeast, ignoring a right turn and heading into pine trees as the path becomes a forestry track. Cross over another track, continuing straight on past two left turns back.

Another 1km from the pass, turn right down a track and then almost immediately left onto a small path heading into the trees. This widens out to a small track and you get views of Pórtugos ahead and glimpses of Pitres below you. Pass through cherry trees on a well worn path and, by a fountain off to your left, come into the hamlet of Capilerilla (1440m, population 30, drinking fountain) 2.4km from the pass by a sign to Pitres (0.5km). Turn left through the houses and then, on the other side, right to head round and downhill on a track with somewhat incongruous lampposts to rapidly arrive into the outskirts of **Pitres**.

PITRES 1250M, POPULATION 500

Accommodation, campsite, restaurant/bar/café, drinking fountain, food shop, cashpoint, telephone, PO, pharmacy, tourist information, transport.

Accommodation and food
Balcón de Pitres has (A) camping and (B) cabins in a large, shady campsite to the northwest of the village with restaurant, shop, laundry service and swimming pool, and information on local walks, about 500m out of the village. Carretera Órgiva-Ugívar, Km52, tel 958 766 111, www.balcondepitres.com. **Hotel San Roque** (B) is a friendly hotel with free wi-fi and a good restaurant, at the entrance to the village: Paseo Maritimo 57–59, tel 958 857 528.

Further information
Town hall: Plaza del Ayuntamiento, tel 958 766 061, www.latahamunicipio.blogspot.com.

Transport
Taxi: tel 958 766 005.

Bustling and very pretty, Pitres perches high on the hillside overlooking Altabéitar and the other smaller villages of La Tahá, the municipality of which it is the capital. It is a lively place with lots going on and a sizeable community of British expats (evident from the marmite, Hellmann's mayonnaise, baked beans and Bisto section in the supermarket).

STAGE 22B
Pitres – Trevélez

Start	Hotel San Roque in Pitres
Distance	15.2km
Time	5h45
Highest point	1758m
Height gain	955m
Height loss	675m

Leave Pitres on a path through lush vegetation past streams, passing through the tiny hamlet of Atalbéitar to climb to Pórtugos. Visit the colourful iron-rich spring then take the oak woodland route to Trevélez.

Pitres to Pórtugos (2.5km, 1h)
Head east out of Pitres on the main road past the Hotel San Roque and, before leaving the village, turn right down C/Agua Agria. Cross the road and you will see a GR7 sign. The road rapidly turns into a dirt path as you leave the houses behind passing the Refugio los Alberges. Pass through a gateway in an old wall and then take two left turns to go down to a stream, El Bermejo. Cross over it on stepping stones or by wading and then, a short distance on, cross a second stream surrounded by lush vegetation.

Follow the path round and up to the right and after 300m it brings you to a small tarmac road along which you turn right. Ignore a turning to the right to a ceramic workshop shortly after, following the road into **Atalbéitar** (1250m, population 30, drinking fountain), which is now in sight (1.5km, 30min).

> The **hamlet's name** comes from the Arabic word *haratalbaitar* which means 'veterinarian's neighbourhood'. It was apparently once the home of a wise man known throughout all of the La Tahá area for his extensive knowledge of the healing properties of plants and herbs.

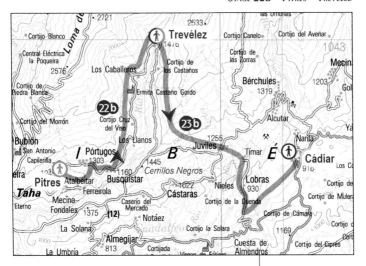

Leave Atalbéitar to the east by the laundry on a small path (signposted Camino de Pórtugos). After 200m, the path crosses a small bridge over the Barranco de los Castaños and carries on through figs and broom. Another 300m later, when you come to a T-junction, turn left onto a wider track.

Almost immediately turn right and then left again after another 200m to bring you back onto a small path by an old sweet chestnut tree. Climb for another 300m to arrive at a big wall on the edge of **Pórtugos**. ▶ The route heads right and up to the road and a viewpoint which looks back towards Pitres and down to the other villages of La Tahá. Turn left along the road and take the first right to enter the centre of the village.

> To the left you can see the rear of the Hostal Nuevo Malagueño.

PÓRTUGOS 1,300M POPULATION 320

Accommodation, restaurant/bar/café, drinking fountain, food shop, cashpoint, telephone, PO, pharmacy, tourist information, transport.

Accommodation and food
The village has plenty of hotels and restaurants:

Hostal Mirador de Pórtugos (B) is central with balconies looking down onto Plaza Nueva, with lively restaurant with good reasonable menu of the day, tel 958 766 014. **Hostal Nuevo Malagueño** (B) is a smart hotel and restaurant on C/Sierra Nevada where the GR7 exits the village, tel 958 766 098.

Further information
Town hall: C/Sierra Nevada, tel 958 766 001, www.portugos.es.

Transport
Taxi: tel 958 766 006.

Pórtugos started life as a Roman settlement. It is famous for its red waterfall, El Chorreón, which is worth a short detour even if you're not stopping here. If you have more time to spend make sure you stroll through its three plazas: La Nueva, La Vieja and La Churriana, the last with a waterfall and laundry inside a cave.

Pórtugos – Busquístar (1.7km, 45min)

If you went into Pórtugos (or are starting from here), the route out leaves from the centre opposite the bank at a GR7 sign (Busquístar 45min) and heads southwest to rejoin the road. Turn left.

The road passes by the Agua Agria de Pórtugos, possibly the most famous mineral water spring in the Alpujarras. Just down off the road to the left, its iron-rich water is red, orange and yellow. It is supposed to be very good for you but the taste is not unlike drinking liquid rust! You then pass a small, shady picnic area to your right. Look out for a difficult to spot small track off and up to the left after 700m on the road.

This track takes you up and cuts off a corner of the road. Where this track divides soon after you join it, take a small path to the right. It follows the edge of fields and a hedge and, after only 200m, the village of Busquístar comes into sight.

When the path divides stay on the lower of the two branches to walk in front of a house. The path then becomes a track which takes you down onto the road. Turn left along the road to come to Busquístar entering the upper part of Albaicín – the *barrio alto* of Busquístar. The route continues up to the left and the main village is down to the right.

BUSQUÍSTAR 1150M POPULATION 400

Accommodation, restaurant/bar/café, drinking fountain, food shop, telephone, transport.

Accommodation
The limited available accommodation is nice but pricey:

El Castañar Nazarí (D) has five bright rooms with wi-fi and fireplaces, a library and a courtyard: Ctra A-4132 km. 39, tel 958 343 613, www.castanarnazari.com.

For further information
Town hall: C/Mezquita 1, 958 766 031, www.busquistar.es.

Transport
Taxi: tel 958 766 036.

Beautiful and tranquil, Busquístar is situated in the Río Trevélez valley, opposite the imposing rock faces of the Sierra de Mecina. It has typically Alpujarran Berber-style whitewashed buildings, slate roofs and steep narrow streets. Sites of interest in the village include the 15th-century parish church (earlier than most in the area) and the remains of an ancient mosque.

Busquístar – Trevélez (11km, 4h)
Leave Busquístar on a small path heading north off the main road. It takes you round the front of a building and then right to come to a concrete road and the village's basketball court. Turn left up the concrete road which rapidly turns into a dirt track. When it divides take the right fork.

The track gets smaller and divides again, 500m from leaving the village. After a sharp left-hand bend take the right hand fork climbing through chestnuts and oaks and cross the Acequia de Busquístar on a small bridge. ▶

This has water all year round and is a lifeline for the village.

Continue uphill and, 1.5km on, the path comes to a wide track. Turn left up the hill and then turn left after an isolated house, as you pass through some oak trees. A further 500m on (2.4km from the start), take the small well marked path to the right.

Throughout the relatively **young oak woodland** there are rich smells of lavender, oregano and thyme. You will come across rock roses, gorse and Spanish broom.

Climb steeply for 100m then, where the path splits, take the right fork to level out and contour around the hillside through trees. After about 1km you will emerge into a more open bushy landscape with views of the Sierra Nevada beginning to appear. The path then crosses a small track and heads along and down through pine trees to a gully. Cross over it and climb, steeply at first and then more gently.

The path follows the edge of the pine forest for 1km before arriving at a loftily located *cortijo* 5.5km from Busquístar. Here cross over the track and stay on the small path heading in the same direction as before, taking a left fork when it divides almost immediately.

After 500m on this path you come to a wide forestry track on the Parque Nacional de Sierra Nevada boundary along which you turn right. After 300m, turn right off the track onto a small path.

Serious landslides and flooding during the winter 2009–2010 made this track (which is signposted GR240 Sulayr) impassable just beyond the turning and have made the terrain for the rest of the GR7 route to Trevélez more difficult.

Having turned right off the track, you head steeply downhill into pine and oak trees. The path zigzags down for 400m through the trees to meet the line of an old *acequia*, which you cross straight over and then continue downhill for another 400m to come to a stream, the Barranco de la Bina, a permanent water source which flows into **Río Trevélez**. Cross the stream on an improvised log bridge, follow along the left bank for 30m then begin the climb up the other side.

Note: Due to **recent landslides**, the path has been diverted here. The terrain is unstable and further diversions should be expected.

As you climb, the path splits many times, but continues to climb and is always clearly marked.

Soon afterwards you pass through two gates and cross an *era* (threshing platform). Just before reaching a ruined farmhouse the path has again been eroded and you need to climb a little and cross a rough meadow. Pass behind the farmhouse. Just after this take the left and higher of two paths which goes steeply uphill heading north. ◄

This takes you back into pine trees and much more gently uphill. Pass through a further gate and across a streambed taking the left of two paths just afterwards, to come through the woods and out onto the open shoulder of the hillside. Head north uphill and through a gate to take a right fork among some striking rock formations.

This path climbs, takes you through a final gate and brings you back to the wide forest track. Trevélez can be seen down to your right. Walk along the track for 500m then start to lose height, turning off onto a small path downhill to the right.

Another 400m further down cross over the track for the last time and keep descending, the path now heading

Trevélez

through fields. Ignore a small path off to the left after 300m then turn right just after you cross a footbridge over the Río Chico de Trevélez, named after the larger Río de Trevélez which the route crosses in its next section.

This area is home to the best-conserved traditional Alpujarran architecture in the village.

Arrive at the top edge of **Trevélez**, the *barrio alto* at 1600m, by a GR7 sign pointing back to Busquístar. ◄ From here, head down C/Charquilla and between the houses to come to a wider street. Turn left along this to enter the main part of the village.

TREVÉLEZ 1400M POPULATION 830

Accommodation, campsite, restaurant/bar/café, drinking fountain, food shop, cashpoint, telephone, PO, pharmacy, tourist information, transport.

Accommodation and food
A good number and range of hotels including:

Camping Trevélez has (A) camping and (B) cabins on a pleasant, terraced site which is open year-round with friendly owners, great views and a restaurant: 1km southwest of the village on the main road, tel 958 858 735, www.campingtrevelez. net. **Bar-Hostel Mulhacén** (B) has well-maintained and equipped rooms: just before the bridge at the bottom of the town, tel 958 858 587. **Hotel Rural Pepe Álvarez** (B) has clean heated rooms with balconies, on the main road through the village: Pza Don Francisco Abellán, tel 958 858 503, www.hotelpepealvarez. es. **Hotel Restaurante La Fragua I and II** (B) are two friendly guesthouses on the eastern side near the top of the 'middle' section of the town with a popular restaurant and great views over the village from its roof terrace. La Fragua II has a pool: C/San Antonio, tel 958 858 626/958 858 512, www.hotellafragua.com.

Further information
Town hall: C/de la Cárcel 8, tel 958 858 501.

Transport
Taxi: tel 609 911 657.

Vegetarians should be warned that Trevélez seems to be the ham capital of the world, with ham-curing specialists on almost every street and few restaurants or shops not adorned by multiple legs of ham hanging from the ceiling. While similar to the other beautiful Berber-style villages in the area, it is larger and more touristy than those you'll have already passed through. Notable, but contested, as the highest village in Spain, it is an excellent starting point for climbing in the Sierra Nevada, especially Mulhacén.

STAGE 23B
Trevélez – Cádiar

Start	A4132 in Trevélez
Distance	18.7km
Time	6h
Highest point	1757m
Height gain	615m
Height loss	1150m

After a steep climb out of Trevélez, this is an attractive, gentle route on forestry tracks and little paths which winds its way between sleepy hamlets passing through beautiful oak woodlands, pine forest and fertile market gardens. (NB: throughout this section the unconventional red arrow markings do mark the correct route.)

Trevélez – Juviles (9.7km, 2h50)
Leave on the A4132 heading east out of the *barrio bajo* of Trevélez, crossing the river on a road bridge. After 70m, just after the town limit sign, take a left turn up a little path (Juviles 9km) surrounded by plane trees. ▶

Climb steeply up through gardens and walnut trees. Cross a wide *acequia* (Acequia de Cástaras) on a little stone bridge after 500m, and continue into pines. The track flattens out a bit here heading downhill gently, crossing a stream, through a gate and then up less steeply, looking down on Trevélez to your right. The route is marked with red and white marker poles, but is not signed for the GR7 at this point.

After 1.2km, leave views of Trevélez behind as you round the edge of the hill and head into landscape of scrubby gorse with some solitary oaks dotted around and pine trees ahead of you. ▶ Continue on the same path gently undulating, but contouring around the hillside heading south into the valley. The path is well signed and you cross the Barranco de los Castaños on a little wooden bridge. At the split immediately after it, head left uphill under a walnut tree. The path then splits again, but either branch is fine as they shortly rejoin.

See map in Stage 22B.

Note that the GR7 shares the same route as the GR240 marked with a star shape – be careful to take the GR7 when they divide.

The route is now signed for the GR7 again.

Cross another streambed on a cobbled path and climb, passing through oaks to pine trees to meet the start of a forestry track, now 3km from the start.

Turn right when it meets another track. You will come to the point where the two GRs separate – the GR240 signed to the left to Bérchules and the GR7 to Juviles straight on along the wide main track. After 500m pass another track back to the left, continuing along the main track, which runs through the firebreak, until it reaches a crossroads 1km on. Here you go straight on into more open countryside. After about 100m turn right down a small signed track which almost instantly bears left and heads south-east.

This takes you into brushy landscape with yellow flowering shrubs in spring. You cross over several gullies and continue on the main path. Descend on this path for over 2km, initially with a hill on the left but, after a while, down a ridge with a deep valley on the left, until you meet a wider dirt track and cross over it heading in the same direction as before (and not down the track just on the left).

The path brings you to a junction of three tracks, bear left and then right continuing downhill in the same direction. Rejoin the signed path after a bend. This brings you down to join the track just before an *acequia* and a water tank.

Head downhill and cross a cattle grid next to a gate and fence, then round the left side of the water tank to meet another track along which you turn right and then, very soon after, leave on a little path down to the left into gardens and orchards. ◄ It comes out at a small white building which you go round to the left and then turn right onto a concrete track heading steeply downhill. Pass a fountain and laundry, then descend further to arrive on the main street in **Juviles**. If you want to go to the bar with accommodation, turn right along the road; otherwise head left for the other bars and to carry on along the route.

The path is cobbled in parts and passes through lush vegetation including mint, figs, brambles and broom alongside an acequia.

JUVILES 1255M POPULATION 170

Accommodation, restaurant/bar/café, drinking fountain, food shop, telephone, pharmacy, tourist information, transport.

Accommodation and food
A few bars with food and one with beds.

Bar-Pensión Tino (A). A friendly family-run bar with basic rooms above, slightly set back from the main street through the village: C/Altillo Bajo, tel 958 769 174. **Apartamentos de Juviles** (B) has tourist flats with fireplaces and terraces, minimum two night stay: tel 958 816 904, www.apartamentosdejuviles.com. **Apartamento-Cortijo Casa Rural Ismael** has whole houses to let: tel 659 267 748, www.juviles.net/casasrurales/ismael.htm.

Further information
Town hall: Plaza Francisco Rodríguez Ríos, tel 958 769 032, www.juviles.net.

Transport
Taxi: tel 958 753 038.

A small village with great views down from its chestnut-surrounded plateau. It was important in the Arab era when it was capital of a group of villages in the area. You can see the ruins of the 18th-century castle which was an important refuge for inhabitants of surrounding villages in times of danger.

Juviles – Tímar (2km, 40min)
Leave Juviles heading east along the main street to Alcútar (A4130 C/de la Ctra) and come to a GR7 sign (Tímar 2.5km) pointing you down to the right at the edge of the village as you pass Jamones de Juviles on your right. ▶ Take a left fork after 50m signed to Fuente Agria onto a dirt track which heads downhill to a little stream (Barranco de la Umbría).

The road out is also signposted to the Fuerte de Juviles and Fuente Agria.

The route crosses over this, but you can also take a short diversion to the left to the Fuente Agria. At the next divide take the lower right path alongside a high dry stone wall passing olive and almond trees on a shady little path. At the split just after this, keep right again through cherry trees.

Where the path widens into a small track, take the left fork and continue on the same path round the hillside with crags above you to the right, brambles and broom bordering the path on both sides and lush green vegetation in the valley below. A spectacular gorge opens out on your left. The path descends an eroded gully steeply and then climbs towards a striking small pass.

Walk up to pass between two rocky crags with panoramic views across olive-clad hills. ▶ Take the right fork traversing the hillsides down the other side and descend steadily into the top of **Tímar** (950m, population 50, drinking

Below, the roofs of the first houses of the village are visible.

Looking back up at Tímar

fountain). Turn right and take streets downhill and to the right to arrive at the plaza.

Tímar – Lobras (2km, 30min)

Head west from the plaza (which has a drinking fountain in front of the church) and come to a GR7 signpost (Lobras 2km). Go down the concrete street and continue along it as it turns to tarmac, with the last houses of the village on the right and fruit trees on your left. Walk for about 10min and, when you come to ruins of a mercury mine on your right, turn left down a dirt track off the road.

Be careful not to get lost here as there are many other small paths and the route is not clearly marked.

Continue round an era (a circular stone threshing floor typical of the region) on your right, follow the track downhill and pass a small turning up to the right into a field 250m further on. At the next junction keep right, hugging the hillside. ◄ Climb a little and when you come to a small track at a pass turn left. **Note**: this section is steep and eroded.

This takes you steeply downhill and you turn right onto an unsigned little path just before you get to the valley floor. Look behind you for good views back to village above. Cross the river and continue on the other side, zigzagging uphill to meet a path next to an *acequia*. Continue round this path which is green with figs, almonds and fruit trees. Ignore a track down to the right and continue round the hillside as a street light comes into view, onto a tarmac road (GR9027) and into **Lobras** (930m, population 130, restaurant/bar/café, drinking fountain).

> There has been considerable **path development** between Timar and Lobras, shown on a signboard in Tímar village. Interesting unmarked routes drop down from about 20m after you leave the village; these cross the river and traverse alongside the hill before rejoining the main route just outside Lobras. These are shorter, and avoid the steep eroded hillside, but are unmarked and harder to find.

Lobras – Cádiar (5km, 2h)

Continue downhill through Barrio el Chorro to a fountain and laundry down the road with wooden handrails and then along the tarmac road out of the bottom of the village. Just at the edge of the village come to a GR142 signpost for the Sendero Ventilla on your right. Pass this and stay on the newly surfaced road before turning left off it just after a playground (about 500m outside the village) with a GR7 sign (Cádiar 5km).

Follow the dirt track into almond trees and then, 100m on, turn right down a marked path. Descend and after another 500m pass a ruined *cortijo* on your right. Here you come to a crossroads where the GR7 crosses the GR142. Continue straight on ignoring the GR142 signed to Cídiar. ▶ Cross the stream and keep left along the valley ignoring a track heading steeply uphill to the right. Climb steeply for 15min and reach the top of Loma de San Agustin. Cross straight over a larger track onto another little path which goes round and down into the broad valley of the Río Cádiar. When it splits, take the right fork to follow an overgrown path alongside an *acequia* on the right.

Cross over the *acequia*, passing a ruined building and at the crossroads just next to it continue straight on. For a 500m diversion for food or a bed follow the sign to the Alquería de Morayma hotel-restaurant. From this point you follow a broad track with an *acequia* running alongside it first on the right and then on the left. Pass through figs and vegetable and fruit plots with raspberries and kiwis. Continue on the track alongside the river on your right for over 1.5km. You pass some bamboo and after a broken wooden bridge the track

The GR142 is marked with the same red and white marks as the GR7.

becomes tarmac and crosses the river. Turn left and walk alongside the river until you pass a football ground where you can turn right to climb up in to **Cádiar** to emerge near the centre by the church.

CÁDIAR 919M POPULATION 1650

Accommodation, restaurant/bar/café, drinking fountain, food shop, telephone, pharmacy, transport.

Accommodation and food

A few options for beds and food; the restaurant at **La Alquería de Morayma** (B), supplied by its own kitchen garden, is something special: this lovely family-run complex of rooms and flats runs courses including massage and relaxation, set among organic almonds, vines, figs, olives and fruit trees, 2km walk out of the village: Ctra A-348, Cádiar-Torvizcón, tel 958 343 221, www.alqueriamorayma.com.

Hostal Cadi (A) has basic cheap accommodation near the church with small ensuite rooms, bar downstairs: C/Real, tel 958 768 064. **Ruta de la Alpujarra** (B) is a comfortable place with good restaurant: Ctra Ugíjar, tel 958 768 059, www.rutadelaalpujarra.com.

Further information

Town hall: Pza de España 12, tel 958 768 031, www.cadiar.es.

Transport

Taxi: tel 958 768 703.

Cádiar is divided into an older area with traditional architecture, including the 16th-century parish church, and a *barrio alto* with new buildings. It is one of the most commercial villages in the area. The 3rd and 18th of each month are usually the market days and you will see farmers from all around coming into town.

STAGE 24B

Cádiar – Yegen

Start	Church in Cádiar
Distance	16.5km
Time	5h
Highest point	1459m
Height gain	1030m
Height loss	910m

Another day where you never stray far from civilisation, picking your way over and around hillsides and across streams to reach a string of little white villages. There is a steep climb and descent between Bérchules and Mecina Bombarón that takes you from one river basin into another.

Cádiar – Narila (1.6km, 30min)

To rejoin the GR7, from the west side of the church take the street to the right of the fish market and head west, then north-west down towards the river, where you will see a GR7 sign at the bottom, directing you right and into a small plaza with a

fountain and a palm tree. Continue out of the plaza, heading north between stone walls, then turn left to come to a refurbished mill and a GR7 post where the road becomes a track.

After 200m the track ends at a field and you take a small path to the right crossing over an *acequia* to follow the line of the wall and the edge of the fields north for 200m. After this it arrives at a track by a water tank beside the river bed.

Follow the track to the right alongside the river bed. Stay on the track for 500m and then, as you become level with the first buildings of Narila at a large open area of ground, take a small unmarked path to the right. This takes you up a partially cobbled path next to an *acequia* between walls and into **Narila** (980m, population 170, drinking fountain). ◄

> **Note**: Although the **track by the river** is currently in good condition, in some years it gets severely eroded. If this is the case, then the alternative route is by the small country road between Cádiar and Narila.

Narila – Bérchules (3.2km, 1h)

Head out of Narila by the plaza next to the church following a sign west to Agua Agria. Stay on the main street which comes around the side of a gorge on C/Pajares which brings you to a sign (Alcútar 1h) 200m from the plaza.

This sign directs you west along a small concrete road and you go left when it divides soon after. Carry on, ignoring another turning down to the left. After approx 250m, pass a water control system on the river, and shortly after, a sign points you to Agua Agria (5min) and you go left (signpost Alcútar 50min) and cross the river on a log bridge.

Turn right at a divide soon after and continue through almonds as the track becomes a path and starts zigzagging uphill. At a small divide 500m from the river go right. The path is now cobbled in parts. A further 250m on, you stay on the main path, ignoring one off to the left into the fields. Then cross over a track and keep climbing until you come to a wider track after 400m.

Turn right along the track, but quickly leave it again on a path up to the left. Ignore a left turn just after this and then climb steadily to meet a wider track at gates to a garden and turn right along it.

Climb to meet a concrete track and take it uphill, ignoring a little path to the right and looking back on increasingly

If you have time to wander round the village, its claim to fame is being home to the ruins of the Moorish King Aben-Humeya's house.

good views of Narila and Cádiar as you gain height. Head left into **Alcútar** (drinking fountain), climbing the street past the laundry and fountain.

Alcútar is a satellite settlement of the larger **Bérchules** which is just 700m and 10min away. The signs to leave Alcútar are a little confusing. At the laundry a large metal sign indicates that the GR7 is right up a little path, contradicting a red and white mark on the wall directing you up to the left through the village. Ignore the signpost and follow the marks steeply upwards to C/Churre, then head right and uphill along C/Real and then Cantera to the church plaza. ▶

The route just heads up the short stretch of tarmac road to **Bérchules** which is visible ahead as you set off. On entering the village, pass Fuente de los Carmelos and continue up the same road into the centre.

There's a fountain in front of the church (17th-century Iglesia Santa María la Mayor).

BÉRCHULES 1322M POPULATION 800

Accommodation, restaurant/bar/café, drinking fountain, food shop, cashpoint, telephone, PO, pharmacy, transport.

Accommodation and food
A few good choices for places to stay and eat:

Hotel Los Bérchules (B) is the first hotel-restaurant you come to, up to the left as you enter the village, good value but a luxurious-feeling place to relax, with friendly owners, a pool, balconies and shared terrace with great views and a cosy lounge: tel 958 852 530, www.hotelberchules.com. **Casa Rural El Paraje** (B) has comfortable clean rooms in a peaceful location with gorgeous views, run by a friendly multilingual couple who love walking: Ctra. Granada – Bérchules (A4130 Km23), tel 958 064 029, www.casa-rural-el-paraje.blogspot.co.uk. **El Mirador de Bérchules** (B) has attractive flats in a complex offering activities including horseriding, with meals also available: Pza de Zapata 1, tel 958 769 090, www.miradordeberchules.com.

Further information
Town hall: Pza Constitución, Bérchules, tel 958 769 001, www.berchules.es.

A beautiful old village which is the capital of the municipality. It has a great vantage point with views across the surrounding area. Important in Moorish times, it was once a centre for the silk trade and there are some lovely examples of traditional Alpujarran architecture. There are other walks in the area detailed on information boards in the village.

Bérchules – Mecina-Bombarón (6km, 2h)

Head out of Bérchules northeast on C/Agua, a little concrete street that turns to dirt as you come to a GR7 sign (Mecina Bombarón 2h). The GR7 and the Sendero Veréica Misa follow the same route through lush greenery beneath figs, hazels and chestnuts until you come to the first split where you head left, other walking routes head right: take care, this turn is easy to miss.

You then cross a wider track under a large chestnut tree and cross over a stream heading downhill on a shady path into the gorge. After crossing another little stream surrounded by ferns, you descend to the river, looking out at the dramatic rock face to your right.

While stopping for breath, enjoy great views back towards Bérchules and Alcútar.

Cross the river on a bridge to begin climbing steeply up the other side of the gorge on a rocky path. Where the path divides into a few little goat tracks about 500m further on you can take either, as they rejoin, and continue climbing. ◄

At the next divide in the path 250m on, take the right fork and pass a ruined stone building. The path then joins another flanked by dry stone walls and comes to a wide track heading right about 750m further on which you take, now ascending less steeply.

After nearly another kilometre you meet another track and again head right, curving round and passing smaller side tracks off into the pines and two wide tracks off to the right, the first after 300m and then another 500m further on.

After the second right turn, watch out for a barely visible path about 400m later heading into an almond grove. This takes you down a dry stream bed between trees. It may be hard to spot the route but keep going southeast and aim for the house below and you should emerge next to the house and a post.

Skirting to the left of the house, continue in the overgrown streambed in the direction you've been going and it brings you down to a path that runs alongside a cool and shady *acequia*. Follow this left and you soon come to a track to the right which you take, leaving the *acequia* behind. Descend past a building on your right and **Mecina Bombarón** comes into view ahead. Continue down to the road and turn left onto it to enter the village.

MECINA BOMBARÓN 1110M POPULATION 700

Accommodation, restaurant/bar/café, drinking fountain, food shop, cashpoint, telephone, PO, pharmacy, transport.

Accommodation and food

There are a few bars and places to eat and there is accommodation in very nice self-catering *casas rurales*. Two good choices are:

Alojamientos Rurales Los Macabes (B): C/Santa Teresa 2, tel 696 472 678, www. casasruralesmacabes.com; and **El Benarum** (C), a range of well-equipped little houses with jacuzzis, and activities on offer: C/Casas Blancas, tel 958 851 149, www.benarum.com.

Others are listed on the town hall website: www.alpujarradelasierra.es/casas-rurales.

Further information

Town hall: Pza Nueva, tel 958 851 001, www.alpujarradelasierra.es.

Another village established by the Berbers, Mecina Bombarón has a bloody history. It is thought to have been home to Abén Aboo, the last Moorish King in Spain, who assassinated his cousin the previous King Aben Humeya to become ruler of the Moors for a short period before he himself was assassinated by Philip II. Lots of circular walking routes start from the village.

Mecina Bombarón – Yegen (5.7km, 1h30)

From the middle of the main street, leave on a street to the south next to a restaurant, signposted to Los Macabes. After passing the school, turn left and go down the hill on a small concrete road, C/Santa Teresa. Turn right at a T-junction and continue on downhill going left around a building. The road soon becomes a dirt track and you see the hamlet of Golco ahead.

After 200m, when you meet a stream, ignore a left turn and continue straight on along the lamppost-lined track. Cross an *acequia* then take a small unmarked path to the left that zigzags downhill before running parallel to the main track then along another *acequia*.

After a short distance you come back up on the main track then take the left fork at a divide. Pass another two turns, one off to the right and then to the left, to come into **Golco**. ▶ A sign directs you downhill on a small concrete road to **Montenegro** (50min).

This tiny hamlet is notable for its large church, one of the oldest in the region.

Distinctive barren rock gullies on way into Yegen

Follow the small road downhill, turning left where it divides. It takes you very steeply down to a small picnic area before becoming a dirt track. After 500m take a path to the left, with fruit orchards on your left.

This little path heads east passing an *era*, on your left, before heading downhill to meet another track. Go left along the track, ignoring another left and continue downhill. Shortly after it becomes concrete, you take a small path off it to the right just at the gate to what look like new holiday cottages (1km from Golco). Cross the small Río de Mecina and continue on the same path through poplars. After another 100m cross a dry stream and then pass a ruined building. ◄

The landscape here is barren and almost desert-like with vividly coloured scree slopes and dry brushy vegetation.

Pass another abandoned building on your left 1.5km from Golco, still on the same path, with Montenegro now visible ahead. After 300m at a crossroads of small paths, go straight on to come to a T-junction.

Right will take you to the **Ermita de la Virgen Fátima de Abén Aboo** in Montenegro, an abandoned *cortijo* which is thought to have belonged to the Moorish king. Left takes you on the continuation of the route to Yegen (30min).

Take the left track and at a split soon afterwards turn left to pass over a little stream and under a weeping willow where there is a mini picnic area with little child-sized seats. Another 700m on you see the white walls of Yegen's cemetery above you. Climb to join a concrete road and follow it into **Yegen**, passing a fountain and a GR7 sign at the entrance.

YEGEN 1087M POPULATION 500

Accommodation, restaurant/bar/café, drinking fountain, food shop, cashpoint, telephone, PO, pharmacy, transport.

Accommodation and food

There are a couple of options for accommodation and food:

Café-Bar Pensión la Fuente has (A) rooms and (B) apartments that are straightforward, good value accommodation just off the plaza: C/Real 46, tel 958 851 067, www.pensionlafuente.com. **Hostal el Tinao** (A) is run by a very friendly Irish lady, has clean, cheap rooms with great views over the valley and the option of a Guinness in the bar: La Ctra, tel 958 851 212. **El Rincón de Yegen** (B) is a hotel/restaurant which has whole *casas rurales* for 4–6 people to let as well as individual rooms, on the main road as you leave the village: Camino de las Eras, tel 958 851 270, www.elrincondeyegen.com.

Yegen's main claim to fame is having been home to the British writer Gerald Brenan (1894–1987) whose work, including *South from Granada*, gave a detailed account of life in the village in the 1920s. His house, just off the main plaza, now has a plaque outside and there is a walking route named after him leaving the village on a path below the road.

STAGE 25B

Yegen – Laroles

Start	Barrio de Arriba, Yegen
Distance	17.2km
Time	5h10
Highest point	1359m
Height gain	950m
Height loss	1000m

Leave Yegen and pass some remarkable fizzy natural springs, then loop in and out of gullies and ravines to visit three of the four villages of the municipality of Nevada and arrive in its capital, Laroles.

See map in Stage 24B.

Yegen – Válor (4.5km, 1h15)

Leave Yegen from the top of the village, the Barrio de Arriba, where Gerald Brenan lived. The GR7 follows the road heading east out of the village. Stay on the road, which then crosses the Barranco de las Eras and climbs gently for just over 1km.

At this point, just after a bend when the road begins to go downhill, and opposite a big plane tree, take a track off to the left (there is a small GR7 mark on a rock) then almost instantly turn right onto a smaller track heading towards Válor, which you can now see ahead of you.

You pass through grasses and wildflowers between almond groves.

The slightly overgrown track takes you downhill between fields for 200m before crossing the road and continuing on, as a path, in the same direction. ◄

On meeting a track, turn left and pass a ruined building 500m after crossing the road and continue downhill gently to come to a picnic site and the Cuesta Viñas fountains 300m later, four natural springs with varying degrees of natural fizziness and iron.

From the fountains, head left uphill and follow the track as it bends round to the right, passing beneath the houses which make up Cortijo de Doña Loreto. Climb on this track through almond groves to the concrete road, ignoring tracks

off to either side. At a bend in the road 500m on from the
fountains, turn right onto a dirt track.

Pass turnings to the right and then left, and when you
reach a T-junction turn left, ignore the next left, but continue
along the dirt track, then left at the next T-junction, still walking through almond and olive trees.

Finally you meet a concrete track with the road visible
up to the left. Turn sharp right down this concrete track, then
left to cross an old stone bridge, the Roman Puente de la
Tableta. ▶ Climb to enter **Válor** on the other side.

Beneath the bridge
is another *agua
agria* (mineral spring
fountain).

VÁLOR 909M POPULATION 850

Accommodation, restaurant/bar/café, drinking fountain, food shop, telephone,
pharmacy, transport.

Accommodation and food
A few bars/restaurants with outdoor seating and a couple of accommodation
options:

Hostal-Restaurante Las Perdices (A). A comfortable little *pensión* with restaurant
below, serving good home cooking on the route out of the village: C/Torrecilla,
tel 958 851 821, www.balcondevalor.com/restaurante-hostal-las-perdices-
alojamietos-rurales-granada. **Balcón de Válor** (C) has *casas rurales* with the same
owner as Los Perdices, a little out of the village on the GR7 route: tel 958 851
821, www.balcondevalor.com.

As the birthplace of Aben Humeya who lead the 1568 revolt against the Christians,
Válor was an outpost of Moorish resistance until the beginning of the 17th century. The village's annual Moros y Cristianos festival, a lively recreation of battles
between the Moors and the Christians, held in September, is one of Spain's most
famous. There are a couple of other marked walking routes around the village
including three circular routes which are described on an information board.

Válor – Nechite (1.5km, 35min)
Head through the village, and just before the Restaurant de
Fuente on the main road, turn left up a concrete road with a
GR7 marker and head steeply up hill.

Alternatively, if staying at the Hotel las Perdices, pass the
hotel and head up to the left on the road signposted to Ermita
de la Torrecilla, but not signposted for the GR7 till a little
further up (Nechite 35min).

The way is marked with yellow posts for the Sendero del Agua circular route, and with sparser, less obvious GR7 posts and marks.

Climb on this road which turns to gravel as you pass the Balcon de Válor *casas rurales*. Pass two tracks off to the right, staying on the same gravel track, which then becomes concrete again, joining the main route.

Pass to the right of some apartment buildings, then take a little path off to the right that passes between fields, leaving the village behind. ◄

Immediately after turning onto the little path, pass other small paths off to either side and, as you head uphill, also pass a small track off to the right. Cross over a drive leading to some gates and keep ascending. The path levels out as you follow the line of an *acequia* and then turn left between walls.

Walk along the edges of fields, following yellow posts and taking in the views back down over the valley. Join another *acequia* and come to a water tank after about 700m on the little path. Here the path becomes a track and when it divides you go right and then pass another path off to the right. Continue on in the same direction, again next to an *acequia*, passing beneath shady chestnuts.

Don't be confused by the metal sign here which seems to direct you up to the right to the fountain – you can actually see it down below.

As you pass the first house of **Nechite**, with the rest of the village visible down to the right, ignore little paths off to either side. Cross over a track at a small electricity substation and come to the cement road and a GR7 sign pointing back the way you've come. Cross over this road and go down to the left to the village passing the Fuente Martín drinking fountain. ◄

Nechite (980m, population 100, drinking fountain) has three neighbourhoods clearly separated by pretty gardens, vegetable plots and a ravine full of vegetation. The only accommodation available is a 2 bedroom flat (Casa Jasmine (B), tel 958 851 516, www.casa-jasmine.co.uk.)

Nechite – Mairena (5km, 1h15)

Continue down into the village till you come to a sign to the Fuente Rojo, where you turn left to pass in front of a small ruin and come back onto a little path which curves round next to a wall, heading north into the gorge. Pass one track off to the right which ends at a gate, and another back to the left just after 200m.

Once you've left the village behind, the path runs into a track. Continue straight on and you meet another track along which you turn right at a GR7 signpost (Mairena 1h15). Stay

right at the next divide immediately after this and ignore a driveway up to the left. The track becomes a path again and you cross a stream by a waterfall heading down into the ravine and across the **Río Nechite** over stones.

Zigzag up the other side of the ravine. ▶ Continue south, then east, parallel to the valley, reaching the highest point after nearly 3km. After 200m, the path becomes a track and you turn right to keep heading east, with the town of Ugíjar visible down to the right.

Take a track on the left a few metres on, and bend round to go uphill to the left and keep going in the same direction on another path, crossing a small stream beneath a sweet chestnut tree. At this point there seem to be two shortcuts across bends, each about 20m long. Ignore them, and just keep on the track. When you see the road and village ahead, the route goes left up into a small ravine and then climbs into **Mairena**.

The view down to Mecina Alfahar from the route

Once you're high up there are great views back over Nechite (and the village of Mecina Alfahar below).

MAIRENA 1082M POPULATION 300

Accommodation, restaurant/bar/café, drinking fountain, telephone, transport.

Accommodation and food

There is one option for food and accommodation:

Las Chimeneas (C). B&B and a range of self-catering flats comfortable rooms in beautiful old house and little flats, with packed lunches and friendly dinner around shared big table available on request: C/Amargura 6, tel 958 760 352, www.alpujarra-tours.com.

Further information
Town hall: C/Real, tel 958 760 007.

Mairena is also known as 'El Balcón de las Alpujarras' because of its stunning panoramic views, and as the gateway to the high Alpujarras. Like other villages in the area, it was inhabited since long before the Islamic era, but it is the Moors that have left their mark on it.

Mairena – Júbar (1.2km, 15min)

Head up through Mairena to the church and then east along C/Iglesia to meet the road, along which you go left. A small path marked with a post leaves the road at the bend just after you join it. Head uphill steeply on the path, which is partially cobbled, and when it divides go right on a wider track under fig trees. It meets another track and you take it to the right to come back to the road. Again go left along it and then take the road turning to the left signposted Júbar 0.5km.

A small path takes you off to the left of this road at the first bend. Head up it steeply and turn right to climb more gradually and come round the hillside to a wide track. Cross this track twice carrying on in the same direction on the small path, the Camino de las Eras, to enter the village of **Júbar** (1140m, population 60, restaurant/bar/café, drinking fountain, transport by the old laundry and fountain).

Júbar – Laroles (5km, 1h50)

Head for the church, the Iglesia de Santo Cristo de la Columna XII – one of the oldest in the Alpujarras and notable for having traces of the three main religions of the area in its architecture: its roof has a Christian cross and a Jewish star of David and its main doorway is of the traditional Hispanic–Muslim style.

Take the track up to the left before the church as you enter the plaza, passing a GR7 signpost (Laroles 1h15) and continuing up this track. A further 200m on, pass a left turn and then a right turn climbing uphill and over an *acequia*.

After another 350m, at the brow of the hill, Laroles comes into view. Pass a left turn and then continue straight on at a crossroads of tracks heading away from Laroles north into the gorge. Another 350m on from your first view of Laroles, pass a right turn, then a left a further 100m on and then two rights, the second marked with yellow and white signs by Cortijo de las Encinas.

At a split, just after passing the *cortijo*, turn right and cross a stream. Keep heading north into the gorge, with Laroles now behind you. Pass a left turn, 800m after the *cortijo*, and at an abandoned farmhouse turn off the track onto a little path down to the right towards a big chestnut tree.

Now heading back towards Laroles, the path continues down into a lush valley full of poplars and chestnuts. You come to a stream next to a waterfall surrounded by ferns. Cross the stream 600m down the little path and continue along the same path up the other side. Climb up the other side of the valley, with views of another waterfall opposite and the road below you.

Climb more steeply and, 600m on from the second waterfall, Laroles comes into view again. Join a track 200m further on and head left along it walking on mica-rich rocks. When you come to an old ruined mill turn off to the right onto a little path which rejoins the track after 100m. After 200m the track then meets the road at a GR7 sign on the edge of the village. Turn left up the road to enter **Laroles**.

LAROLES 1100M POPULATION 750

Accommodation, campsite, restaurant/bar/café, drinking fountain, food shop, cashpoint, telephone, PO, pharmacy, tourist information, transport.

Accommodation and food

A touristy place with a handful of options for food and beds including:

Alpujarras Camping. Camping (A) and cabins/flats (B) about 1km out of Laroles (signposted from village centre), lots of space with good plots separated by trees, swimming pool and bar/restaurant: Ctra la Puerta, tel 958 760 231, www.laragua.net. **Hostal Refugio de Nevada** (B) is small family hotel with 12 rooms, seven with fireplace and small lounge, breakfast included and bed for third person added for an extra fee, swimming pool and garden: Ctra Mairena 2, tel 958 760 320. **Balcón de Alpujarras** (B) is a restaurant with rooms and flats on the route out: Ctra Puerto de la Ragua, tel 958 760 217.

Villa Rural la Ragua (B). Flats for rent near campsite, minimum two night stay: tel 950 483 703, www.aldearural.com/villalaragua.

Further information
Town hall: C/Pósito, 1, tel 958 760 007.

Transport
Taxis: tel 958 760 183/958 760 183.

A bustling little place, Laroles is one of the oldest settlements in the Alpujarras and capital of the Nevada municipality. It has a variety of craft workshops making and teaching handicrafts including esparto grass work, wickerwork, tapestry and rug making. For architectural interest visit the 16th-century parish church with its 18th-century red brick Mudéjar tower and take a look at some of the grand old *casas señoriales*.

STAGE 26B
Laroles – Puerto de la Ragua

Start	Centre of Laroles
Distance	16km
Time	6h
Highest point	2040m
Height gain	1385m
Height loss	380m
Note	The *albergue* (hostel) at Puerto de la Ragua is not always open

Climb up to Bayárcal and cover the 12km of route in Alméria, passing back in to Granada province over a high pine-forested pass.

Laroles – Bayárcal (4.5km, 1h30)
Come out of the village on the road heading west taking the turning to the right signposted to Cherin on the appropriately named Camino de Bayárcal then, just past the Balcón de

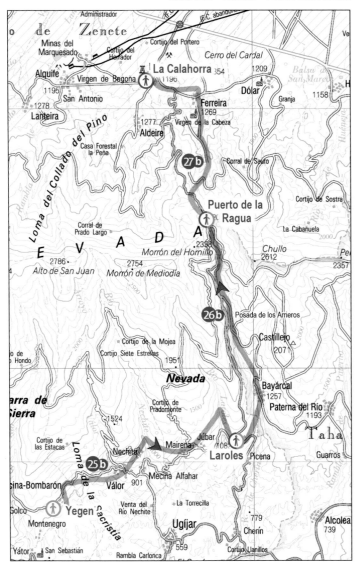

Ascending to Bayárcal

Alpujarras restaurant, turn off to the left onto a track with a GR7 sign (Bayárcal 1h30).

After 600m, at a divide in the track where there is a dry stone building above you built into the rocks, turn right into orchards and olive groves. The village of Bayárcal comes into view above you ahead, and you pass a right turn (which may have a chain across it) and a left turn just afterwards and continue, heading through holm oaks. ◀

There are no markings for this section.

Where the track bends up to the left, about 2km from setting off, you leave it on a little path to the right, passing a GR7 signpost of an unfamiliar type as you cross the province boundary into Almería (Bayárcal 1h15).

Leave the path soon afterwards to head down a little dry streamed to the right between two walls. It turns into an attractive little path taking you steeply down to the bottom of the valley where the vegetation is lush and green with ferns and poplars.

You pass a small building hidden in the undergrowth 200m from where you joined the little path and cross the Río Bayárcal on big boulders. Climb up the other side on a path that becomes cobbled and, at the split 100m on, take the left fork still climbing uphill. Emerge out of the trees at a small water storage reservoir and head left onto a wide track which is concrete in places.

Just after an apple orchard turn left onto a path next to a dry stone wall. You climb on this up to some ruined buildings, passing a left turn and continuing straight on uphill. Turn right at the next fork to come to the village laundry and fountain, and head steeply past them uphill to the left into **Bayárcal**.

BAYÁRCAL 1255M POPULATION 400

Accommodation, restaurant/bar/café, drinking fountain, food shop, telephone, pharmacy, transport.

Accommodation and food
There are a couple of straightforward *hostales* but they are not always open off-season:

Hostal Restaurante Hermanos Navarro (A) is a simple hostal: C/José Antonio, tel 950 512 873. **Sol y Nieve** is another simple hostal (A) on the route out of the village: C/Granada 3, tel 950 512 813.

Further information
Town hall: Pza Mayor, tel 950 512 848, www.bayarcal.es.

Transport
Taxi: tel 950 512 813.

Like many villages in the area, Bayárcal was an Arab settlement which was severely depopulated and destroyed when the area was 'Christianised' in the 16th century. There are still ruins of an Arab castle. Also worth a visit is the 16th-century Mudéjar-style church which was destroyed during the Alpujarran rebellions but reconstructed by the end of the same century by the Archbishop of Granada

Bayárcal – Puerto de la Ragua (12km, 4h30)

Leave the village heading north on the AL5402 road and after about 200m there is a sign sending you off the road to the right. Ignore this and continue on the road for a further 200m. When you get to a junction, follow a sign on the right which sends you uphill. ▶

Follow the path up behind the building, zigzagging uphill to meet a track which you follow to the left to rejoin

From here the GR7 and the GR140 follow the same route up to Puerto de la Ragua.

the road. Leave the road again on a signposted track (4h) to the left 200m on.

When the path divides after a further 200m, take the lower left path staying next to the wire fence with orchards behind it. Pass between gardens, orchards and buildings, following the line of the gorge, and pass below a stone farmhouse on a little undulating path.

You then start climbing more steeply with great views back into the gorge. At a divide 200m after the farmhouse, head left on the lower path which begins to level out a bit, passing through old holm oaks. A further 200m on, the path divides again and this time you take the upper right path under some craggy rocks.

You emerge from the trees and at the point when you can see a dry stone building on the other side of the gorge take the right fork at a divide. Bend up to the right and, before you get to another dry stone building built into the crags ahead, climb steeply heading northwest on an unclear path, but with lots of marks to follow. This takes you up past an era, and back into oaks. Climb more gently through these coming up close to the road which is above you on the right.

Stay on the same path as it levels out more and comes out of the trees at a profusion of signs. You have two options here to reach the inn, the **Posada de los Arrieros**. The simpler route, which does however involve a couple of km of road walking, is to follow new wooden posts uphill to the right on a zigzagging route to the A337 road then follow it to the inn.

The other route is to continue straight on to pass below a ruined building to a GR7 sign just past it (2h back to Bayárcal). You then pass above another *era* and descend below more crags with beautiful pools in the river down to your left. Another 300m on from the GR7 sign you come to a divide: the left, marked with the new posts, takes you down to a bridge over the river, but don't go this way. Instead, take the unmarked path up to the right to continue through brambles and under crags along and up the gorge, with the edge of the road visible ahead. This brings you up onto the road (the A337) just before the Posada de los Arrieros at 1800m.

The **hotel–restaurant** is built on the site of the ancient resting point, the Venta del Zamburino on the Camino de los Arrieros, which was an important trading route from the 16th century onwards between the Alpujarras and the Almerian coast.

The Posada (C) offers 20 comfortable bed-rooms, three lounges with fireplaces and a restaurant serving up traditional dishes. Winter adventure sports are available (tel 952 583 945, www.posa-dadelosarrieros.com).

A GR7 sign (Puerto de la Ragua 1h40) directs you through the gate of the Posada and onto a little path around the left-hand side of the building. Follow it along the line of the gorge, now on the left bank of the river. ▶ After 1.2km briefly enter shady pines coming out at a meadow to cross the stream for the first of many times heading up the gorge. From here you simply follow the line of the stream all the way to Puerto de la Ragua.

The path is very pretty with hawthorn, elder, brambles and dog roses.

The path takes you for 1.7km past a dry stone building and through cow pastures and in and out of pine trees on both sides of the stream. After this you then begin to climb above the stream going in the same direction, but slightly higher up, coming close to the road on the other side of the stream.

Don't cross over to the road but continue uphill, still following line of the gorge, with a small natural stone arch up to your right. ▶ 1.5km on you come to the picnic area of **Puerto de la Ragua**, through which the path passes. On the other side of the road is the Pilas de las Yeguas fountain. Continuing along the path through the picnic tables you come to the *albergue* and information centre at 2000m.

The path here is less clear, but posts direct you along and the route levels out as you begin to approach the pass.

PUERTO DE LA RAGUA 2000M

Accommodation, restaurant/bar/café, drinking fountain, telephone, tourist information.

Accommodation and food
There is not much here and the *albergue* is not always open. The only food available if it is shut is from vending machines.

Puerto de la Ragua Albergue (A). A youth hostel with a bar–restaurant and two 16-bed dorm rooms is the only place to stay at the pass itself. It is worth checking that it is open before you go as it tends to be at its busiest in winter when people flock to the pass for skiing. It is run by the same people as the campsite in Laroles, tel 958 345 528, www.laragua.net. Otherwise, you may need to camp or carry on to La Calahorra.

Further information
www.puertodelaragua.com.

A mountain pass and hub for a range of outdoor activities, especially cross-country skiing in the winter. A network of walking routes spans out from here including a 13.5km, 5h route to Doctor where there is a refuge; and a 9.7km, 3.5h route to Dílar along an old *camino real* between Dílar and the Alpujarras. There is also a circular route to the Laguna Seca and an alternative route back to Laroles on forest tracks on the other side of the gorge (7h, 18.3km).

STAGE 27B
Puerto de la Ragua – La Calahorra

Start	Puerto de la Ragua Albergue
Distance	11.4km
Time	3h20
Highest point	2055m
Height gain	121m
Height loss	958m

A couple of hours' descent on paths and tracks through pine forest and farm land bring you to Ferreira, and from there it's a gentle amble to La Calahorra, dominated by its impressive castle.

The Provincial authority does not actively promote this final section of the GR7 in Andalucía, from Puerto de la Ragua to Puebla de Don Fadrique. FAM is considering rerouting some of this section of the route but has no fixed plans at the time of writing. It would be worth checking their website www.fedamon.com and the Cicerone website (www.cicerone.co.uk) for any changes and updates.

See map in
Stage 26B.

Puerto de la Ragua – Ferreira (8.6km, 2h20)
Pass the *albergue* and head down along the road to the right, turning left off it after just a few metres to cross a wide

wooden bridge, made of old railway sleepers, and enter the pine forest. At the edge of the forest you come to a GR7 signpost (Ferreira 2h) directing you down the forest track. Follow the track out and back into trees where a signpost (not GR7) marks two routes to Ferreira. You take the one to the right, climbing gently on the track then leaving it for a small path off to the right marked by a GR7 post, 600m from the start and just before the track bends to the right.

Follow the path down into and then out of a small ravine to go round the hillside heading south above the road. ▸ After 600m, the path comes down to cross over the road.

Breaks in the trees here give amazing views over to the mountains of the Parque Natural de la Sierra de Baza, through which the GR7 continues.

On the other side of the road head north downhill, and after 300m you come to a cow shed. Go round the right-hand side of it, then head straight on to some ruined buildings. Keeping the ruins on your left, head downhill to the right on a path which runs alongside a wall. Stay on this path going through rocky and scrubby landscape for 600m before entering a firebreak in the pine forest. ▸ Keep to the left edge of the trees to come to a wide track lined with poplars.

There are no marks in this section but the occasional post.

Turn right along the track and then take the first left soon after, the village of Ferreira now visible down and ahead in the distance. At the first bend of the new track head off onto a small path which takes you back over to the edge of the pine trees and then bends to the right to go down the side of them.

Follow this path as it heads down between trees into the gorge and comes to a stream, the Arroyo Chico, on the left in an alder-filled gully. Cross the little stream three times among brambles, more alders and chestnuts in a little lush, grassy pocket amidst the pine forest. Stay by the stream with old stone walls to your left, crossing it one final time to come to a track at Venta Natalio (4.4km from start).

Head along the track, carrying on down the valley in the same direction as before. When it divides, take the track which is forward to the left (the middle of three). It soon becomes more path-like and enters the woods, passing a small white building on the left.

Continue along this path, joining a track which carries on in the same direction, and take the left fork when it divides, onto a smaller path again. ▸ Another 300m on, the path divides and you stay left to pass in front of some ruined buildings, carrying on along the path which then goes between some walls and crosses an *acequia*.

There are no markings from Venta Natalio to this point.

Soon afterwards, you arrive at a wider track which you turn right along, passing the pretty Virgen de la Cabeza church on your left and a fountain on your right. Just at the church the track becomes a tarmac road and you stay on it until it meets another at the start of the village beside a GR7 sign. Go left along the road to enter the village of **Ferreira** (population 320, restaurant/bar/café, drinking fountain, food shop, telephone, transport.).

> **Ferreira** is so named because of large iron deposits found here. It is built on the site of a historic passing place of travellers. If you have time, visit the prehistoric burial site and the 14th to 15th-century Arab baths in the north of the village.

Ferreira – La Calahorra (3km, 40min)

Leave the village by the gates to the Monte Chullo school, heading for the cemetery on a cement track which goes down to a water storage pool.

Approaching La Calahorra

Go round the pool and come to a junction. Take the track to the left and continue on this track which is an old camino real with a stone wall on your left and orchards on your right. When you arrive at the river bed of the Río Barranco Hondo, cross over it and continue straight on until you cross another dry river bed.

From this point onwards the track turns into path which is overgrown by plants and shrubs. You need to climb, staying between the edges of the orchards to arrive at a junction with the road which goes to Puerto de la Ragua.

Cross the road and come to a track on the edge of a pine forest. You can see **La Calahorra** from here and you continue along the same track to enter the village.

LA CALAHORRA 1192M POPULATION 800

Accommodation, restaurant/bar/café, drinking fountain, food shop, cashpoint, telephone, pharmacy, transport.

Accommodation and food
There are a couple of reasonably priced hostales in town, both with restaurants, and there is a more luxurious option on the outskirts:

Hotel Manjón (A) has nice rooms with air conditioning and bar/restaurant downstairs and information on outdoor activities in the area: C/Los Caños 20, tel 958 677 346. **Hostal Labella** (B) has spacious rooms with air conditioning, some with large balconies above a good bar/restaurant: C/Aldeire, tel 958 677 241, www.hostallabella.com. **Hospedería del Zenete** (C) is a grand establishment on the edge of the town, with luxury flats and jacuzzi, gym and sauna available: Ctra de la Ragua, tel 958 677 192, www.hospederiadelzenete.com.

Further information
Town hall: Pza del Ayuntamniento, tel 958 677 040, www.lacalahorra.es.

Transport
Taxis: 958 677 062

La Calahorra is famous for its huge fairytale castle which was built in the 16th century for the Marquis de Zenete as a palace and a fortress. It is worth going inside to see the well-conserved and ornate decorations. It was the last castle built in Spain before more sophisticated weaponry made this style of fortress redundant.

STAGE 28B
La Calahorra – Narváez

Start	Main road through La Calahorra
Distance	53.3km
Time	14h
Highest point	2047m
Height gain	1660m
Height loss	1485m
Note	A tent is essential to break the journey: see 'Sierra De Baza Natural Park' below

This is a walk full of contrasts. You leave the Sierra Nevada behind to cross the flat, dry plains of the Marquesado de Zenete before re-entering more rugged countryside in the Parque Natural de la Sierra de Baza, heading deep into woodlands of pines, oaks, maples and juniper then descending to the Hoya de Baza.

Note that there is no accommodation, but wild camping is permitted in two areas of the park.

To leave La Calahorra turn off the main street onto C/San Antón just opposite Mesón la Orca. At the end of the street turn right. The street soon becomes a gravel track and leaves the village.

Follow the gravel track, turning left when it divides soon after and then ignore tracks off to either side, the right-hand one of which passes between farm buildings. After the buildings, ignore another track to the left, taking the right turn towards the last farm before the plains. ◄

From here there is a large flat expanse between you and the foothills in which Charches sits and the walking is along long, straight farm tracks.

After 1.4km you come to a crossroads and turn right. Then 750m later, go straight across another crossroads. You cross the **railway line** at a pedestrian crossing 350m later, and another 600m on pass beneath a major road, turning left after the underpass onto a small tarmac road. It goes alongside the major road for 150m before you take the first right turn onto a long, straight track.

After 1.3km the track ends at a T-junction where you go left and, 250m later, right. Another 2.4km on, still on same track, cross a concrete bridge and continue straight on passing a couple of little tracks off to the right and then going straight over a crossroads. ▶

Fruit trees in the fields to your left mark the first real change in vegetation all day.

Come to a small tarmac road and a level crossing at the **Estación de la Calahorra-Ferreira**. Then, 150m after crossing the tracks, turn off onto a track to the left just after a red brick ruined building covered in bird boxes. This wide track, which looks as though goats use it more often than people, heads north and you ignore a track off to the left. After 1km the track splits and you take the left fork and then turn left again 200m on.

Another 1km in among fruit trees brings you to a right turn which you ignore to come to the Rambla de Alquira, a dry river bed. Go left along it briefly and then take the track up to the right finally beginning to leave the flat plains behind.

Come to another track and turn right along it with the hills now closer up ahead. Follow this track through the almost abandoned hamlet of **La Trinidad** and, when it divides

Crossing the plains to Charches

269

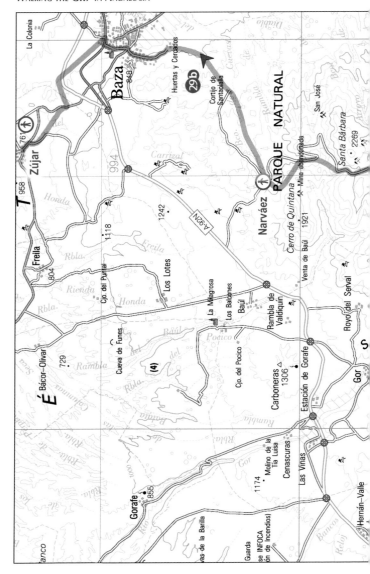

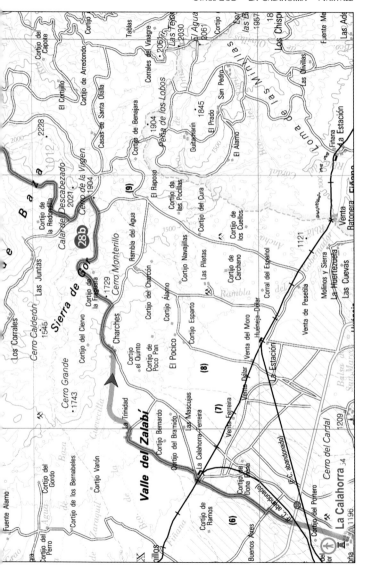

200m later, take the track to the left and head right up the dry river bed. Follow the course of the river bed until you meet another track and then turn right along it.

This takes you east and around behind some farm buildings. After these, turn off to the left onto a very small unmarked path heading directly for **Charches**. ◄ It brings you down and across a dry river bed after 250m and then up onto a wider track. Head between two farm buildings onto another unmarked, unclear path still heading in the direction of the village.

The path becomes much clearer after you've crossed two fields and then it rejoins a wider track to come down to cross another dry river bed. Go up the river bed to the left and then take another very small path uphill to the right heading straight for Charches. Pass between farm buildings to come out on a wide track. Head uphill as the track turns to concrete to enter **Charches** (1426m, population 500, restaurant/bar/café, drinking fountain, food shop, cashpoint, telephone, transport) which sits on the edge of the **Parque Natural de la Sierra de Baza**, 20km from La Calahorra.

Leave Charches on the road heading east past a fountain and laundry and follow the road until it turns into a track and divides. Take the right fork signposted to La Rambla del Agua, La Fraguara Encinar Pino Mediterráneo and Gor. ◄

Take the left fork at the first and second divides, staying on the main track. After almost 1km, pass another turn to the left, climbing steadily, the track taking you higher into the Sierra de Baza through scrub vegetation.

3km from the start, pass a turning down to the right to the small hamlet of **Rambla del Agua**, and 450m further on the track levels out as you enter pine trees. As you continue, pass a track off to the left with yellow and white markings for the PRA116 Rambla del Agua–Charches route.

You pass a stone cattle shed and ruined building on your right, 5.5km after leaving the village, and come to the Fuente La Alfaguara on your left beneath a weeping willow. Pass a left turn just after it and then ignore the continuation of the PRA116 which goes down to your right.

Pass by a further track up to the left, this one small and very steep near an unlikely hand-painted sign to Arizona, and continue on to the next fork in the main track. The fork to the right would take you to the Casa Forestal el Raposo (4km); you take the left fork to continue on the route. ◄

At points the path is unclear but keep going towards the buildings.

You come across the first GR7 signpost of this section here (Prados del Rey 5h).

There are no marks at this junction or the next.

SIERRA DE BAZA NATURAL PARK

One of the lesser-known natural parks, the Sierra de Baza (536km²) is part of the Cordillera Penibética. It is known for its dramatic limestone and dolomite geology of jagged crags. The porous limestone results in a lot of underground water, which emerges at many fountains and springs.

The whole area is known as a 'climatic island' with up to 1000 litres of rain per square metre falling every year in sharp contrast with its hot, dry surroundings. It is a verdant landscape between two arid plains – the Llanos del Marquesado (which the route crosses to reach the park) and the Hoya de Guadix.

Wildlife
There are thought to be 100 plant species endemic to the southern Iberian penisula in the park. The vegetation ranges from cultivated cereals at lower altitudes to pine forest (including patches of native woodland) and, in the highest parts, tough thorny shrubs. Other notable trees in the park include holm oaks, gall oaks and junipers. There are also patches of deciduous forest with Italian maples and Lusitanian oaks and lots of Mediterranean scrub which includes Kermes oaks, laurel and sloes. You're also likely to catch the scents of thyme, lavender, marjoram and rosemary.

The park is rich in animal life including impressive big birds of prey such as golden eagles, hawks and Egyptian vultures; over 100 other bird species including woodpeckers and turtle doves in the woodland areas; and hoopoes, crested larks and red-legged partridges in cultivated fields. About 30 species of mammals have been catalogued in the park, among the most common being deer, badgers, genets, beech martens, wildcats and foxes. You are also likely to see game animals including roe deer and, if you're lucky, wild boar.

Camping
From November to May camping is allowed at the Tablas and Fuente del Pino picnic areas (but is banned in summer because of the risk of forest fires). You need to apply for permission in writing from the Consejería de Medio Ambiente, C/Marqués 1, Granada, tel 958 026 000.

Further information
The Centro de Visitantes de Narváez (tel 670 943 910), which the route passes, has lots of information on the park and on walking routes, many of which leave from the centre.

Less than a kilometre on you come to another major divide in the track (now 11.5km from Charches). Here the right fork would take you to the Mirador de Barea (10km), Caniles (36km) and Escúllar (37km). The left fork, which you take, is signposted to Los Prados del Rey, but its stated distance of 20km should be more like 12.5km.

Begin to descend with the hills and rocky outcrops of the natural park all around you. After 250m you pass another fountain and, at the next junction, 2km from the last, you turn right. GR7 markings reappear here and you begin to climb again.

Pass two turnings off to the left after 1.2km and then, 600m after that, continue uphill. A kilometre on you pass a turning to the right just before crossing a bridge, then 700m further on also pass a smaller turning to the left which goes to the Cortijo de los Pollos. Just opposite this turning there is a water fountain on the right side of the main track.

The route continues along the forestry track passing a left turn 1.2km from the fountain to come to a well-marked junction. A signpost here pointing left indicates it is 3.5km to Los Prados del Rey, 11km to the picnic area at La Canaleja and 15km to Narváez. You will pass through all three before arriving in Baza. Right is the route to the El Pinarillo picnic area (7km).

Take the left to head uphill on a long, straight and enthusiastically marked section of track, ignoring a track down to the left to the Casa Forestal el Cascajar (3km). Pass a little house on your right and then mine workings and some caves down to your left.

From here the path levels out and you enter an area of natural pine woodland. Pass by a turn on your left that leads back to the caves and a right turn just after. A few hundred metres on, a small side track down to the right leads to a fountain (which does not always have water).

This area is a great place to look out for birds including raptors.

Staying on the main track, ignoring a further track to the left, you come to a GR7 signpost indicating that you've arrived at **Los Prados del Rey** and the highest point of the route, at almost 2050m and 24km from Charches. A track up to your left would take you into ancient natural pine woodland of great ecological importance. ◂

The signpost directs you along the main track still to Narváez (2h15) and then on to Baza (4h30). The track now heads downhill with great views opening up before you over the peak of Jabalcón and the *altiplano* through which you are about to walk. After going down the track for almost 2km, turn off to the left onto a tiny path just after a stone bridge.

There is a post, but it is a little difficult to spot so be careful not to miss it.

Descend steeply on a well-marked and pretty little path through pines, zigzagging down for 1.5km before levelling out slightly and then arriving at the Canaleja Alta picnic area, a pleasant shady spot to stop with picnic tables and a fountain. ▸

You are now 7h from Charches.

Head left around the picnic area, now briefly back on the main track, before taking a little path off up to the left after 300m (signposted Narváez 1h30). This takes you uphill through pines, levelling out a bit after 1.5km and entering some hawthorn, oaks and dog roses as well as pines.

The path emerges into a firebreak which you follow down to the right before re-entering trees on the other side. Continue on the small path as it goes down the left side of another firebreak and, 3km from the start of this path, a large building comes into view ahead and below you. This is the Cortijo de Narváez, which now houses an information and education centre for the park and a tourist complex with outdoor activities. You are heading for it, although not in a direct line.

At the next junction, take the left fork passing by, or making use of, stone and wooden benches, then descend further on what becomes a wider track. Ignore a track down to the right and continue on past the Fuente del Olvido passing more picnic benches, crossing over a small stream and around a hillside.

Ignore another track down to the right and continue for 500m before turning down to the right into the trees onto a small path just beside an open water storage tank. This brings you down to a tarmac road just to the right of a bridge (almost 5km from the Canaleja Alta).

Cross over the road and onto a wide gravel track where there is a GR7 sign (Baza 2h15) – 2h50 is a more realistic estimate. A park sign directs you up the next track to the visitor centre in **Narváez**, but you can also get to it by taking the first right turn off the track you are following.

The Cortijo de Narváez (B) offers dorm beds and (B) wood cabins. The hostel also runs a range of outdoor activities and there is a bar/restaurant: Ctra de Murcia Km175, tel 958 34 20 35, www.cortijonarvaez.es.

STAGE 29B
Narváez – Zújar

Start	Cortijo de Narváez
Distance	24km
Time	6h
Highest point	1373m
Height gain	300m
Height loss	900m

This stage passes through the sprawling city of Baza and then into the unique landscape of the Subbética, walking along a section of unmarked route across the tracks and gullies of the high plateau to arrive in Zújar.

See map in
Stage 28B.

Narváez – Baza (14km, 3h30)
Next to the centre are the starting points of three marked walks including the Sendero Mirador de Narváez, a gentle 1km walk to a viewpoint along a fire break. To continue along the route to Baza stay on the main track passing the turning into Cortijo Narváez.

Ignore a right turn for one of the other walking routes after 700m, but do take a right at the next divide just over 1km further on. Pass a right turn almost immediately and cross a dry stream beside a small concrete building. The route then continues through small oak trees and bushes and you pass three more right turns before the track turns into a small path 3.5km out of Narváez.

The path follows the course of a dry stream, crossing it for the first time after 500m and then recrossing it a further nine times in the next 1.3km before ending up on a wider track on the left-hand side. This track heads uphill past a dam, then back down and across the streambed. After passing a small white building on your right you arrive at the **Cortijo de Santaolalla** (now 5.5km from Narváez).

Follow the track round to the right between the buildings of the *cortijo*. Take the left fork when it divides just beyond the buildings before turning off to the right almost instantly onto a smaller track heading north. Another 400m further on turn right onto a small path which goes along the edge of a field then brings you to the dry river bed of the Barranco de Antonio Sánchez, where the path continues up and along its right-hand side.

As with the streambed, the path then re-crosses the river bed several times for the next 600m before ending up on the left-hand side. From here it climbs and the river bed becomes more of a gorge. You get your first views of the outskirts of Baza and go through a gate and along the top right edge of field before descending back into the river bed, along which you turn left.

Ignore two tracks out but take the third which heads uphill to the right. When it meets a crossroads, go straight across heading directly for **Baza**. Cross the river bed for the last time then follow the track between almond trees until you arrive at a tarmac road and a pizza restaurant. Continue along the road for 3km into the town.

BAZA 847M POPULATION 22,100

Accommodation, restaurant/bar/café, drinking fountain, food shop, cashpoint, PO, telephone, pharmacy, tourist information, transport.

Accommodation and food
There's a good range of hotels and a choice of places to eat ranging from pizza places and typical bar fare to more upmarket restaurants including seafood:

Pensión los Hermanos (A) has basic rooms with dated décor, air conditioning, TV, restaurant downstairs and free internet access: Ctra de Murcia, Km176, tel 958 701 880, www.hostalloshermanos.com. **Hotel-Restaurante Anabel** (B) has ensuite, air-conditioned rooms with comfortably long beds, not particularly good value for the price and not the friendliest service: C/Maria de Luna 3, tel 958 860 998, www.hotelanabelbaza.com. At **Cuevas al Jatib Hospedería Troglodita** (C) you can stay in your own fully-equipped cave in a cave village with Arab baths, tea house and a cave for children: Arroyo Cúcar, tel 958 342 248, www.aljatib.com.

Further information
Tourist office: Museo Municipal de Baza, Pza Mayor 1, tel 948 861 325.

Transport
Taxi: tel 659 454 066/659 458 864/958 700 555/958 736 122.

Now a busy town and the capital of the Hoya de Baza region, Baza has been an important settlement from prehistory up to Christian times and many cultures have left their mark there. Visit the archaeological museum to see examples of finds from the 3rd- to 4th-century Bastetan civilisation which founded the town, then 'Ciudad Basti'. The ruins of a Moorish castle and surrounding neighbourhoods are reminders of its past as a frontier town in the time of the Nasrid kingdom, and the town's 10th-century Arab baths in the old Jewish quarter are among best preserved in Spain.

Baza – Zújar (10km, 2h30)

The GR7 leaves Baza along the road to the cemetery reached by going down C/Ingeniero Gutiérrez Segura from the bus station and then left along Ctra de Granada. The road to the cemetery leaves the Ctra de Granada at the final roundabout.

Leaving Baza, Jabalcón in the distance

Go down the small concrete road between olive trees and buildings ignoring all side roads. After 1.5km you pass the cemetery and carry on as the road becomes more track-like. Just over a kilometre further on you come to the motorway and

go through an underpass. **Note**: from this point to Zújar is a rerouted section of the GR7 that has not been marked.

Where the track divides into three on the other side, you take the left fork, starting a gentle climb on a dirt track, the Cañada del Camino Real de Lorca. About 900m from the junction you arrive at a high flat plateau and you can see the motorway down below you. From here you leave the track which keeps climbing and continue on an unclear path to the right. Keep the dry stream bed of the gully 100m below you on your right. ▶

You can see wind turbines in the distance and you head towards them.

Keep climbing to come to the edge of a field of crops. From here you continue for 700m, keeping the edge of the field to your left and the gully to your right. When the edge of the field bends sharply to just leave a narrow strip of crops, you leave the field edge to head west towards two wind turbines. This brings you down to the bottom of the dry gully.

After about 200m in the bottom of the gully, you come out of it to emerge onto an old abandoned train line. From here you go under a bridge and continue for 30m to come out onto the A-315 road. Turn right along it to head towards Zújar. About 300m on you can see a small tarmac road off to the left. Take this to leave the road and continue until you cross a bridge and then immediately take a track on the left. From here the track descends passing a water pool and greenhouses.

After just less than 3km the track brings you to the roundabout at the entrance to the village by a big sign for **Zújar**.

ZÚJAR 760M POPULATION 2900

Accommodation, restaurant/bar/café, drinking fountain, food shop, cashpoint, telephone, PO, pharmacy, tourist information, transport.

Accommodation and food
A range of shops, a few bars, and restaurants including a pizzeria and a couple of *hostales* to choose from:

Hostal Restaurante Jaufil (B) is a family-run restaurant with 11 rooms, all with air conditioning and TV: Ctra Pozo Alcón, tel 958 716 191, www.altipla.com/jaufil. **Hostal-Café Bar Jabalcón** (A) is a simple hostal: Av. de los Baños 27, tel 958 716 043.

Further information
Town hall: C/Jabalcón 10, tel 958 716 017, www.altipla.com/zujar.

Transport
Taxi: tel 958 716 105.

Parts of Zújar are modern with a lot of new housing, but it also has a historic centre where many Arab-style buildings survive. There are also many cave houses. Although the limestone landscape here is bare and dry, the centre of Zújar lies in an area rich in subterranean waterways. The many springs have encouraged the development of a lush area of fertile land.

STAGE 30B
Zújar – Benamaurel

Start	Centre of Zújar
Distance	20.8km
Time	5h15
Highest point	886m
Height gain	440m
Height loss	525m

A gentle climb out of Zújar soon rewards you with stunning views of the Embalse de Negratín. You descend to the spa on the reservoir and then climb again for a panoramic view across the Hoya de Baza flanked to the north by the Sierra de la Sagra. Track walking through strange dry landscape and then a road walk bring you to Benamaurel.

Heading out of the village turn right off the main street onto the Camino del Pasillo (the second turn on the right along the main street if you entered Zújar on the GR7). This turns into a track as you pass the last houses of the village and heads into fields of olives and walnuts. Where the track forks at a stone wall, take the left fork and stay left on the main track next to a wire fence and around a farmyard. After 500m, at a fork after passing vines on the left, pass the first turning to the right, but take the second, ignoring another track off to the left just after a house.

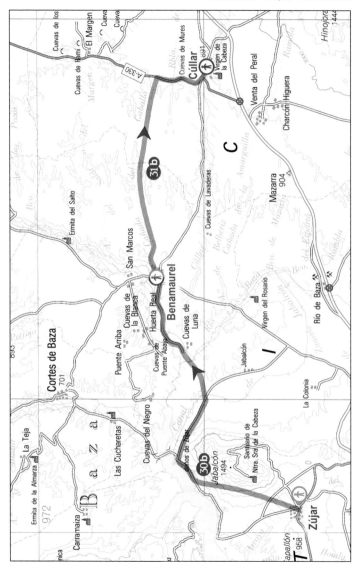

The Embalse de Negratín

There are beautiful views ahead of the Sierra del Pozo, the Sierra Harana and the Sierra Mágina.

Continue straight on beside an *acequia* and then stay on the main track as it bends round to left and across another *acequia*, ignoring a track off to the right.

From here you stay on the main track, ignoring smaller ones off into fields. Stay left at a wider fork after 500m where 'El Chopo Camino los Baños' is written on the wall, and then take the right fork at the next junction. ◄

This brings you to a confusing GR7 post which is marked with a cross and seems to indicate that you should turn off the main track to the left. **Don't** – the route continues along the main track.

You start to climb here heading further up the western slope of **Jabalcón**, with the **Embalse de Negratín** coming into view. This huge reservoir has the third largest capacity in Andalucía. You can also see the deep ravines and sharp-edged ridges which give this area its unique character.

As the track begins to level out, pass by a right turn and come up to meet another track which you go left along. Pass another left then continue straight on at a staggered cross-roads, heading uphill towards pines. There are no markings here but stay on the main track and soon it begins to descend, passing another right turn. ▶

Continue down the same track, taking the left fork at the junction just as you're passing above the greenhouse. This brings you down and across the canal on a small concrete bridge to descend on the track on the other side. Follow it down until you reach the road and then continue right along the road to **Baños de Zújar** (8km, 1h45).

> The **thermal waters**, which are heated by hot air under the ground beneath the volcanic Jabalcón, have been in use since Roman times. There is now an outdoor spa where for just €2 you can experience the healing waters (closed Mondays). There is also a friendly bar/restaurant.

Continue along the road past the Baños de Zújar and the last GR7 marking, passing a large mansion down to your left. The road climbs, leaving behind the shores of the **Negratín** reservoir and gaining views down to where the Castril, Guardal and Baza rivers join the huge reservoir.

After 1.4km the road joins the one which runs alongside the canal and you continue along in the same direction (now with the canal on your right). ▶

The road leaves the side of the canal briefly 2km on, but returns to it after 600m. From here stay on the road for just over a kilometre more before turning off to your left, where there are two tracks. The left track is signposted with an alternative route to Benamaurel, Cuevas del Negro and Cortes de Baza. You take the right of the two, signed to Cortijio del Médico, which heads downhill into a strange landscape of scrub and heavily irrigated agricultural plains.

Ignore a track off to the left after 400m and another off to the right 500m further on. Stay on the main track between the fields, ignoring smaller ones, and at a divide 600m later take the right fork, with the hamlet of Cuevas de Luna now straight ahead. Another 500m on, stay right and then left when it forks, soon after making your way across the maze of farm tracks.

Go right at a crossroads then left and across a small bridge to leave the fields behind. The track bends up to the right and then splits. The right fork takes you into **Cuevas de Luna**, which as the name suggests is made up almost entirely

You can now see more of the reservoir and, below you, a power station and a large greenhouse.

From this height you can see Jabalcón's north side and a wide panorama over the Sierra de la Sagra and the other mountains of the national park.

The unusual terrain and climate in this area has led to a cave-dwelling lifestyle.

of cave dwellings and set in such arid surroundings that it could be the moon. ◄

The left fork is the continuation of the route and takes you the remaining 4.5km (1h) to **Benamaurel** on the road, which soon becomes tarmac. To your left you will pass some of the other cave hamlets of Benamaurel: Cuevas de Puente Abajo, San Marcos, **Cuevas de la Blanca** and **Huerta Real**.

CAVE HOUSES

Cave dwelling has been common in the northeast of the Granada province since the Moors arrived in the eighth century. It is especially common around Baza and across the *altiplano*.

In the recent past (up until the 1950s) the caves tended to be used by farmers as temporary accommodation during harvest times, or for housing livestock. However, in the last few decades they have become more and more popular as homes and holiday homes. Many are being renovated, and there are architects and estate agents specialising in cave renovation rental and sales.

Apart from their current popularity, the appeal of cave dwelling has a lot to do with the ability to self-regulate their temperature to a comfortable year-round 18–20°C. Their thick limestone walls and vaulted shape offer perfect insulation from heat and noise and make them a very environmentally friendly form of housing.

BENAMAUREL 720M POPULATION 2,500

Accommodation, restaurant/bar/café, drinking fountain, food shop, cashpoint, telephone, PO, pharmacy, tourist information, transport.

Accommodation and food
There are a couple of options for eating out, including a pizzeria and some nice tourist flats:

Apartamentos Turísticos Alhanda (B). Luxurious, well-equipped tourist flats around a pool: Plaza Mayor 8, tel 958 104 271, www.alhanda.com.

Further information
Town hall: Pza Mayor 1, tel 958 733 011, www.benamaurel.es.

Transport
Taxi: 610 880 450.

A historic village set on an outcrop with great views down on the bizarre contrast of the lush valley of the Río Guardal and the desert-like plains. There are many ancient cave houses here: some of them date from the 12th century. Try to make time to visit the ancient Almohad cave dwellings in Las Hafas del Salto where there are caves containing a beautiful Roman columbarium and a dovecot dug into the rock face.

STAGE 31B
Benamaurel – Cúllar

Start	Bottom of Benamaurel
Distance	12.9km
Time	2h30
Highest point	908m
Height gain	260m
Height loss	40m

A stretch of flat, easy walking through more bizarre lunar landscapes brings you to the Río Cúllar valley with the Sierra de Orce as a beautiful backdrop.

Leave from the bottom of the village on the road past the plaza and the park and come to a left turn at the end marked with a GR7 sign (Cúllar 2h15) and a sign for a walking route to Puente Arriba.

See map in Stage 30B.

Turn up to the left along this small tarmac road and stay on it, ignoring turnings up to the left to houses, including some interesting cave houses. Then at a U-bend after about 500m, leave the road, taking a gravel track to the right. This takes you along next to small flat fields bordered by low hills covered in scrubby undergrowth and, at a divide after 400m, you take the right fork.

Pass another right turn soon after, then stay on the same track, the **Cañada del Caballo**, heading east. The peaks of the Sierra de Orce are visible in the distance ahead and you

285

Leaving Benamaurel (Jabalcón in distance)

Esparto, which is a local crop, has been used in handicrafts since prehistoric times.

continue through the yellows and greys of the dry hills and esparto grass. ◄

After almost 3.5km you pass a right fork and then a left about 200m on. Stay on the same track, which is easy, fairly flat walking, and look back for views of Jabalcón. Then just over 4km later meet another track and head right, leaving behind the small hills and walking through open farmland.

Just over a kilometre further on you come to a farm and continue straight on past it. At the next junction just beyond it, turn left. After passing another farm to the left you soon come to a tarmac road. Turn right onto it towards the outskirts of the town which are visible ahead, and when this road meets a bigger road, the **A-330**, turn right onto it and follow it into town.

This road turns into Av. Andalucía, which is the main street across the bottom of the town and contains most of its accommodation. If you want to head into the centre, turn left turn onto a smaller road with a GR7 mark as you enter **Cúllar**.

CÚLLAR 890M POPULATION 5000

Accommodation, restaurant/bar/café, drinking fountain, food shop, cashpoint, telephone, PO, pharmacy, tourist information, transport.

Accommodation and food
A few eateries and a couple of hotels to choose from:

Luna Mar (A), a hostal with 8 rooms with air conditioning: Juan Pérez Arcas, tel 958 732 392. **Hostal Ventas del Peral** (B) is a straightforward hotel and restaurant on the street of the same name: Ventas del Peral, tel 958 730 288, www.ventadelperal.es.

Further information
Town hall: Pl. Constitución 1, tel 958 730 225, www.cullar.es.

A historic village with an architectural legacy from many different cultures since prehistoric times. There are many Paleolithic and Neolithic archaeological remains and the major Bronze Age archeological site El Malagón, where the Idolo de Malagón, a fine ivory figure carving thought to date from 2700–2300BC, was found. It is now in the archaeology museum in Granada.

Almost half of the population live in cave houses. At the end of April, the Fiesta de los Moros y Cristianos is an impressive sight.

STAGE 32B
Cúllar – Orce

Start	C/Vieja in Cúllar
Distance	24.2km
Time	5h30
Highest point	1060m
Height gain	310m
Height loss	305m

Easy walking, although very poorly marked, along farm tracks skirting the edge of the dry plains with good views of the Sierra de Orce and back to Jabalcón, arriving in Orce after a brief road walk.

Leave Cúllar from C/Vieja, the old road, at the top of the village. Heading east along it, take the second track on the left past the large red-and-white pylons/antennae just opposite a large farm shed, the last building on the road.

The track takes you downhill and towards fields. After 400m, pass a track off to the right as the track bends round on itself. Then, when you join another track 200m on, turn right along it passing both a left then a right turn. Continue on the same track heading uphill and east through broom. ◄

There's an impressive panorama of the Sierra del Periate ahead and corn fields and olives all around.

Take the left at a divide, 800m after joining this new track, and then turn right at a crossroads 300m further on,

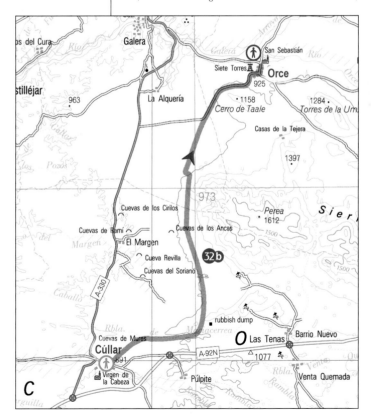

heading along a dry river bed. A track comes off the river bed 900m along and you take it up to the right. It crosses the river bed a couple of times, following its course, and then at the crossroads of the river bed and a track 400m further on, you head left uphill towards a **rubbish dump**.

You pass the tip 3km after leaving Cúllar and, at the next junction, take the right fork. Continue with young olive groves on your right and young pines on your left. A further 1.3km on, go straight over crossroads heading east, and 500m later, when you meet another track, turn left and shortly come to a large abandoned *cortijo*.

Carry on between the buildings of the *cortijo*, now heading north along a tree-lined track. When you come to the next cortijo 1km on, head straight on again behind the buildings and, where the track forks just beyond, take the left fork. Continue along this track, which bends round to head north, parallel to the road a couple of kilometres to the left, and alongside the Sierra del Periate, now to the right. ▶

You stay on this main track now almost all the way to Orce, ignoring all turnings off for 10.5km. You pass two large greenhouses and eventually arrive at the tarmac road

Passing through cereal fields leaving Cúllar

Jabalcón is still visible to your left.

289

to **Orce**, 1.2km from a warehouse and 19km from your start. Turn right and walk along it for just over 5km to arrive in Orce.

ORCE 928M POPULATION 1300

Accommodation, restaurant/bar/café, drinking fountain, food shop, telephone, pharmacy, tourist information, transport.

Accommodation and food
A couple of places to stay, a few bars with food and great, good value meals on offer at the *albergue*:

Albergue Villa de Orce (A). A great new youth hostel in centre with option of a private room, friendly staff and good home-cooked food including vegetarian fare: C/Mercedes Ortiz 6, tel 625 341 725. **Cuevas de Orce** (C). Fully-equipped caves in a restored cave village, panoramic views, BBQs and garden furniture, mountain bike hire: Ctra de María, tel 958 746 281/678 869 121, www.cuevasdeorce.com.

Further information
Tourist information office: C/Tiendas, 18 (Palacio de Los Segura), tel 958 746 171.

Transport
Taxi: 958 746 196/958 746 086.

Orce claims to have been inhabited by the first ever human beings in Europe, by virtue of a piece of bone found in 1982 which is thought to be a one to two million-year-old fragment of the skull of the famous 'Hombre de Orce'. Although this is disputed, Orce is unquestionably one of the most important prehistoric sites in Europe. Stone remains and fossils of a wide variety of animals have been found here and many of them can be viewed in the museum in the Arab castle, the Alcazaba de las Siete Torres.

STAGE 33B
Orce – Huéscar

Start	Plaza Nueva in Orce
Distance	17.2km
Time	4h
Highest point	949m
Height gain	230m
Height loss	210m

The route as far as Galera crosses the *vega* (fertile plain) following a little oasis-like channel in the arid landscape as you walk next to reed-filled *acequias* and green crops. After Galera, you return to crossing arid landscape with patches of cultivation to enter the historic town of Huéscar.

Orce – Galera (9km, 2h10)

Leave the Plaza Nueva, heading towards the castle and turn down to the right past the church, continuing down C/Chalud as it leaves the village which brings you to a GR7 sign (Galera 2h10).

Stay on the tarmac road for 500m until you come to the white walls of the cemetery, then turn left just before it to go along the road for 150m before turning left again onto a gravel track heading north. Pass through fields of crops with craggy hills ahead then, after 550m, turn left at a crossroads. ▶ After 1.2km you come to a divide and go left, passing another turn down to the left, and then at the next divide keep left.

Pass by some abandoned **cave houses** 4km from the start and, at the junction just afterwards, keep left heading towards some buildings with the road down to your left. Continue between the buildings and beneath a rock face on your right. Another 400m later, when the track divides again, continue straight on.

Stay on the same track as it turns into a path. After about 500m it passes through a farmyard. Stay to left of the farm buildings to re-emerge on a track along which you turn

You walk alongside reed-filled irrigation channels passing more crops including sunflowers with the village up to your left.

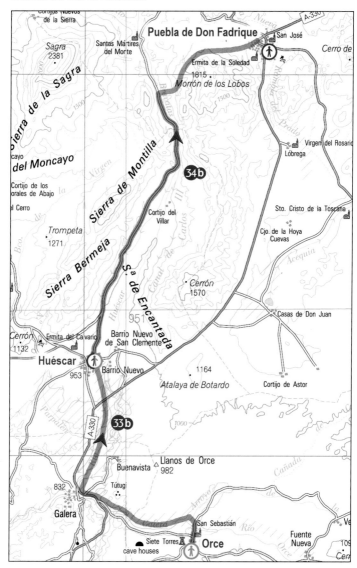

right passing a grand, but now empty, cave house, before it becomes a small path again. Descend on this small path heading around the hillside, passing more abandoned cave houses, before meeting another wide track along which you turn left, 1.3km after the farm buildings.

A line of pines with a row of basic cave entrances behind them between Galera and Huéscar

Go downhill gently to meet another track and follow it round to the right ignoring a little turn up to the right soon after. Continue along main track parallel to the Cúllar–Huéscar road which is on your left. The village comes into view just around the corner, and at the junction just after some newly renovated caves turn left to come down to the road passing the Molino de Morillas at a GR7 sign. Now 8km from start, turn right along the road and follow it past a turning to the Necrópolis Ibérica de Tútugi to your right. After 900m turn down to the left if you want to enter **Galera**.

GALERA 830M POPULATION 1200

Accommodation, restaurant/bar/café, drinking fountain, food shop, telephone, transport.

Accommodation and food
Several cave accommodation options and a couple of bar/restaurants:

El Molino de Morillas (B) has lovely flats in renovated old flour mill, indoor and outdoor swimming pool, pool room and internet room: C/Iglesia 4, tel 958 739 068, www.molinomorillasgalera.com. **Cuevas la Morada** (B). Five caves with 2–8 rooms, fully equipped with kitchens, wood fires, TV, minimum 2-night stay, meals to order, visits in 4x4 arranged: C/San Isidro 30, tel 660 862 044, www.lamoradagalera.com. **La Pisá del Moro** (B). Five recently refurbished caves with air conditioning, wood fires and fully-equipped kitchens: Av. Nicasio Tómas 6, tel 958 739 061, www.altipla.com/lapisadelmoro.

Further information
Town hall: Plaza Mayor 8, tel 958 739 115, www.galera.es.

Like Orce, Galera boasts important prehistoric and Iberian archaeological sites, of which the most important is the Necrópolis Ibérica de Tútugi, where the Phoenician Goddess La Dama Ibérica de Galera was found (now housed in el Museo Arqueológico Nacional in Madrid). You can also visit the Mudéjar church, declared a national monument, and the cave museum.

Galera – Huéscar (8.2km, 1h45)

Take the first right off the road on which you entered the village, going up to and across a bridge over the big road. Just at the end of the bridge take an unmarked track off to the left. Follow this dirt track, and come to what at the time of writing was the one and only post you see all the way to Huéscar.

Ignore a couple of turnings off to the left to houses and, after about a kilometre on the same main track, continue straight on, passing a track downhill and a right uphill. Then, at a divide immediately after, where Huéscar's 15th-century church spire comes into view briefly in the distance, take the left fork.

Cross over a little bridge and at the next junction just over a kilometre further on, take the left fork. Then at a divide just after this take the right fork at an impressive walnut tree. Stay on this same track passing a couple of houses to the right then, 400m after joining the track, a turn steeply up to the left (marked no entry).

After another 300m and a line of pines with a row of basic **cave entrances** behind them, another track joins yours from back to the right and you continue to the left and pass another house. Ignore a right turn down to farm buildings, but then at the next fork, 250m after the house, turn right.

Stay on this main dirt track, ignoring more minor tracks off to both sides and 400m further on come to a T-junction with a big house up to the left. You go right, staying next to the *acequia*, heading generally northeast then east. ▶

Again stay on this main track ignoring small turns off to either side.

After 2km come to a major road and pass through an underpass, continuing straight on the other side on a track that heads towards **Huéscar**, now clearly visible ahead. At the divide a kilometre on from the underpass, take the right fork and meet a small tarmac road after 450m. At the next divide turn right again back onto a gravel track which brings you up to the village. It becomes concrete and you turn left where you meet the road, then right into the Paseo de San Cristóbal to head into the centre of town.

HUÉSCAR 953M POPULATION 9500

Accommodation, restaurant/bar/café, drinking fountain, food shop, cashpoint, telephone, PO, pharmacy, tourist information, transport.

Accommodation and food

A range of places to eat and a few hotels to choose from. For longer stays, there are also many good caves and casas rurales on the outskirts:

Hotel Rural Patri (B). Hotel-restaurant with 17 smart, comfortable rooms set around sunny central patio area, all with TV, air conditioning and heating, restaurant with good range of dishes including a good value daily set menu: Av. de Granada 18, tel 958 742 504, www.hotelpatri.com. **Hostal Ruta del Sur** (A) has pleasant clean rooms with satellite TV and air conditioning and a restaurant downstairs, friendly English-speaking owner: Av. Granada 41, tel 958 741 289. **Hotel El Maño** (B). Nice airconditioned rooms with wi-fi and café/restaurant: the same owners have a hostal; C/Morote 11, tel 958 723 005, www.grupohosteleroelmano.es.

Further information

Town hall: Plaza Mayor 1, tel 958 740 036, www.aytohuescar.com.

Transport

Taxi: tel 958 740 801/958 742 313/616 903 020.

www.huescar.org, www.comarcadehuescar.com.

Huéscar is rich in history. The area around it has been inhabited since prehistoric times and it was an important settlement in Roman times and then a frontier town, changing hands between Christians and Muslims for several centuries.

There are a few sites worth visiting, including the ruins of the castle and its 15th-century watchtowers, some of the grand residential palaces, churches, the Santo Domingo Convent, and the 16th-century chapel which was converted into a theatre in the 19th century. Make time to visit the thermal baths which make use of a natural source of hot water at 18°C.

STAGE 34B

Huéscar – Puebla de Don Fadrique

Start	C/Mayor in Huéscar
Distance	25km
Time	6h30
Highest point	1488m
Height gain	640m
Height loss	375m

A 15km walk along the cyprus-lined tarmac road Ctra de las Santas followed by a delightful forested climb and descent into the final village on the Andalucian GR7.

See map in Stage 33B.

The road is pleasant and quiet and your only other option is a taxi.

Leave the centre of Huéscar heading north along C/Mayor. When you get to the edge of the town take the Ctra de las Santas marked with a road sign and a GR7 post. Going along this small tarmac road you immediately enter cyprus trees which line either side of the road for 10km and stay on the road for this whole distance getting good views of hills on either side as you climb gently. ◄

Pass a sign for Piedra del Letrero, where there are cave paintings (shut for conservation work at the time of writing). Further on there is a solitary, strangely shaped rock popularly known as the Salto del Moro, the Moor's jump. Ahead is the Sierra de Jurena and, to the left, the **Sierra Bermeja**. The valley opens up and becomes the Campo de Jurena with fruit plantations and fields.

After 10km you come out of the trees into more open landscape but stay on the road as it climbs more, crosses several small bridges and enters pine trees. Another 5km further on, you finally leave the road for a forestry track off to your right. A large GR7 signpost here tells you the **Ermita de las Santas** is 30min further along the road and that Puebla de Don Fadrique is 3h45 up the forestry track. ▶

Turn up the track heading into the pine forest ignoring a left turn after 300m. Another 600m on, pass by a semi-ruined *cortijo* with the buildings on your left and fields of almonds to your right. From here stay on the main track still heading uphill.

The track levels out as you pass a stone picnic table on your left 1km on from the *cortijo* and you get great views over the hills. Almost 2km on, the track divides and you take the right fork to climb again, heading part way up the north side of **Lobos**, which stands at 1815m. Ignore a track off to the right a kilometre on. A further 800m on the track divides again. The right fork would take you all the way to the top of Lobos, but you take the left to begin the descent to Puebla de Don Fadrique.

Head downhill with the views opening out ahead of you, but Puebla de Don Fadrique still hidden. At the next divide, stay on the main track to the left leaving the pines behind for scrub and pasture land, now in the foothills of the Cerro del Calar and passing almond trees on your right.

The Puente de las Tablas picnic area is also less than a kilometre further.

The view on route to Puebla de Don Fadrique

At the next junction, 2km from the start of the descent, take a right turn and keep left, ignoring a right turn heading uphill. The town comes into view a kilometre later, sitting in a big valley surrounded by hills.

Ignore another right turn 500m later to head downhill straight for **Puebla de Don Fadrique**, past a rubbish dump to your right, then turn off the track to your left to follow a small path down alongside a stone wall to arrive in the town on C/Ramblica. Follow this down and into the town.

You'll find a **GR7 signpost** pointing you on to the continuation of the route into Murcia or celebrate the end of the route in Andalucía at the strange roundabout in the centre of the town which has used GR7 posts to prop up its 'keep off the grass' signs!

From Puebla de Don Fadrique there is a daily bus (on weekdays only) to Granada (3h45) and Málaga (5h15).

PUEBLA DE DON FADRIQUE 1164M POPULATION 2400

Accommodation, restaurant/bar/café, drinking fountain, food shop, cashpoint, telephone, PO, pharmacy, tourist information, transport.

Accommodation and food
The hotel is the main place to stay and eat although there are a few bars.

Hotel Puerta de Andalucía (B) has spacious, bright but characterless rooms, with bar and restaurant downstairs: Ctra Granada-Valencia 1, tel 958 721 340/958 721 076. **Apartamentos Don Fadrique** (B) has well-equipped tourist flats with kitchens, heating and TV: Ctra Granada, behind petrol station, tel 958 721 116.

Lots of *casas rurales* – information available on the town hall website: www.puebladedonfadrique.com/turismo/alojamientos-rurales.

Further information
Town hall: Av. Duque de Alba, tel 958 721 011, www.puebladedonfadrique.com.

A pleasant little town with white houses and its 16th-century church of Santa María surrounded by fields of cereals and almonds. It has a rich past, first as a Muslim settlement and later a Christian one.

Puebla de Don Fadrique

APPENDIX A

Summary of route itineraries

Where symbols are in brackets the facilities require a small detour to a nearby town or village.

Route	Facilities at end point					Highest point/ height gain/ height loss	Length	Time	Description	Page
	accommodation	camp site	restaurant/ café/bar	drinking fountain	food shop					
PART 1										
CÁDIZ PROVINCE (6–9 days, 161.5km, 46h)										
1 Tarifa – Los Barrios (2-day section with tent or detour/ transport)	Y		Y	Y	Y	241m/820m/ 810m	45km	12h	A beach walk followed by a gentle climb up into the green hills. Very long so worth having a tent to split in two.	47
2 Los Barrios – Castillo de Castellar (optional 2-day section no tent needed)	Y		Y	Y	Y	250m/750m/ 520m	33km	9h30	Hill tracks and a road walk ending at the hilltop castle of Castellar. A 1km detour at Almoraima on the route would take you to Castellar de la Frontera and shorten the route by 4km and 1h30 or you could stop at hotel along route.	53
3 Castillo de Castillar – Jimena de la Frontera	Y		Y	Y	Y	250m/170m/ 340m	20.5km	6h	Flat route along a railway line through pretty rural landscapes.	58
4 Jimena de la Frontera – Ubrique (optional 2-day section with tent)	Y			Y	Y	840m/1160m/ 995m	35km	10h	Small paths passing over lofty passes and through cork trees. Worth having a tent – wild camping permitted.	61

Stage					Ascent/Descent	Distance	Time	Description	Page
5 Ubrique – Montejaque					1044m/1230m/880m	28km	7h30	Steep climbs over limestone crags and beautiful paths though the spacious valleys of the Grazalema Natural Park.	65
Ubrique – Benaocaz	Y	Y	Y	Y		4km	1h		65
Benaocaz – Villaluenga del Rosario	Y	Y	Y			5.5km	1h20		68
Villaluenga del Rosario – Montejaque (optional 2-day section, no tent needed)	Y	Y (en route)	Y	Y		18.5km	5h10		69

MÁLAGA PROVINCE (7–8 days, 108km, 32h)

Stage					Ascent/Descent	Distance	Time	Description	Page
6 Montejaque – Arriate					761m/525m/615m	16.5km	5h	Steeply up and over the El Puerto pass and across the wide valley floor to Arriate. Worth splitting to spend time in Ronda.	74
Montejaque – Ronda	Y	Y	Y	Y		8.5km	3h		75
Ronda – Arriate	Y	Y				8km	2h		78
7 Arriate – Ardales					894m/765m/1005m	32.7km	9h30	Very long route through remote hilly landscapes and beneath rocky outcrops which can be split by taking a detour to spend a night in nearby Cuevas del Becerro.	79
Arriate – Serrato	Y	Y	Y			20km	5h20		79
Serrato – Ardales						12.7km	4h10		83
8 Ardales – El Chorro	Y	Y			583m/580m/840m	15.8km	5h	Cross hilltops and then descend a zigzagging mountain path.	85
9 El Chorro – Valle de Abdalajís	Y	Y			679m/590m/450m	10km	3h	A long steep climb up beneath the Sierra del Huma.	89
10 Valle de Abdalajís – Antequera	Y	Y			781m/560m/400m	18.5km	5h30	Easy route with some road walking and views of El Torcal.	91
11 Antequera – Villanueva de Cauche	Y	Y			942m/520m/350m	14.5km	4h	Small, pretty paths make up for an early uphill road walk.	95
TOTAL FOR PART 1						269.5km	78h	**13–17 days**	

Route	Facilities at end point					Highest point/ height gain/ height loss	Length	Time	Description	Page
	accommodation	camp site	restaurant/ café/bar	drinking fountain	food shop					
PART 2 NORTHERN FORK – Málaga, Córdoba and Jaén										
MÁLAGA PROVINCE (5–6 days, 107.4km, 25h40)										
12A Villanueva de Cauche – Villanueva del Trabuco						819m/330m/ 340m	15.3km	4h10	Gentle route between fields and olive groves with mountains on the horizon.	100
Villanueva de Cauche – Villanueva del Rosario	Y		Y	Y	Y		11.3km	3h	Lots of it next to a busy road.	100
Villanueva del Rosario – Villanueva del Trabuco	Y		Y	Y	Y		4km	1h10		103
13A Villanueva del Trabuco – Villanueva de Tapia (optional 2-day section with wild camp)	Y		Y	Y	Y	957m/550m/ 600m	30.6km	8h30	Loop around village then through open farmland and olives. Wild camping is possible to break the day up or there is an option to cut the route shorter)	104
14A Villanueva de Tapia – Villanueva de Algaidas	Y		Y	Y	Y	900m/520m/ 660m	16.9km	4h30	Pretty undulating tracks through seemingly endless olive groves.	107
15A Villanueva de Algaidas – Cuevas de San Marcos	Y		Y	Y	Y	540m/295m/ 440m	17km	5h	Overgrown route alongside a riverbed.	110
Villanueva de Algaidas – Cuevas Bajas	Y		Y	Y	Y		8.5km (or 8km by road)	3h (or 2h by road)		115
Cuevas Bajas – Cuevas de San Marcos	Y		Y	Y			8km	2h		113

Route						Ascent/Descent	Distance	Time	Notes	Page
16A Cuevas de San Marcos – Rute	Y		Y	Y	Y	679m/560m/345m	12.3km	3h30	A beautiful section crossing from Málaga into Córdoba.	115
CÓRDOBA PROVINCE (3 days, 55.5km, 16h30)										
17A Rute – Priego de Córdoba	Y	Y (en route)	Y	Y	Y	1000m/1020m/1050m	23.2km	7h20	Magical woodland paths passing through pine and oak.	121
18A Priego de Córdoba –Almedinilla	Y	Y	Y	Y	Y	290m/195m/755m	10.4km	2h40	Through trees and rocky landscape then into olives.	126
19A Almedinilla – Alcalá La Real	Y	Y	Y	Y	Y	1109m/930m/610m	21.9km	6h30	Small section of road walking followed by a steady climb through olive groves before a lovely descent.	129
JAÉN PROVINCE (13–15 days, 285.4km, 76h15)										
20A Alcalá La Real – Frailes	Y	Y	Y	Y		1010m/235m/240m	9km	1h50	Gentle route through open countryside.	135
21A Frailes – Carchelejo	Y	Y	Y	Y		1497m/1755m/1870m	35.5km	9h30	A climb in beautiful wild hills then through a rocky gorge. (Worth having a tent to divide this section.)	139
22A Carchelejo – Cambil	Y	Y	Y	Y		834m/420m/470m	11.8km	3h30	Half road walk, half riverside stroll.	143
23A Cambil – Torres	Y	Y	Y	Y		1655m/1155m/995m	26.7km	8h	A beautiful stretch in the heart of the Sierra Mágina.	147
24A Torres – Bedmar	Y	Y				1162m/570m/875m	15.3km	4h50	A climb to the Albánchez pass then around the Sierra Mágina foothills.	151
Torres – Albánchez de Úbeda			Y	Y	Y		4.6km	1h20		152
Albánchez de Úbeda – Bedmar			Y	Y			10.7km	3h30		153
25A Bedmar – Jódar	Y	Y	Y	Y	Y	1125m/500m/470m	7.8km	2h20	Steep climb over the Serrezuela de Bedmar and gentle descent through olives to Jódar.	155

Route	Facilities at end point					Highest point/ height gain/ height loss	Length	Time	Description	Page
	accommodation	camp site	restaurant/ café/bar	drinking fountain	food shop					
26A Jódar – Quesada	Y		Y	Y	Y	665m/670m/ 630m	34.4km	9h30	A long road walk then an easy, pretty stretch through grassland and olive trees. You can wild camp in Hornos de Peal.	157
27A Quesada – Cazorla	Y		Y	Y	Y	1199m/930m/ 760m	17.4km	4h30	Dramatic rugged mountains of the Cazorla Natural Park.	163
28A Cazorla –Vadillo de Castril	Y	Y	Y	Y	Y	1394m/1080m/ 960m	15km	5h30	Wide tracks through vast pine forests and below rocky crags.	167
29A Vadillo – Coto-Ríos	Y	Y	Y	Y	Y	1446m/1675m/ 1975m	34.5km	8h	Forest tracks bring you out next to the pretty Río Guadalquiver.	171
30A Coto-Ríos – Pontones	Y		Y	Y	Y	1733m/1710m/ 1060m	30.3km	7h30	Ascend into peaceful pine woodlands and rocky peaks.	173
31A Pontones – Santiago de la Espada	Y		Y	Y	Y	1632m/490m/ 485m	13.5km	3h15	A gentle pretty route following tiny paths in open farmland.	177
32A Santiago de la Espada – Puebla de Don Fadrique	Y		Y	Y	Y	1662m/980m/ 1100m	34.2km	8h	Nice route to Cortijo de las Cuevas then very long road walk.	181
NORTHERN FORK TOTAL							448.3km	118h25	21–24 days	

PART 3 SOUTHERN FORK – MÁLAGA AND GRANADA

MÁLAGA PROVINCE (2 DAYS, 46KM, 11H30)

							Ascent/Descent/Alt	Distance	Time	Notes	Page
12B Villanueva de Cauche – Riogordo	(Y)	(Y)	Y	Y	Y		936m/670m/820m	20.8km	5h	Unmarked, but fairly easy to follow, section over a high pass. (Accommodation on route or in nearby Colmenar.)	186
13B Riogordo – Ventas de Zafarraya			Y		Y		946m/1000m/630m	25.2km	6h30	Mostly track walking then along an old railway in lovely scenery.	190
Riogordo – Guaro								17.5km	4h5		190
Guaro – Ventas de Zafarraya	Y			Y	Y			7.7km	2h25		192

GRANADA PROVINCE (22–23 days, 419.5km, 119h)

							Ascent/Descent/Alt	Distance	Time	Notes	Page
14B Ventas de Zafarraya – Alhama de Granada	Y	(Y)	Y	Y	Y		1100m/440m/460m	19.5km	5h30	Pass into Sierras de Tejada, Almijara and Alhama Natural park.	196
15B Alhama de Granada – Arenas del Rey	(Y)	(Y)	Y	Y	Y		1138m/535m/555m	22km	6h	Beautiful route through a dramatic gorge and cork oak groves.	201
16B Arenas del Rey – Jayena	Y	(Y)	Y	Y	Y		1080m/1550m/640m	16.6km	6h	Forestry tracks back through pines in the natural park.	205
17B Jayena – Albuñuelas (optional 2-day section)	Y		Y	Y	Y		1331m/980m/1150m	31.1km	8h30	Remote pine forest track into the hills with great views. (You could split this by wild camping if you have a tent.)	208
18B Albuñuelas – Nigüelas							938m/575m/400m	15.1km	4h30	Pretty, winding path orange groves and along ancient irrigation channels.	214
Albuñuelas – Restábal	Y		Y	Y				5.1km	1h15		215
Restábal –Nigüelas	Y		Y					10km	3h15		217
19B Nigüelas – Lanjarón	Y		Y	Y	Y		1282m/840m/1060m	5.1km	5h	Forest tracks high up through pines then a long descent.	220

Route	accommodation	camp site	restaurant/café/bar	drinking fountain	food shop	Highest point/height gain/height loss	Length	Time	Description	Page
20B Lanjarón – Soportújar										
Lanjaron – Cáñar	Y		Y	Y	Y	1128m/700m/400m	12.4km	4h50	Zigzags round ravines passing Cáñar and across a dam, Dique 24.	223
Cáñar – Soportújar	Y		Y	Y	Y		7.8km	2h50		223
							4.6km	2h		226
21B Soportújar – Pitres										
Soportújar – Pampaneira	Y		Y	Y	Y	1531m/955m/635m	11.9km	3h45	Pass between villages, through the stunning Poquiera Valley with views of the Sierra Nevada.	227
Pampaneira – Bubión	Y		Y	Y	Y		6km	2h		228
							1.4km	20min		229
Bubión – Pitres	Y	Y	Y	Y	Y		4.5km	1h25		230
22B Pitres – Trévelez										
Pitres – Pórtugos	Y		Y	Y	Y	1748m/955m/675m	15.2km	5h45	Through lush vegetation past streams to climb to Pórtugos then on up through beautiful oak woodland.	232
							2.5km	1h		232
Pórtugos – Busquístar	Y		Y	Y	Y		1.7km	45min		234
Busquístar – Trévelez	Y	Y	Y	Y	Y		11km	4h		235
23B Trevélez –Cádiar										
Trevélez – Juviles	Y		Y	Y	Y	1757m/615m/1150m	18.7km	6h	Gentle route on forestry tracks between sleepy hamlets through beautiful oak woodlands.	239
							9.7km	2h50		239
Juviles – Timar				Y			2km	40min		241
Timar – Lobras			Y	Y			2km	30min		242
Lobras – Cádiar	Y		Y	Y	Y		5km	2h		243

Stage						Ascent/Descent/Altitude	Distance	Time	Notes	Page
24B Cádiar – Yegen						1459m/1030m/910m	16.5km	5h	Walk round hillsides and over streams to reach a string of beautiful white villages.	245
Cádiar – Narila				Y			1.6km	30min		245
Narila – Bérchules			Y	Y	Y		3.2km	1h		246
Bérchules – Mecina Bombarón			Y	Y	Y		6km	2h		248
Mecina Bombarón – Yegen			Y	Y	Y		5.7km	1h30		249
25B Yegen – Laroles						1359m/950m/1000m	17.2km	5h10	Pass some amazing fizzy natural springs then loop in and out of gullies and ravines to each of the villages.	252
Yegen – Válor							4.5km	1h15		252
Válor – Nechite							1.5km	35min		253
Nechite – Mairena							5km	1h15		254
Mairena – Júbar							1.2km	15min		256
Júbar – Laroles							5km	1h50		256
26B Laroles –Puerto de la Ragua						2040m/138m/380m	16km	6h	Along the 12km of route in Alméria, through its highest village then further up to the pass	258
Laroles – Bayárcal	Y			Y			4.5km	1h30		258
Bayárcal – Puerto de la Ragua	Y*			Y			12km	4h30		261
27B Puerto de la Ragua – La Calahorra						2055m/121m/958m	11.4km	3h20	A pleasant descent on paths and tracks through pine forest and farm land. Marking is poor from here to end of route.	264
Puerto de la Ragua – Ferreira			Y	Y	Y		8.6km	2h20		264
Ferreira – La Calahorra	Y		Y	Y	Y		3km	40min		266
28B La Calahorra – Narváez (2-day section)	Y			Y		2047m/1660m/1485m	53.3km	14h	Across the flat dry plains of the Marquesado del Zenete then climb through the green rugged hills of the Sierra de Baza. (No accommodation – you need a tent – wild camping permitted in two areas of the park.)	268

* check accommodation is open or take tent

Route	Facilities at end point					Highest point/ height gain/ height loss	Length	Time	Description	Page
	food shop	drinking fountain	restaurant/ café/bar	camp site	accommodation					
29B Narváez – Zújar						1373m/300m/ 900m	24km	6h	Through the sprawling city of Baza and then into the unique landscape of the Subbética, walking along a section of unmarked route across the tracks and gullies of the high plateau to arrive in Zújar.	276
Narváez – Baza	Y	Y	Y		Y		14km	3h30		276
Baza – Zújar	Y	Y	Y				10km	2h30		278
30B Zújar –Benamaurel	Y	Y	Y		Y	886m/440m/ 525m	20.8km	5h15	Twinkling reservoir, great spa baths then strange arid lands.	280
31B Benamaurel – Cúllar	Y	Y	Y		Y	908m/260m/ 40m	12.9km	2h30	Flat easy walking through odd lunar landscapes.	285
32B Cúllar – Orce	Y	Y	Y		Y	1060m/310m/ 305m	24.2km	5h30	Gentle walking, though terribly marked, along farm tracks.	287
33B Orce – Huéscar						949m/230m/ 210m	17.2km	4h	Following oasis-like channel next to acequias and green crops.	291
Orce – Galera	Y	Y	Y		Y		9km	2h10		291
Galera – Huéscar	Y	Y	Y		Y		8.2km	1h45		294
34B Huéscar – Puebla de Don Fadrique	Y	Y	Y		Y	1488m/640m/ 375m	25km	6h30	15km road walk then lovely forested up and down to the end.	296
SOUTHERN FORK TOTAL							**465.5km**	**130h30**	**22–25 days**	

APPENDIX B
Spanish–English glossary

A few useful walking-related words which you may see on maps or signs.

Spanish	English
acequia	irrigation channel
agua (potable/no potable)	(drinking/non-drinking) water
albergue	hostel
alcazaba	castle
aldea	hamlet
arroyo	stream
ayuntamiento	town hall
atalaya	watchtower
baños	baths
barranco	gully/ravine
Barrio (alto/bajo)	neighbourhood (upper/lower)
Calle (abbreviated to C/)	street
camino	path
Carretera (Ctra)	road
casa forestal	forest house/cabin
castillo	castle
cerro	hill
comarca	region
cordillera	mountain range
cortijo	farmhouse
coto privado de caza	private hunting reserve
cruz	cross
cuesta	hill/slope
cueva	cave
desfiladero	gorge
embalse	reservoir

Spanish	English
era	threshing circle
ermita	chapel/hermitage
estación	station
fábrica	factory
finca	farm/estate
fuente	fountain
garganta	ravine
hoya	hollow/plain
iglesia	church
laguna/lago	lake
lavadero	laundry
llano	plain
mina	mine
mirador	viewpoint
montaña	mountain
parque natural	natural park
parque nacional	national park
plaza (pza)	square
prohibido el paso	no entry
puerto	pass
rambla	watercourse/stream
río	river
senderismo	walking/cycling
sierra	mountain range
tajo	cliff/cleft
torre	tower
vega	fertile plain
venta	country inn

APPENDIX C
Further information

Useful websites

www.alsa.es
Bus timetables and online ticket purchase from the main bus company, Alsina Graells

www.autobuses.costasur.com
Useful site for searching buses from over 50 companies

www.andalucia.com
A good all-round information source on the region

www.andalucia.org
The region's official tourist information site

www.ecologistasenaccion.org
Andalucía's main environmental group

www.era-ewv-ferp.com
European Ramblers Association

www.fedamon.com
Federación Andaluza de Montañismo, the agency which is responsible for the route (with gps route downloads and updates on the route)

www.iberianature.com
A wealth of information on Spanish nature, environment and wildlife

www.johnhayeswalks.com
A personal account of walking the whole of the E4 route in 2011

www.juntadeandalucia.es
Site for the Regional Government (Spanish)

www.paginas-amarillas.es
Spanish Yellow Pages, useful to look up accommodation and facilities

www.rutasyviajes.net
Download GPS tracks for all stages of the route and many other GR and local routes

Additional reading

Boyd, A *The Sierras of the South: Travels in the mountains of Andalusia* (HarperCollins, 1992)

Colwell, A *Common Wildflowers of Spain* (Santana, 2008)

Brenan, G *South from Granada* (1st edn 1957, Penguin Books, 1992)

Butler, J *Bird Watching on Spain's Southern Coast* (Santana, 2004)

Gill, J *Andalucia: A Cultural History* (Landscapes of the Imagination, 2008)

Irving, W *Tales from the Alhambra* (1st edn 1832, Editorial Everest, 2005)

Stewart, C *Driving over Lemons* (Sort Of Books, 1999)

INDEX

DOWNLOAD GPS TRACKS
OF THE ROUTE

Up-to-date GPS tracks for the GR7 in Andalucía can be downloaded for free from

www.rutasyviajes.net

which is managed by Miguel Ángel Santaella, contributing author to this book.

To get to the tracks, first click on 'Rutas' and then follow links to 'Senderos de Gran Recorrido (GR)' and 'GR7'. This takes you to a list of all the individual GPS tracks available for the route – Part 1, Part 2 and Part 3 of this guidebook.

To download a track, just click in the right-hand column, headed 'Ver etapa y Descargar' (See track and Download). The first time you download you will be asked to register with the website by giving a username and password but no payment is required.

NOTES

NOTES

LISTING OF CICERONE GUIDES

Tour of the Oisans: The GR54
Tour of the Queyras
Tour of the Vanoise
Trekking in the Vosges and Jura
Vanoise Ski Touring
Walking in the Auvergne
Walking in the Cathar Region
Walking in the Cevennes
Walking in the Dordogne
Walking in the Haute Savoie
  North & South
Walking in the Languedoc
Walking in the Tarentaise and
  Beaufortain Alps
Walking on Corsica

GERMANY

Germany's Romantic Road
Walking in the Bavarian Alps
Walking the River Rhine Trail

HIMALAYA

8000m
Annapurna
Bhutan: A Trekker's Guide
Everest: A Trekker's Guide
Garhwal and Kumaon: A
  Trekker's and Visitor's Guide
Kangchenjunga:
  A Trekker's Guide
Langtang with Gosainkund and
  Helambu: A Trekker's Guide
Manaslu: A Trekker's Guide
The Mount Kailash Trek
Trekking in Ladakh
Trekking in the Himalaya

ICELAND & GREENLAND

Trekking in Greenland
Walking and Trekking in Iceland

IRELAND

Irish Coastal Walks
The Irish Coast to Coast Walk
The Mountains of Ireland

ITALY

Gran Paradiso
Sibillini National Park
Stelvio National Park
Shorter Walks in the Dolomites
Through the Italian Alps
Trekking in the Apennines
Trekking in the Dolomites

Via Ferratas of the Italian
  Dolomites: Vols 1 & 2
Walking in Abruzzo
Walking in Stelvio National Park
Walking in Sardinia
Walking in Sicily
Walking in the Central
  Italian Alps
Walking in the Dolomites
Walking in Tuscany
Walking on the Amalfi Coast
Walking the Italian Lakes

MEDITERRANEAN

Jordan – Walks, Treks, Caves,
  Climbs and Canyons
The Ala Dag
The High Mountains of Crete
The Mountains of Greece
Treks and Climbs in Wadi Rum,
  Jordan
Walking in Malta
Western Crete

NORTH AMERICA

British Columbia
The Grand Canyon
The John Muir Trail
The Pacific Crest Trail

SOUTH AMERICA

Aconcagua and the
  Southern Andes
Hiking and Biking Peru's
  Inca Trails
Torres del Paine

SCANDINAVIA

Walking in Norway

SLOVENIA, CROATIA AND
MONTENEGRO

The Julian Alps of Slovenia
The Mountains of Montenegro
Trekking in Slovenia
Walking in Croatia
Walking in Slovenia:
  The Karavanke

SPAIN AND PORTUGAL

Costa Blanca: West
Mountain Walking in Southern
  Catalunya
The Mountains of Central Spain
The Northern Caminos

Trekking through Mallorca
Walking in Madeira
Walking in Mallorca
Walking in the Algarve
Walking in the
  Cordillera Cantabrica
Walking on the Sierra Nevada
Walking on La Gomera and
  El Hierro
Walking on La Palma
Walking on Tenerife
Walking the GR7 in Andalucia
Walks and Climbs in the
  Picos de Europa

SWITZERLAND

Alpine Pass Route
Canyoning in the Alps
Central Switzerland
The Bernese Alps
The Swiss Alps
Tour of the Jungfrau Region
Walking in the Valais
Walking in Ticino
Walks in the Engadine

TECHNIQUES

Geocaching in the UK
Indoor Climbing
Lightweight Camping
Map and Compass
Mountain Weather
Moveable Feasts
Outdoor Photography
Polar Exploration
Rock Climbing
Sport Climbing
The Book of the Bivvy
The Hillwalker's Guide
  to Mountaineering
The Hillwalker's Manual

MINI GUIDES

Avalanche!
Navigating with a GPS
Navigation
Pocket First Aid and
  Wilderness Medicine
Snow

For full information on all our
guides, and to order books and
eBooks, visit our website:
www.cicerone.co.uk.

Walking – Trekking – Mountaineering – Climbing – Cycling

Over 40 years, Cicerone have built up an outstanding collection of 300 guides, inspiring all sorts of amazing adventures.

 Every guide comes from extensive exploration and research by our expert authors, all with a passion for their subjects. They are frequently praised, endorsed and used by clubs, instructors and outdoor organisations.

All our titles can now be bought as **e-books** and many as iPad and Kindle files and we will continue to make all our guides available for these and many other devices.

Our website shows any **new information** we've received since a book was published. Please do let us know if you find anything has changed, so that we can pass on the latest details. On our **website** you'll also find some great ideas and lots of information, including sample chapters, contents lists, reviews, articles and a photo gallery.

It's easy to keep in touch with what's going on at Cicerone, by getting our monthly **free e-newsletter**, which is full of offers, competitions, up-to-date information and topical articles. You can subscribe on our home page and also follow us on **Facebook** and **Twitter**, as well as our **blog**.

Cicerone – the very best guides for exploring the world.

CICERONE

2 Police Square Milnthorpe Cumbria LA7 7PY
Tel: 015395 62069 info@cicerone.co.uk
www.cicerone.co.uk